CRASH COURSE

Pushkar Raj Thakur

Invincible Publication Pvt Ltd.

Published by:

Invincible Publication Pvt Ltd.
1103-A, 11th Floor, SAS Tower, Sector 38, Gurugram,
Haryana – 122003
Phone: +91-124-4034247, +91 9599066061
Website : www.invinciblepublishers.com

Sales Office : - 4760-61/23, Basement, Pratap Street, Ansari Road,
Daryaganj, New Delhi - 110002
Phone: +91-11-40198405
Email: invinciblepublishers@gmail.com

ISBN : 978-81-962775-1-2
Book Name : Stock Market - Crash Course

Revised Edition: October 2023

Preface

"Stock Market Crash Course" is an informative guide that delves into the world of stock market investing, curated for both beginners as well as experienced investors.

Ranging from basics of investing to advanced trading strategies, this book is an all-encompassing crash course. This book provides a distinct and taut analysis of the stock market, comprising of its workings, trends, and investment strategies. Additionally, the author provides practical advice on how to analyze stocks, read financial statements, use fundamental & technical analysis, as well carrying out strategies to attain success in investment and trading ventures.

"Stock Market: Crash Course" is here to be your essential guide that offers valuable insights and advice on navigating through the complex world of the stock market!

About the Author

Pushkar Raj Thakur is India's leading Finance Educator & Business Coach with millions of followers on all leading social media platforms. He is known for his versatile knowledge of financial education, personal mastery, sales, marketing, human psychology & business development.

He is multiple Guinness World Record holder & is committed to make Bharat #GoSelfMade.

Contents

Disclaimer

This Book is based on research and case studies gathered from different books, media, internet space, etc. Pushkar Raj Thakur and producers do not accept any responsibility or liability for the accuracy, content, completeness, legality or reliability of the information contained in the book.

The book is written solely for educational purpose and is not created with an intent to harm, injure or defame any person, body of persons, association, company or entity. The readers should always do their diligence and anyone who wishes to apply the ideas contained in the book cannot replace or substitute for the services of trained professionals in any field including, but not limited to; financial, medical, psychological or legal matters. Pushkar Raj Thakur and the producers do not take responsibility for any direct, indirect, implied, punitive, special, incident, or other consequential damages arising directly on account of any actions taken based on the book. Pushkar Raj Thakur and the producers of the book disclaims any kind of claim of libel, slander or any other kind of claim or suit of any sort.

"We are not Financial Advisers. Please consult your Financial Adviser before Investing or Trading". We do not give any tips or manage portfolio. Please be safe from anyone impersonating us. We will never take money from you for tips or portfolio management! Readers discretion is advised."

Chapter 1

To Open Free Demat Account, Just Scan the QR Code

BASICS OF SHARE MARKET FOR BEGINNERS

Since a long time, there had been a growing demand for step-by-step guidance on stock market concepts. The foremost questions that trouble beginners are - where to begin and what to learn first. The good news is - this book will help you resolve all your doubts and misconceptions. It's like a crash course in itself on stock market investing and trading.

Ever since I was young, I had a keen interest in investing and trading. When I wanted to learn about the stock market, there were no options available except to join institutes that charged exorbitant fees for such courses and information. However, with the advancements in technology and the widespread availability of information on the internet, social media, YouTube, books, podcasts, etc., learning has become more accessible than ever before. Today, one can learn anything they desire, according to their own time and convenience.

Due to financial constraints, I couldn't join any of the expensive offline institutes back then, instead, I used to analyze the activities of people close to me who traded in the stock market. From my own experience as well as theirs, I realized that a lack of financial & market knowledge increases one's chances of incurring losses.

One of the most common reasons why people are motivated to enter the stock market is due to the claims they see on social media of others around them earning lakhs and crores of rupees. Unfortunately, many individuals jump into the market without any proper analysis, often investing in penny stocks, which can lead to disastrous losses. The main goal of this book is to prevent such speculative gambles and help individuals avoid incurring avoidable losses.

Through this book, I will take you on a journey of the stock market, starting from the basics and progressing towards advanced stages of trading. We will learn the fundamentals, various types of analysis, as well as different techniques, patterns, and strategies that I have acquired through my own experiences. This book has been curated in such a manner to provide all the vital knowledge, in the simplest of language.

Financial education is an essential aspect of our lives that we often overlook. Investing and trading are critical components of financial education that people should understand, if not actively participate in. There are three primary objectives of financial education, akin to the preamble of the constitution. These objectives include earning money, managing money, and growing money steadily.

Financial education has not received the attention it deserves from schools, colleges, or individuals. Therefore, it is crucial for every individual to personally undertake this task of financial education if they intend to grow financially.

Learning any subject requires effort, and the time dedicated to the subject is proportional to the level of learning achieved. With one hour of studying per day, a person can become an expert in a subject in less than five years. However, this learning curve can be shortened if one is willing to dedicate more hours per day, wherein mastery of the subject can be achieved in as little as two years. People often assume trading and investing to be complex, which always reminds of what Warren Buffet said, "There seems to be some perverse human characteristic that likes to make easy things difficult." In the stock market arena, simple concepts work wonders if understood and practiced well. Simple approaches worked for me and that is exactly what I intend to share with my readers.

If I were to offer you a large sum of money, let's say Rs. 5 Crores, your mind would immediately jump to how you would spend it. Only after that initial excitement would you begin to consider investing some of the money for the future. Some might argue that they would save the entire amount, but where would they keep it? Banks offer interest rates of only 3-6%, while fixed deposits might earn interest rates of 6-8%. Others may consider simply keeping the money in a safe at home, but what about inflation? Just like termites hollow out wood, inflation eats away at the value of money over time. Inflation is a common and observable economic phenomenon. The prices of commodities you bought three years ago are likely much different than their current prices due to the declining purchasing power of money. So, how can we beat inflation? By making the right investments!

Success in investing begins with the ability to distinguish between the right investment opportunities and speculative ones. I often encounter people from all walks of life who have invested in various schemes and plans, ranging from unregistered real estate to ULIP policies and cryptocurrency. But is it enough to simply invest in anything? This question used to trouble me as well. I wondered endlessly how I could double my money through the right investments.

The answer lies in the Rule of 72. This formula is used to calculate how many years it will take to double your investment based on the annual rate of return. For example, if you are earning a 12% rate of return on your investment, it will take at least 6 years to double your investment (72/12=6). This minimum time period should ideally be 3-4 years. The goal of this book is to help you achieve this ideal return rate.

When I advise young people to start investing, they often complain that they don't have enough money to invest. But it's important to start somewhere in order to grow and make money over time. Trading can even become a full- time profession, but it requires dedication and study. By devoting 4 hours per day to studying the subject, you can shorten the learning curve from 5 years to just 1 year. In the next chapter, we will delve into concepts that will help you make the right investments.

Chapter 2

To Open Free Demat Account, Just Scan the QR Code

FUNDAMENTAL ANALYSIS

Analyzing a company's financial data is a crucial task that must be undertaken before investing your hard-earned money. Simply dumping your money into the first company you come across without perusing and comprehending various aspects is not surely advisable. In this chapter, we will discuss what needs to be analyzed and how to do it. Before investing, you must undertake two important tasks: Fundamental Analysis and Technical Analysis. Fundamental Analysis is the most basic yet the most important task you can run before investing your money. It is the way of knowing whether you can buy a good or a service at a fair price or whether it is costlier than it should be. Warren Buffet refers to this as 'Value Investing.' The purpose of this analysis is to determine whether you are buying a stock at a price lower than its intrinsic value or above it. The goal is to ensure that you are paying a fair price for the value you will receive. For example, if you paid Rs. 50 for a haircut and received excellent service and benefits, you got good value for your money. However, if you paid Rs. 1000 for a haircut and did not receive satisfactory service or benefits, you did not get value for your money. When buying a property, you would analyze various aspects such as location, construction, and total area to estimate its value. Peer comparison involves comparing the property to others with similar benefits to determine its worth. Similarly, when investing in stocks, analyzing various aspects and peer comparisons are crucial steps in making the right investment.

It is common to observe stock prices increase beyond their intrinsic value. In such a situation, the question arises as to whether one should buy the stock or not. To answer this question, it is essential to understand how prices tend to exceed intrinsic value. Ratios play a significant role in the grand scheme of investing, and there are four primary ratios to focus on: PE ratio, PB ratio, debt ratio, and current ratio. These ratios are often portrayed as complicated and challenging to understand, leading many to believe that they are only for finance professionals. However, in this chapter, my goal is to explain these terms in the simplest way possible, just as I came to understand them.

PE RATIO (PRICE/EARNINGS RATIO)

This ratio involves calculating the price-to-earnings ratio. In simpler terms, it is a calculation based on the price you pay for a stock compared to the amount of money the company is earning. It is possible that the price you pay today is higher than the intrinsic value of the stock, which implies that the company is doing something to increase its earnings, or its earnings are expected to increase eventually. Future trends and market expectations play a significant role, and people invest based on these future trends rather than the current scenario. Therefore, we can say that the stock market is futuristic in nature.

For example, let's say you assume that Google will dominate the market in the future based on certain calculations. In this case, the PE Ratio will give a higher price for its stock because it is expected that its earnings will significantly increase. For instance, if you pay Rs. 100 for a stock, and the company is earning Rs. 10 per share, the Price/Earnings (PE) ratio will be calculated as 100/10 =

This means that you are paying Rs. 10 to earn Rs. 1 per share. If the earnings or profits of a company increase, the PE ratio will decrease, which means that you will have to pay less to earn more. In other words, the lower the PE ratio, the more beneficial it is.

PB RATIO (PRICE/BOOK RATIO)

The PB Ratio is a ratio that calculates a company's assets. Its purpose is to determine whether a company possesses sufficient assets that can be liquidated to repay investors in case of a need. As with the PE Ratio, a lower PB Ratio indicates a higher chance of obtaining greater value. The factors that affect a company's book value differ from one industry to another. Certain industries, like IT, may have lower book values but higher prices, which are influenced by various factors that vary from industry to industry.

DEBT RATIO (DEBT/EQUITY RATIO)

The debt ratio represents the amount of money that a

company borrows, which is separate from the money it obtains from selling its equity or shares. Companies often need capital to expand their business, and they can obtain it either by selling shares or by taking out a loan. Taking out a loan is usually cheaper than selling equity to raise capital. Companies that are confident in their ability to generate profits are less likely to sell equity. Some people view a higher debt ratio as a warning sign, but this is not necessarily the case if the company is capable of repaying the debt.

For example, if the debt ratio is 2, this means that the company has borrowed twice as much as the equity it has sold. If the ratio is 10, it means that the company has borrowed ten times the amount of equity it has sold. If a company has taken on debt, its ability to repay it must be evaluated by calculating the current ratio.

CURRENT RATIO (CURRENT ASSETS / CURRENT LIABILITIES = CURRENT RATIO)

The current ratio is a ratio that calculates a company's current assets and liabilities. The emphasis is on the word "current," meaning the assets and liabilities that the company currently holds. Assets are materials that the company can immediately earn money from, while liabilities are the immediate payments the company has to make. For example, if a company has Rs. 20 crore in assets and Rs. 10 crore in liabilities, its current ratio is 2, calculated as CA/ CL=CR; 20 Cr/10 Cr = 2, this value is good enough because the company holds more assets, therefore, it can easily repay its debts. This ratio is considered good because the company has more assets and can easily repay its debts. In general, the higher the current ratio, the greater the company's ability to repay its debts.

BALANCE SHEET

Analyzing a company's balance sheet is one of the most crucial tasks when it comes to investing. While it may seem daunting at first, the elements that make up a balance sheet are actually quite simple to understand. At the heart of every company's operations is the desire to generate profits through the sale of its products or services. The balance sheet primarily consists of two key elements that reflect this: sales and profits.

Sales, often referred to as the "top line," represent the revenue generated from the sales of the company's products or services. Profit, on the other hand, represents the amount of money left over after all expenses have been deducted, and is often referred to as the 'bottom line.' When analyzing a balance sheet, it is important to focus on the steady growth of sales and the amount of profit generated, as this indicates the company's overall financial health.

In addition to sales and profits, a balance sheet also includes a detailed list of all the assets and liabilities held by the company over a specific period of time. Ideally, a company's assets should increase over time, while its liabilities should decrease. By analyzing a company's balance sheet over a period of several years, investors can gain insight into whether the company's assets have been consistently increasing while its liabilities have been decreasing, which is a clear indicator of growth.

CASH FLOW STATEMENT

This is one of the critical aspects of analyzing a balance sheet. This particular statement focuses on the calculation of cash inflow and outflow in a company. It involves a simple calculation of the cash generated by the company through its sales or investments. Although the cash flow statement of a company contains several terms, the most important one to focus on is 'free cash flow,' which represents the cash held by the company. Steady increases in cash flow are considered to be good and beneficial.

The process of analyzing these segments is known as fundamental analysis. By studying these segments diligently, you will have completed 90% of fundamental analysis, and the remaining 10% can be left to experts or gained through steady analysis over time. It's important to not only focus on fundamental analysis or technical analysis but to strike a balance between both to arrive at a sound investment conclusion.

To simplify this task, websites like Screener or Tickertape can be used to access all the above segments with just a few clicks. Check out the below images from Screener:

Profit & Loss

Consolidated Figures in Rs. Crores / View Standalone

RELATED PARTY | PRODUCT SEGMENTS

	Mar 2013	Mar 2014	Mar 2015	Mar 2016	Mar 2017	Mar 2018	Mar 2019	Mar 2020	Mar 2021	Mar 2022	Mar 2023	Mar 2024	TTM
Sales +	395,957	433,521	374,372	272,583	303,954	390,823	568,337	596,679	466,307	694,673	876,396	901,064	925,289
Expenses +	362,802	398,586	336,923	230,802	257,647	326,508	484,087	507,413	385,517	586,092	734,078	738,831	762,384
Operating Profit	**33,155**	**34,935**	**37,449**	**41,781**	**46,307**	**64,315**	**84,250**	**89,266**	**80,790**	**108,581**	**142,318**	**162,233**	**162,905**
OPM %	8%	8%	10%	15%	15%	16%	15%	15%	17%	16%	16%	18%	18%
Other Income +	7,757	8,865	8,528	12,212	9,222	9,869	8,406	8,570	22,432	19,600	12,020	16,057	16,438
Interest	3,463	3,836	3,316	3,691	3,849	8,052	16,495	22,027	21,189	14,584	19,571	23,118	23,199
Depreciation	11,232	11,201	11,547	11,565	11,646	16,706	20,934	22,203	26,572	29,782	40,303	50,832	52,653
Profit before tax	**26,217**	**28,763**	**31,114**	**38,737**	**40,034**	**49,426**	**55,227**	**53,606**	**55,461**	**83,815**	**94,464**	**104,340**	**103,491**
Tax %	20%	22%	24%	23%	25%	27%	28%	26%	3%	19%	22%	25%	
Net Profit +	**20,886**	**22,548**	**23,640**	**29,861**	**29,833**	**36,080**	**39,837**	**39,880**	**53,739**	**67,845**	**74,088**	**79,020**	**78,207**
EPS in Rs	30.31	32.62	34.14	43.03	43.11	53.39	58.55	58.20	77.50	89.74	98.59	102.90	101.61
Dividend Payout %	13%	12%	12%	10%	11%	10%	10%	10%	9%	9%	9%	10%	

Cash Flows

Consolidated Figures in Rs. Crores / View Standalone

	Mar 2013	Mar 2014	Mar 2015	Mar 2016	Mar 2017	Mar 2018	Mar 2019	Mar 2020	Mar 2021	Mar 2022	Mar 2023	Mar 2024
Cash from Operating Activity +	36,918	43,261	34,374	38,134	49,550	71,459	42,346	94,877	26,958	110,654	115,032	158,788
Cash from Investing Activity +	-27,601	-73,070	-64,706	-36,186	-66,201	-68,192	-94,507	-72,497	-142,385	-109,162	-93,001	-114,301
Cash from Financing Activity +	408	13,713	8,444	-3,210	8,617	-2,001	55,906	-2,541	101,904	17,289	10,455	-16,646
Net Cash Flow	**9,725**	**-16,096**	**-21,888**	**-1,262**	**-8,034**	**1,266**	**3,745**	**19,839**	**-13,523**	**18,781**	**32,486**	**27,841**

Balance Sheet

CORPORATE ACTIONS

Consolidated Figures in Rs. Crores / View Standalone

	Mar 2013	Mar 2014	Mar 2015	Mar 2016	Mar 2017	Mar 2018	Mar 2019	Mar 2020	Mar 2021	Mar 2022	Mar 2023	Mar 2024
Equity Capital	2,936	2,940	2,943	2,948	2,959	5,922	5,926	6,339	6,445	6,765	6,766	6,766
Reserves	179,119	195,747	215,556	228,608	260,750	287,584	381,186	442,827	693,727	772,720	709,106	786,715
Borrowings +	107,219	138,761	168,251	194,714	217,475	239,843	307,714	355,133	278,962	319,158	451,664	346,142
Other Liabilities +	73,083	91,395	117,736	172,727	225,618	277,924	302,804	358,716	340,931	399,979	438,346	616,363
Total Liabilities	**362,357**	**428,843**	**504,486**	**598,997**	**706,802**	**811,273**	**997,630**	**1,163,015**	**1,320,065**	**1,498,622**	**1,605,882**	**1,755,986**
Fixed Assets +	133,487	141,417	156,458	184,910	198,526	403,885	398,374	532,658	541,258	627,798	724,805	966,458
CWIP	49,952	91,494	166,462	228,697	324,837	187,022	179,463	109,106	125,953	172,506	293,752	152,382
Investments	42,848	60,602	76,451	84,015	82,899	82,862	235,635	276,767	364,828	394,264	235,560	225,672
Other Assets +	136,070	135,330	105,115	101,375	100,540	137,504	184,158	244,484	288,026	304,054	351,765	411,474
Total Assets	**362,357**	**428,843**	**504,486**	**598,997**	**706,802**	**811,273**	**997,630**	**1,163,015**	**1,320,065**	**1,498,622**	**1,605,882**	**1,755,986**

Shareholding Pattern

Numbers in percentages

Quarterly Yearly TRADES

	Sep 2021	Dec 2021	Mar 2022	Jun 2022	Sep 2022	Dec 2022	Mar 2023	Jun 2023	Sep 2023	Dec 2023	Mar 2024	Jun 2024
Promoters +	50.61%	50.61%	50.66%	50.62%	50.56%	50.49%	50.41%	50.39%	50.27%	50.30%	50.31%	50.33%
FIIs +	25.41%	24.75%	24.23%	23.90%	23.58%	23.48%	22.49%	22.55%	22.60%	22.13%	22.06%	21.75%
DIIs +	13.20%	13.62%	14.23%	14.67%	14.91%	15.26%	16.06%	16.13%	15.99%	16.59%	16.98%	17.30%
Government +	0.18%	0.17%	0.17%	0.17%	0.16%	0.16%	0.16%	0.17%	0.17%	0.18%	0.19%	0.19%
Public +	10.60%	10.85%	10.71%	10.64%	10.78%	10.59%	10.89%	10.76%	10.98%	10.80%	10.46%	10.43%
No. of Shareholders	0,43,511	33,06,662	33,27,847	33,06,732	34,85,825	33,62,915	36,39,396	35,06,867	36,98,648	36,13,814	34,63,276	34,93,125

Quarterly Results

PRODUCT SEGMENTS

Consolidated Figures in Rs. Crores / View Standalone

	Jun 2021	Sep 2021	Dec 2021	Mar 2022	Jun 2022	Sep 2022	Dec 2022	Mar 2023	Jun 2023	Sep 2023	Dec 2023	Mar 2024	Jun 2024
Sales +	139,949	167,611	185,027	207,375	218,855	229,409	216,737	212,834	207,559	231,886	225,086	236,533	231,784
Expenses +	116,618	141,591	155,321	176,009	181,157	198,438	181,728	174,478	169,466	190,918	184,430	194,017	193,019
Operating Profit	**23,331**	**26,020**	**29,706**	**31,366**	**37,698**	**30,971**	**35,009**	**38,356**	**38,093**	**40,968**	**40,656**	**42,516**	**38,765**
OPM %	17%	16%	16%	15%	17%	14%	16%	18%	18%	18%	18%	18%	17%
Other Income +	4,219	4,263	7,016	2,602	2,275	3,656	3,377	2,996	3,813	3,899	4,022	4,534	3,983
Interest	3,397	3,819	3,812	3,556	3,997	4,554	5,201	5,819	5,837	5,731	5,789	5,761	5,918
Depreciation	6,883	7,230	7,683	8,001	8,942	9,726	10,183	11,452	11,775	12,585	12,903	13,569	13,596
Profit before tax	**17,270**	**19,234**	**25,227**	**22,411**	**27,034**	**20,347**	**23,002**	**24,081**	**24,294**	**26,551**	**25,986**	**27,720**	**23,234**
Tax %	20%	20%	19%	20%	28%	24%	23%	11%	25%	25%	24%	24%	25%
Net Profit +	**13,806**	**15,479**	**20,539**	**18,021**	**19,443**	**15,512**	**17,806**	**21,327**	**18,258**	**19,878**	**19,641**	**21,243**	**17,445**
EPS in Rs	19.36	21.58	27.42	23.95	26.54	20.19	23.34	28.53	23.67	25.71	25.52	28.01	22.37
Raw PDF													

Peer comparison

Sector: Refineries   Industry: Refineries

EDIT COLUMNS

S.No.	Name	CMP Rs.	P/E	Mar Cap Rs.Cr.	Div Yld %	NP Qtr Rs.Cr.	Qtr Profit Var %	Sales Qtr Rs.Cr.	Qtr Sales Var %	ROCE %
1.	**Reliance Industr**	**3002.55**	**29.50**	**2031469.44**	**0.30**	**17445.00**	**-5.45**	**231784.00**	**11.67**	**9.99**
2.	I O C L	176.95	8.11	249875.29	6.76	3722.63	-75.56	193844.91	-2.37	21.14
3.	B P C L	349.95	7.84	151825.99	6.04	2841.55	-72.40	113094.92	0.10	32.09
4.	H P C L	392.15	8.36	83442.57	5.38	633.94	-90.63	113888.28	1.61	21.26
5.	M R P L	217.50	14.21	38119.03	1.34	73.22	-92.78	23247.02	10.40	25.75
6.	C P C L	1007.95	5.90	15009.55	5.54	342.60	-37.52	17094.98	15.94	35.44
7.	Gandhar Oil Ref.	212.45	14.77	2079.24	0.00	12.11	-58.81	939.24	-4.81	21.70
	Median: 8 Co.	283.73	11.29	60780.8	3.36	488.27	-72.4	68170.97	1.61	21.48

By using these websites, you can easily analyze the information you need and filter it to make the process more efficient. Take some time to explore the websites and learn at your own pace. The first thing to consider is whether the stock price is higher or lower than its intrinsic value. If the price is significantly higher than its intrinsic value, it may not be a good investment. You can also compare yearly data from the balance sheet in a simple table. Keep an eye out for increasing liabilities, which can be a red flag.

Additionally, it is important to monitor the stock price for any significant drops. If the price starts to decline, you should investigate the Promoter's Pledging. Let's consider an example. Suppose X establishes a frozen food manufacturing business and is the "promoter" of the company. If X does not have enough capital to run or expand the business, he may pledge some of his shares to raise money from the market. There will be shares that X holds, as well as the shares he pledges to gain more capital. It is crucial to analyze whether the company's holdings and pledging are increasing or decreasing. If X's holdings are increasing, it means his company is buying back its own shares, which indicates the company has potential for growth. Therefore, analyzing the pattern of holdings and pledging is important.

Another factor that can help you determine whether it's the right time to invest in a particular stock is by checking whether mutual funds and foreign investors have already invested in the company. If all the financials appear promising, and they haven't invested yet, it suggests that it's the ideal time for you to invest as they are likely to invest in the company in the future. However, if they have already invested, it's important to check whether their investment in the company is increasing over time, indicating potential growth for the company.

Apart from these factors, fundamental analysis also involves assessing the company's business in the broader context of the economy. This means determining whether there is a long-term demand for the product or service offered by the company. For example, coal companies may face challenges in the long run due to the increasing adoption of renewable energy and technological advancements. In contrast, essential goods, which are always in demand, are less likely to be affected by economic fluctuations than luxury goods and services.

Fundamental analysis is a crucial component of stock market investing. One important aspect of fundamental analysis is understanding the concept of 'monopoly.' A monopoly occurs when a company has exclusive control over the supply of a particular commodity or service, which allows it to dominate the market. There can be several reasons for such a monopoly, including unique products, exclusive licenses or patents, advantageous location, political support, and restrictions on the entry of other companies. Additionally, a company with higher sales than another company may earn more profits due to its superior networking capabilities.

A common mistake that people make is investing in stocks based solely on others' claims that prices will rise without conducting their own analysis. Such rash decisions can lead to unforeseeable losses that could have been avoided if a thorough analysis had been performed.

Now that you understand the importance of fundamental analysis, let's delve into technical analysis and how it can complement fundamental analysis to improve your stock market investments.

Chapter 3

To Open Free Demat Account, Just Scan the QR Code

TECHNICAL ANALYSIS

It is widely recognized that mindset and psychology play a significant role in achieving any task we undertake. Our mindset heavily influences how we perceive a challenge. I have encountered many individuals who perceive a simple challenge to be difficult and end up making it so. Similarly, people perceive a paper or screen full of graphs and numbers to be complex and difficult. This is precisely how people perceive technical analysis. When they hear the term technical, their mind immediately assumes it to be complex and challenging. To dispel this notion, I will explain technical analysis in the simplest way possible.

Technical analysis involves studying charts and price action to determine the likelihood of price increases or decreases. Therefore, technical analysis helps determine the best time to buy or sell a stock and how long one should hold onto it.

There are basic goals of technical analysis, such as;

- Identifying the trend
- Identifying the support & resistance

THE TREND IS YOUR FRIEND

The term "trend" is commonly used to describe things that are currently popular or becoming so. In the field of stock markets, investors and traders must be aware of certain types of trends. In simple terms, a trend refers to the fluctuations in the price of stocks. Identifying these trends is crucial, as it's similar to winning half the battle. The price graph we often see is never a straight line; it has zig-zag fluctuations but always heads in a certain direction. There are three types of trends based on the direction of the graph:

- An uptrend is observed when the fluctuations are going up.
- A downtrend is observed when the fluctuations are going down.
- A sideways trend is observed when the fluctuations don't take either direction and remain constant.

It is possible to earn money in all three trends of the market if you can correctly decode the trend. Rule one is - trend is your friend. Rule two is - never trade against the trend, no matter how tempting it may seem. Traders follow different trading styles, such as trend trading, reversal trading, or breakout or breakdown trading. Although people earn a lot from all three, trend trading works the best for me. As you become familiar with trading over time, you can also choose the type of trading that suits you best. Many of you might get a surge of motivation to trade, but hold your horses, I assure you there's much more to learn, that will make you a better trader than you are right now.

Let's begin by understanding the importance of each of the three trends in the stock market and how you can effectively navigate them.

UPTREND

As the graph moves in a zig-zag pattern towards the top, it creates specific points called higher highs and higher lows. As long as the graph continues to form higher highs, we can determine that the trend is moving upwards. By connecting all the higher lows points with a straight line, we can visualize the steepness of the trend. This line is known as the support line or axis.

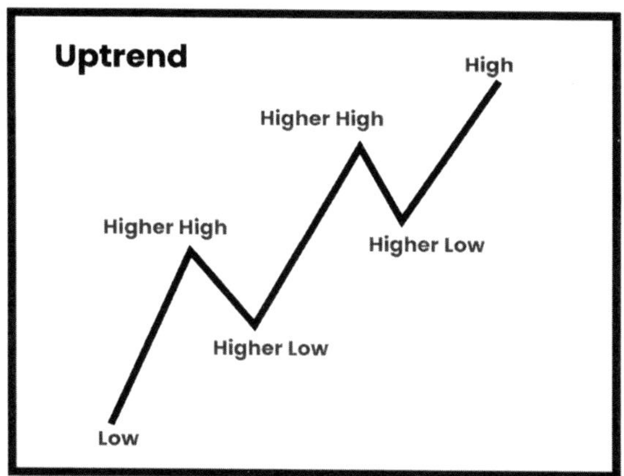

DOWNTREND

When the graph moves downward in a zig-zag pattern, it touches the points of lower highs and lower lows. Connecting the lower high points shows the direction of the trend moving downward, confirming a downtrend. However, if the graph breaks the last lower high and starts moving upwards, creating higher highs, it indicates a potential change in the trend.

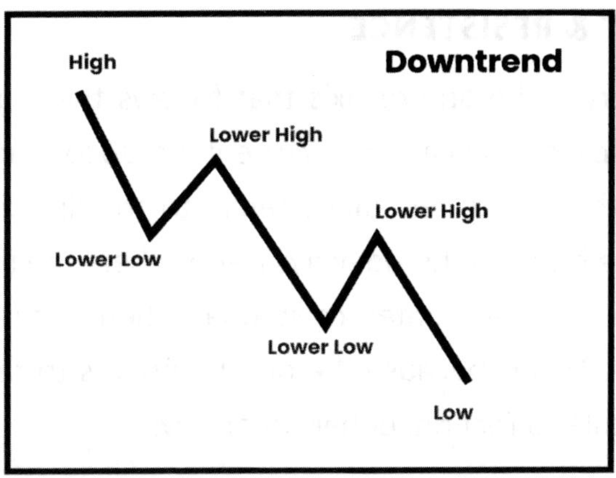

SIDEWAYS TREND

If the graph shows similar levels of highs and lows, and these levels appear to be parallel to each other, then it indicates that the market is moving sideways. In other words, the highs and lows of the price remain fairly consistent, resulting in a horizontal or sideways movement of the price chart. This indicates that there is an equilibrium between buyers and sellers, and the market is lacking a clear direction. Traders often look for breakouts from this range to identify potential new trends in the market.

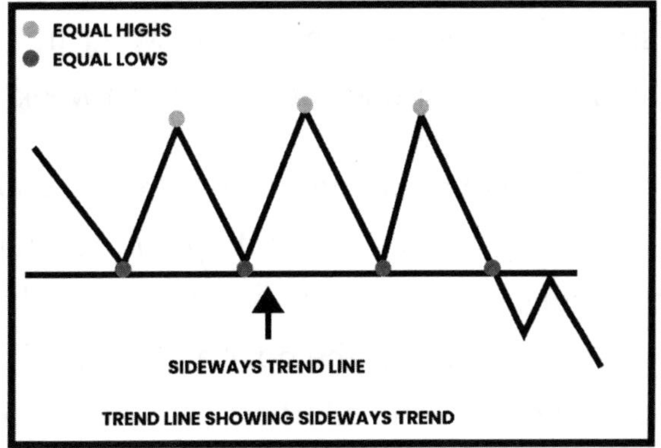

SUPPORT & RESISTENCE

Support is the line or axis that follows the higher highs, which helps to indicate the current or upcoming uptrend. On the other hand, resistance refers to the line or axis that follows the highs of the sideways trend, where the fluctuations appear to be consolidated or stagnant, hence it is known as resistance. This is because the graph appears to resist taking any particular direction, either up or down.

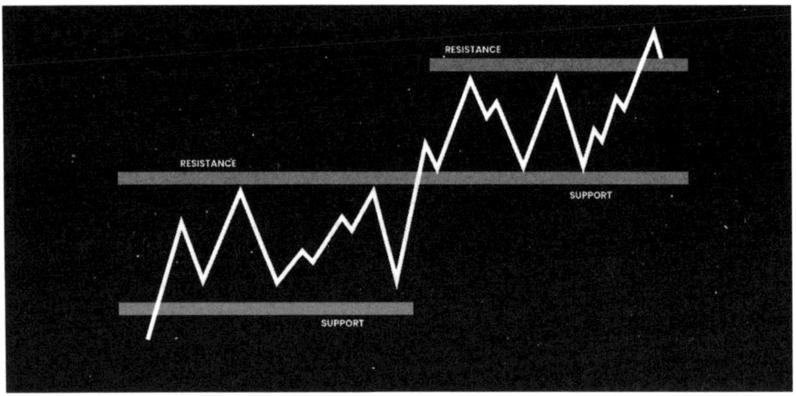

It's worth noting that these trends depend on your trading strategy. For long-term investors, trends are observed over a period of several years or six months, while for short-term traders, such as those who engage in swing trading, trends must be observed accordingly for a day or a week,.

To simplify the observation of these trends, you can select a stock of a company and check its graph to plot the trend lines accordingly. If you don't wish to manually plot the trend lines, you can simply select the option of Super- Trend, which makes observing the trend effortless (see the image below for Super-Trend).

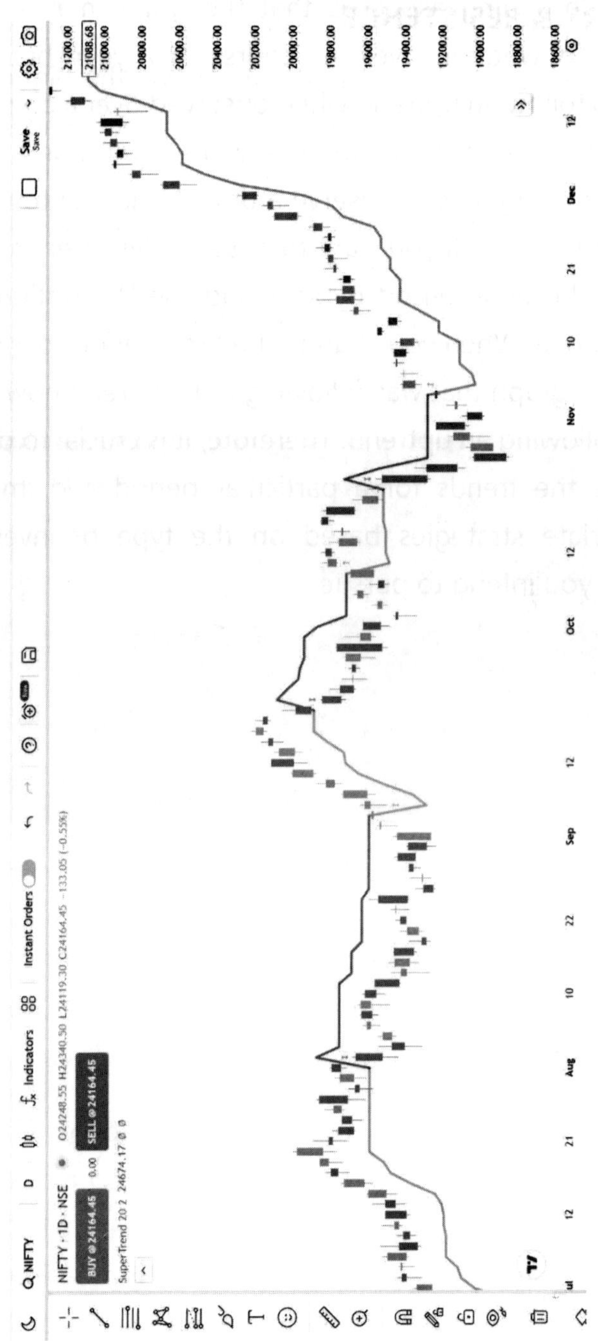

The intriguing aspect is that the graph may appear to follow a downtrend over the course of a year, but it could seem to follow an uptrend when observed over a day or week, and vice versa. In the image below, the time frame is set to one year, and you can observe a downtrend line towards the end of the graph. If you want to observe daily trends, you can change the time period by selecting the "D" option on the panel above. When you change the time period to 5 minutes, the same graph that was following a downtrend now appears to be following an uptrend. Therefore, it is crucial to diligently observe the trends for a particular period and implement appropriate strategies based on the type of investing or trading you intend to pursue.

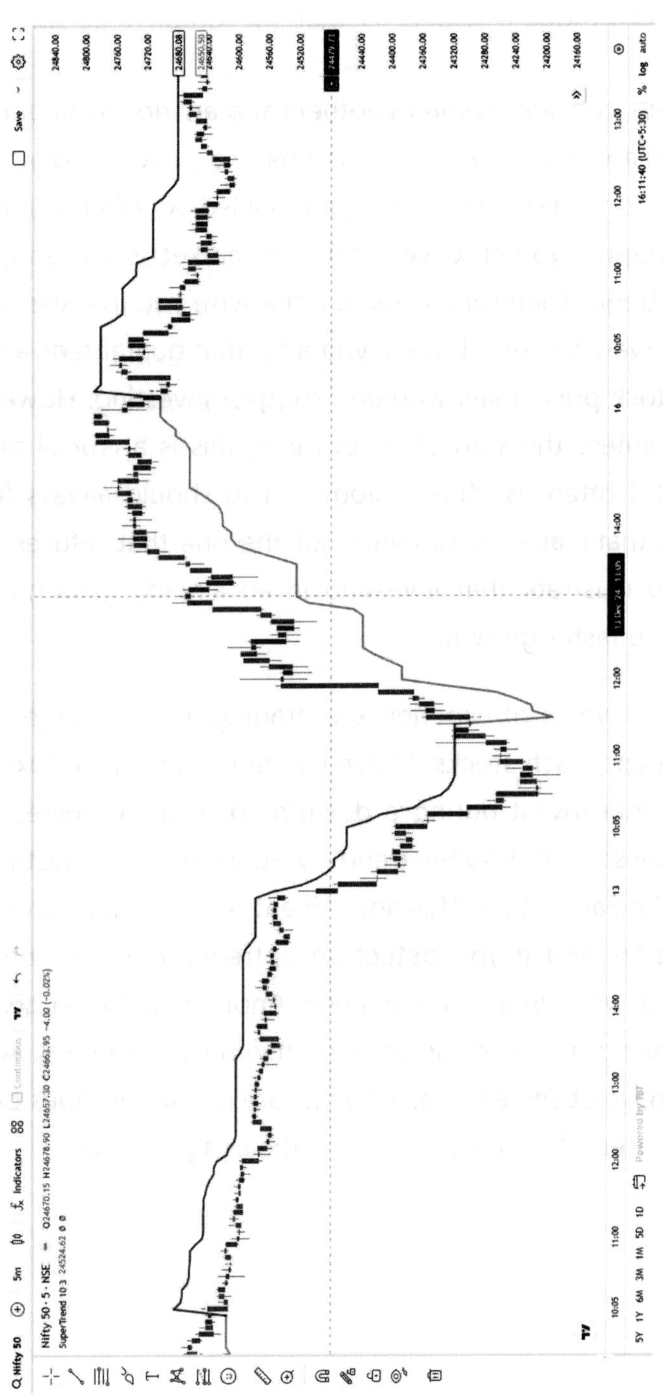
Nifty 50 · 5 · NSE
O24670.15 H24678.90 L24657.30 C24663.95 −4.00 (−0.02%)
SuperTrend 10 3 24524.62
Indicators
Save
16:11:40 (UTC+5:30)
% log auto

Let's consider some hypothetical scenarios to understand how to approach market trends. Imagine you want to purchase shares of a renowned company called X. After examining the graphs, you discover that the market is currently in a downtrend. Therefore, I would not advise you to invest at this time. Even if a friend offers you a tip that guarantees a rise in the stock price, I still wouldn't suggest investing. However, if you witness the start of an uptrend, this is a crucial time to invest. I often use the analogy - 'You should always feed a horse that's already running, not the one that refuses to do so', to illustrate that investing in an already growing stock leads to faster growth.

After years of experience in trading and investing, this is how I approach stocks. I have learned from my mistakes and no longer invest during a downtrend. You can increase the sharpness of the Super-trend by adjusting the Length to 20 and the Factor to 2. This adjustment results in a clearer trend direction, and if you detect an uptrend, you can enter the market with greater confidence. Another factor to consider in making a wise decision is examining the candles. As you may have observed, these graphs are not simply lines but are composed of candles, as seen in the image below.

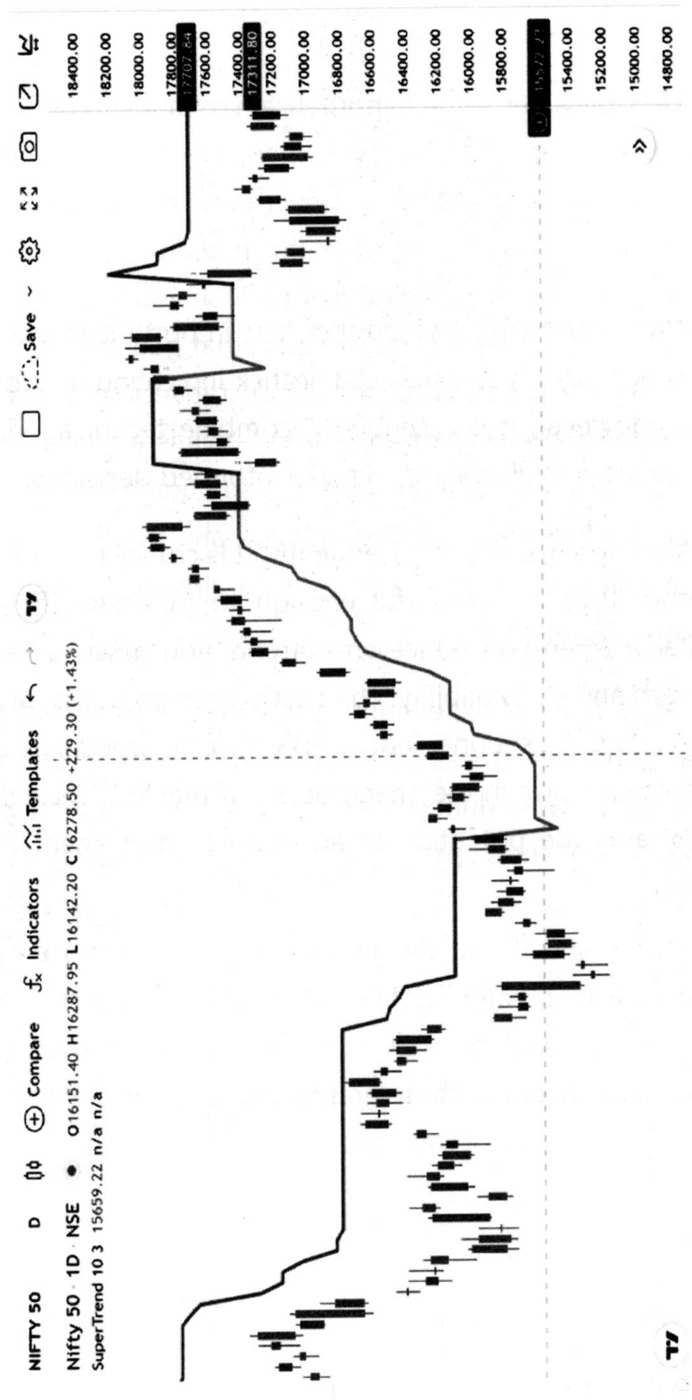
NIFTY 50
D
Compare
Indicators
Templates
Save
Nifty 50 · 1D · NSE
O16151.40 H16287.95 L16142.20 C16278.50 +229.30 (+1.43%)
SuperTrend 10 3 15659.22 n/a n/a
18400.00
18200.00
18000.00
17800.00
17707.84
17600.00
17400.00
17311.80
17200.00
17000.00
16800.00
16600.00
16400.00
16200.00
16000.00
15800.00
15400.00
15200.00
15000.00
14800.00

When observing an uptrend, it is important to consider investing only if you see a candlestick indicating a favorable trend. However, it is essential to combine technical analysis with fundamental analysis to make informed decisions.

Although waves occur frequently, it is crucial to determine whether they are powerful enough to make a difference. Similarly, when you notice an uptrend, you must assess its strength and sustainability. The best way to do this is through the Average Directional Index (ADX), which appears as a line on the waveform in the image below. If the ADX exceeds 25, it indicates the potential for an upward movement in the market.

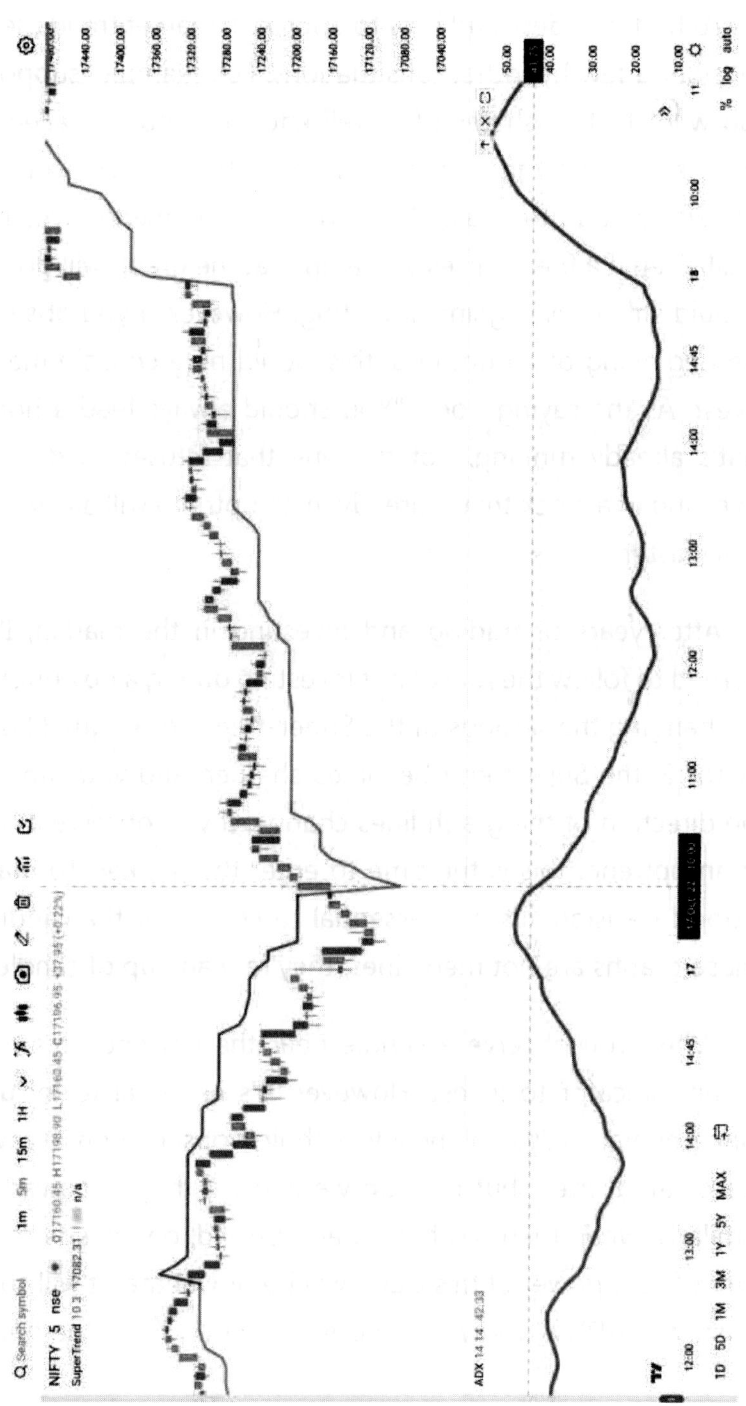
Search symbol
NIFTY 5 nse
1m 5m 15m 1H
ADX 14 14
1D 5D 1M 3M 1Y 5Y MAX
% log auto

To better understand how to approach market trends, let's consider a few hypothetical situations. For example, suppose you want to buy shares of a well-known company called X. Upon examining the graphs, you notice that it is currently in a downtrend. In this case, I would not recommend investing at all. Even if a friend gives you a tip that the graph will go up, I would still advise against investing. However, if you observe the beginning of an uptrend, this would be a crucial time to invest. As the saying goes, "You should always feed a horse that's already running, not the one that refuses to do so." Investing in a stock that's already in an uptrend will allow it to grow faster.

After years of trading and investing in the market, I've learned to follow the rule of not investing during a downtrend. By changing the settings of the Super-trend to Length 20 and Factor 2, the Supertrend becomes sharper, and you can see the direction of the graph lines change. If you observe a hint of an uptrend, this is the time to enter the market. To make a good decision, it's also essential to check out the candles. These graphs are not mere lines; they're made up of candles.

When you observe a candle near the uptrend, this may be an indicator to invest. However, it's essential to include fundamental analysis alongside technical observations. Waves are created often, but how do we know if they're powerful? Similarly, when there's a hint of an uptrend, one needs to be sure of how powerful this trend will be or whether it will soon crash. The ADX is a way to measure the strength of the trend.

If the ADX is below 25, this implies that the market will follow a sideways trend instead of making any sharp moves, and I would not recommend investing. The more the ADX improves on the scale, the more powerful the wave of the trend tends to be. Suppose you're into options trading and enter the market by observing the hint of an uptrend, but the ADX is below 25. In that case, there's a probability that the market may enter a sideways phase, making your investment prone to Theta Decay. This refers to the decrease in the value of the options you've bought as time passes on and the expiration of your options approaches.

It's important to understand that no single indicator is enough on its own, and it's always a set of reliable indicators that allows you to be sure of a certain trend. If you're eager to start trading, you can begin with paper trading or virtual trading.

Chapter 4

To Open Free Demat Account, Just Scan the QR Code

HOW TO EARN THROUGH SIP INVESTMENTS

The chapter offers a valuable lesson for long-term growth that can help you accumulate wealth and increase your earnings significantly. To begin the process, it all starts with Systematic Investment Plans (SIPs), which may sound technical and complex but are actually a straightforward concept. In this chapter, I will explain the fundamentals of SIP in detail to alleviate any confusion or concerns you may have. You may have heard stories of individuals who have made millions in the stock market, but the question remains - how did they do it? Based on my analysis, there are two methods of making money in the stock market.

1. Investing

2. Trading

For now, let's focus on investing and leave trading for the upcoming chapters. Investing is rooted in the fundamental principle of compounding. To illustrate, let's say you invest Rs.5000 in a stock that you carefully selected after conducting fundamental analysis. Assuming you made the right choice and earned a profit of Rs.5000 on your initial investment, your total value would now be Rs.10,000. Although this profit may seem insignificant in terms of creating millions, it doesn't mean that the profit of Rs.5000 is worthless. This is where the principle of compounding comes into play.

FUNDAMENTALS OF INVESTING : COMPOUNDING

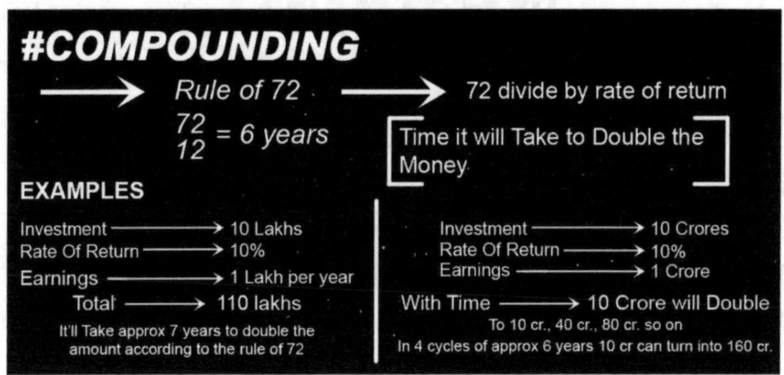

You bathe, eat, and exercise every day, following a routine that produces certain results. Now imagine if your salary was only credited once a year instead of once a month. It's safe to say that you would prefer the latter, right? The bottom line is that consistency is key. When it comes to investing, a systematic plan is essential to maintain balance, regardless of whether the market is experiencing a boom or a dip. The common belief is that investments should only be made during a market boom and caution should be exercised during a dip. However, experts like Warren Buffet advise investing in a dip to reap the benefits later. Returning to SIPs, if you invest Rs.5000 on a specific date each month for an extended period of time, this systematic plan can help you achieve the wealth you desire through the concept of compounding. My initial encounter with compounding left me awestruck, and since then, I refer to it as the financial magician. Every investor's goal should be; to make, manage it, and grow it further, wherein, the Rule of 72 plays a crucial role.

RULE OF 72

The Rule of 72 states that when you divide the integer 72 by the rate of return, you get the number of years required to double your money. This time period can be manipulated by maximizing returns. This rule assists one in understanding the power of compounding in long term. Compounding is a concept used when money is invested in an avenue over a certain period of time, that generates a specific rate of return. For example, as shown in the image above, if my capital is Rs. 10 lakhs and my rate of return is 10%, my principal amount will become Rs. 11 lakhs in a year.

However, instead of using the principle of compounding on this profit, most people spend the money they've earned as a return. The principle of compounding emphasizes that if you spend this sum, your money will never grow. Hence, it is crucial to let this invested money along with its return stay untouched, if you really wish for it to grow ten folds. Now let's assume that the initial sum was Rs. 10 crores or even Rs. 100 crores, so a 10% return will result is Rs. 1 crore and Rs. 110 crore respectively, in a year. Our primary goal is to double the money in the shortest time possible. Even if the money doubles in 3-6 years according to the Rule of 72, Rs. 10 crores will become Rs. 20 crores, 20 will become 40, 40 will become 80, and 80 will become 160. This cycle continues to multiply the money. Understanding and practicing the disciplines of compounding is the primary reason why the rich continue to grow richer every day.

BUILDING WEALTH WITH COMPOUNDING

Through the principle of compounding, an individual with a starting capital of Rs. 10 crores can grow their principal amount to Rs. 160 crores after four cycles of 6 years, totaling 24 years. However, without knowledge of compounding principle, it is impossible to achieve such significant returns. As we have already understood, making substantial profits require consistent investment over time, which can also be made in stocks and other related entities.

INDIAN VS U.S. SOCKS

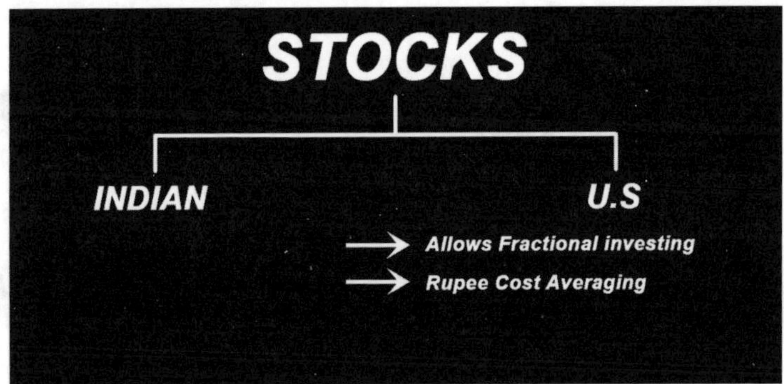

Fractional investing is a major advantage of investing in U.S. stocks. Let me illustrate this with an example: assume that a single share of MRF currently costs Rs. 80,000, which might be beyond the means of a beginner. However, with fractional investing, the buyer can purchase a portion of a share, according to what their financial set up allows. In contrast, in India, one is required to purchase the entire unit quantity of a share.

Another advantage of investing in U.S. stocks is that it allows for dollar cost averaging, in addition to rupee cost averaging that you receive while investing in stocks. For instance, if you had invested $100 at the exchange rate of Rs. 72 per dollar (=Rs. 7,200) in a share, and the share price did not change over the year but the currency conversion rate changed from Rs. 72 to Rs. 82, you would still make a profit of Rs. 1,000 due to the cost averaging.

Apart from Indian and U.S. stocks, one can also invest in mutual funds and Exchange Traded Funds (ETFs). Before we further delve into how fundamental and technical analysis as well as how SIP can lead to wealth creation, I would like to introduce you to stock market index.

STOCK MARKET INDICES

We often hear phrases like 'The market is falling' or 'the market is rising'. The word market here represents a huge segment. This segment comprises of the top performing companies. So, we keep a track on Top 50 companies of NSE

(National Stock Exchange); this top 50 index is also known as NIFTY-50. Other than that, there is another index known as SENSEX in which Top 30 companies of BSE (Bombay Stock Exchange) are listed. These two Indian indexes represent the market movement for us. In case of US Stock Exchange, their top companies are indexed in Nasdeq, S&P 500 and Dow Jones.

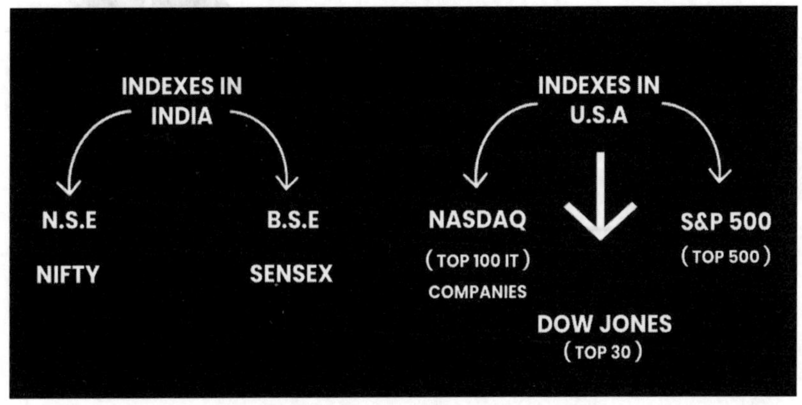

Having learned about indexing, let's apply this concept to our main question: how can SIPs be used to generate crores? The NIFTY has been yielding an average of 15% ROI over the years, and it is expected to continue growing at a similar rate. By using an SIP calculator and considering different combinations of investment amount and years, you can get a fair idea of how to reach your principal goal through monthly SIP contributions. let's assume you want to invest Rs. 5000 a month in a stock SIP. By remaining consistent with this investment and applying the principles we discussed earlier, the magic of compounding can begin. Over a period of 22 years, at a 15% ROI, this investment will generate a wealth gain of approx Rs. 90.3 lakhs, totaling to almost 1 crore with a paid amount of just 13.2 lakhs!

SIP Calculator

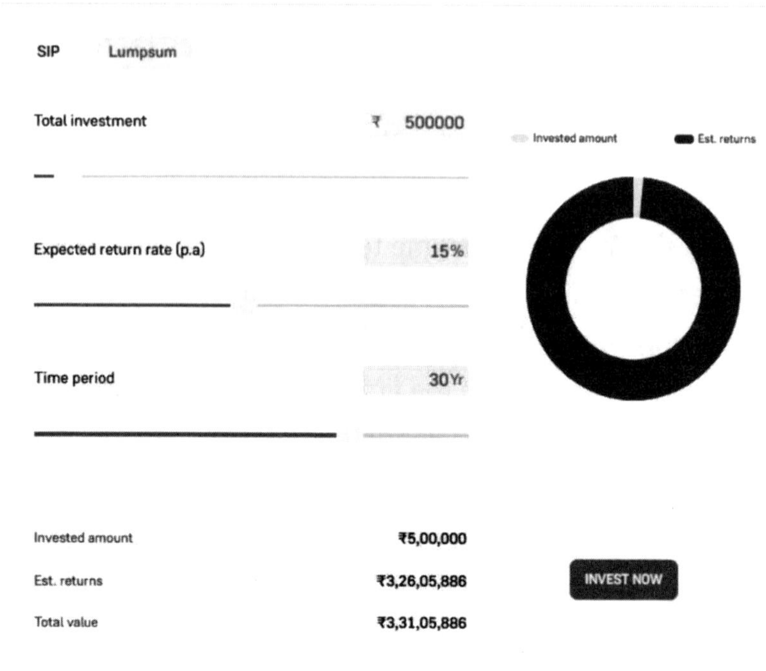

Compounding is so powerful that if an investor starts his SIP of Rs. 20000 a month and then even forgets about it for some 100 years, the final amount over that period can reach to mind boggling amount of Rs. 480000 crores.

This surely sounds hard to believe, so go on, try out the SIP calculator yourself, I'm sure you'll be amazed!

BENEFITS OF SIP

- Beats market volatility - consistency and compounding balance highs and lows of market prices, bringing the sum game that beats market volatility.

- Helps beginners to understand investment and to get familiar with the market.
- Long term game - SIPs are not meant for short term gains, this is about envisioning and broadening your horizons.

Irrespective of where you stand in your professional journey and how much you can save, I strongly recommend allocating 10% of your income towards investments. This may not seem like a significant amount, even if it's just Rs. 500, but in the long run, it has the potential to generate substantial wealth. I urge you to take the first step and allow the power of compounding to work its wonders.

Chapter 5

To Open Free Demat Account, Just Scan the QR Code

MUTUAL FUNDS INVESTMENT

Investing in mutual funds is a commonly recommended piece of advice. Whether it be through TV advertisements or advice from family members, it seems everyone is advocating for mutual funds. But what exactly are they?

When you invest in shares, you select a specific company's shares to purchase. You analyze the company's suitability, market movements, and then proceed to buy their shares. Mutual funds, on the other hand, take this a step further than investing in a single company's shares. With mutual funds, you can use your funds to invest in shares of various companies without requiring knowledge of their active management or risk-reward ratio.

How is this possible?

This is where Asset Management Companies (AMCs) come in. But before delving into AMCs, it's important to understand some background information.

MUTUAL FUNDS

Mutual funds are a type of investment vehicle that pools

funds from individual investors to invest in a diversified portfolio of assets, such as stocks and bonds. These funds are managed by Asset Management Companies (AMCs). When an investor purchases shares in a mutual fund, they entrust the management of their investment to the AMC. The AMC is responsible for selecting and managing a diversified portfolio of securities with the aim of achieving the fund's investment objective.

The idea behind mutual funds is that by pooling your funds with other investors, you can gain access to a wider range of investments than you could on your own. This approach also provides the benefits of professional management and diversification without requiring individual investors to conduct their own research or management.

AMCS AND MUTUAL FUNDS

Understanding how AMCs make money is crucial to fully grasp the workings of mutual funds. Before focusing on potential profits, it's important to comprehend the revenue streams of AMCs. These companies are managed by individuals with significant expertise in their respective fields. AMCs generate income when an investor places their funds with them, primarily through two fees: expense ratio and exit load. Let's first discuss the expense ratio.

The expense ratio is a fee charged by the AMC to manage the mutual fund. This fee covers various costs associated with managing the fund, such as the salaries of the fund managers, research and analysis, administrative expenses, and marketing costs. Typically, the expense ratiocan range from 0% to 2%. For instance, if an investor parks Rs. 1 lakhand the AMC charges a 2% commission, this means the company earns a profit of 2000 rupees. Since an AMC's customer base is not limited to just one investor, their profits can quickly add up.

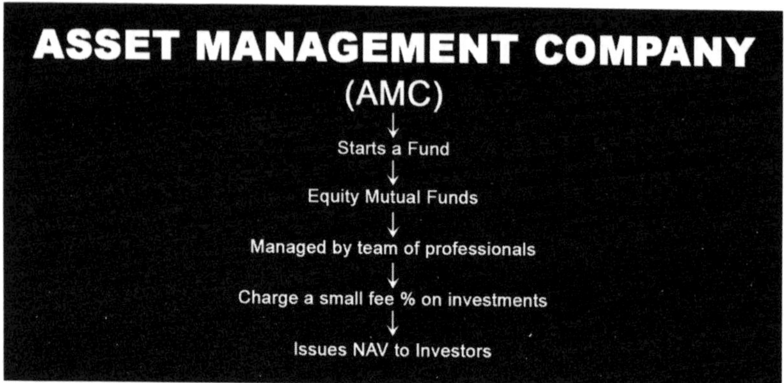

The expertise of fund managers, the security of calculated investments, and the convenience of passive management have contributed to the popularity of mutual funds. Investment diversification is achieved through various means, including debt funds, equity funds, and hybrid funds.

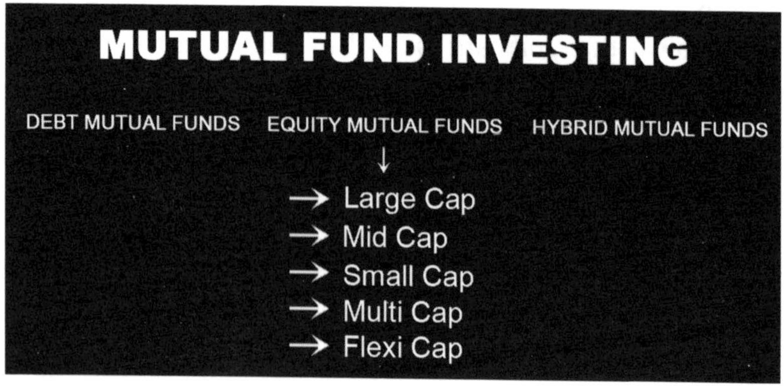

TYPES OF MUTUAL FUNDS-

Debt funds are investment vehicles that mainly invest in fixed income securities, such as bonds, treasury bills, and commercial papers issued by governments or companies. They are suitable for investors seeking a steady stream of income and diversification of their portfolio without taking on excessive risk. Debt funds offer exposure to various fixed income securities and provide a range of investment strategies, including short-term, medium-term, or long-term bonds, based on the fund's investment objectives.

Equity funds on the other hand, primarily invest in equity stocks. These funds can be further classified based on their management approach as either active or passive. Passive management is commonly used for funds like ETFs and Index funds.

Hybrid funds are often assumed to be investment portfolios that combine multiple types of investments, typically stocks and bonds. However, the hybrid structure is based on arbitrage. Arbitrage is the difference in stock prices between the NSE and BSE. Investing heavily in these differences can lead to significant returns.

IPO, NFO & NAV

An IPO, or Initial Public Offering, is when a private company offers its shares to the public for the first time. Conversely, an NFO, or New Fund Offering is when a mutual fund offers its units to the public for the first time. Some people advocate for NFOs because they offer the chance to invest in a new and promising fund at a lower cost. However, NFOs can also be risky for investors, as there is no track record of the fund's performance and it may take time for the fund to build a portfolio of securities. It's important to note that while an IPO is a one-time event, an NFO is a continuous process, as mutual funds take time to grow and reflect their actual performance. Therefore, investing in NFOs may not be a wise decision.

THE SOLUTION TO THIS PROBLEM IS NAVS!

NAV or Net Asset Value is a crucial parameter used by investors to assess the performance of a mutual fund. When you invest your money in a mutual fund managed by an AMC, the AMC invests it in a portfolio of company shares and in return, you receive financial units known as NAVs. NAVs reflect the performance of the underlying stocks over a period of time, making it a comprehensive indicator of investment performance.

TYPES OF EQUITY FUNDS:

LARGE CAP FUNDS

In the previous sections, we discussed the companies listed on NSE and BSE. The companies with the largest market capitalization are included in NSE's top 50 and BSE's top 30. This concept is applied to Large Cap mutual funds as well, which invest in companies with the largest market cap. Therefore, these funds mainly invest in well-established companies in the stock market. These companies are generally well-known, such as Apple, Google, or Microsoft. By investing in large cap mutual funds, investors can potentially benefit from the stability and profitability of these large companies, which may be less volatile than smaller, newer companies. Large cap mutual funds are suitable for investors who are seeking a more conservative investment strategy and looking to diversify their portfolio with safety and security.

MID CAP FUNDS

Mid cap mutual funds invest primarily in companies with medium-sized market capitalization. These companies are often in a growth phase and have the potential for expansion and higher earnings. However, they may be more volatile than large-cap companies.

SMALL CAP FUNDS

Small cap mutual funds invest primarily in small-cap companies, which are more vulnerable to changes in economic and market conditions. These companies may also have limited access to capital, making it challenging for them to sustain growth or withstand downturns in the market.

MULTI CAP FUNDS

Multi cap mutual funds are investment funds that invest in companies with different market capitalization, including large-cap, mid-cap, and small-cap. The objective of these funds is to offer diversification across various market segments, which may provide a balance of growth potential and stability. As a result, multi cap mutual funds can be a suitable investment option for those who wish to gain exposure to a wide range of companies and market capitalization through a single investment.

FLEXI CAP FUNDS

Flexi Cap mutual funds are investment funds that provide investors with the potential to benefit from a wide range of companies and market capitalizations, based on the fund manager's perception. These funds can offer diversification benefits and the potential for higher returns, depending on the fund's composition. Flexi Cap mutual funds can be an attractive choice for investors seeking the flexibility to invest in companies with different market capitalization and who wish to take advantage of the fund manager's expertise in making investment decisions.

Lets go over an example that is well-received by many. There is a comparison between certain animals and the different types of cap funds. A large market cap fund is likened to an elephant, which moves slowly but steadily with a sense of safety and security. A mid cap fund is compared to a camel, which can run faster than an elephant and potentially yield higher returns with slightly increased risk. A small cap fund is compared to horses and donkeys, which can run the fastest among the three but carry a higher risk value. In my opinion, investing solely in large cap funds is not necessary unless the expense ratio is very low. Instead, there is a better option for cumulative benefit of the three types of cap funds, which I will discuss in later sections.

In order to comprehend the fluctuations of these stocks, you can make use of a screener or any other online platform, which can aid you in applying the information in a practical manner. The platforms can provide examples of companies and Asset Management Companies (AMCs) that offer mutual funds in various categories. Additionally, it lists important factors such as exit loads, expense ratios, and Compound Annual Growth Rates (CAGRs).

There are three main factors to calculate the profitability of investing in mutual funds. These are expense ratio, CAGR and exit load. Both of these are forms of commissions as discussed above.

Exit load is a fee that mutual funds or other investment funds may charge investors who sell their shares before the completion of their investment term. It is also referred to as an exit fee or redemption fee. The purpose of this charge is to discourage early exits from mutual fund investments. For instance, if you decide to pull out your investment of Rs. 25,000 after making a certain profit, you may be charged an exit load of 1%, which means Rs. 250 will be deducted from the capital sum. Exit loads typically range from 1% to 4%.

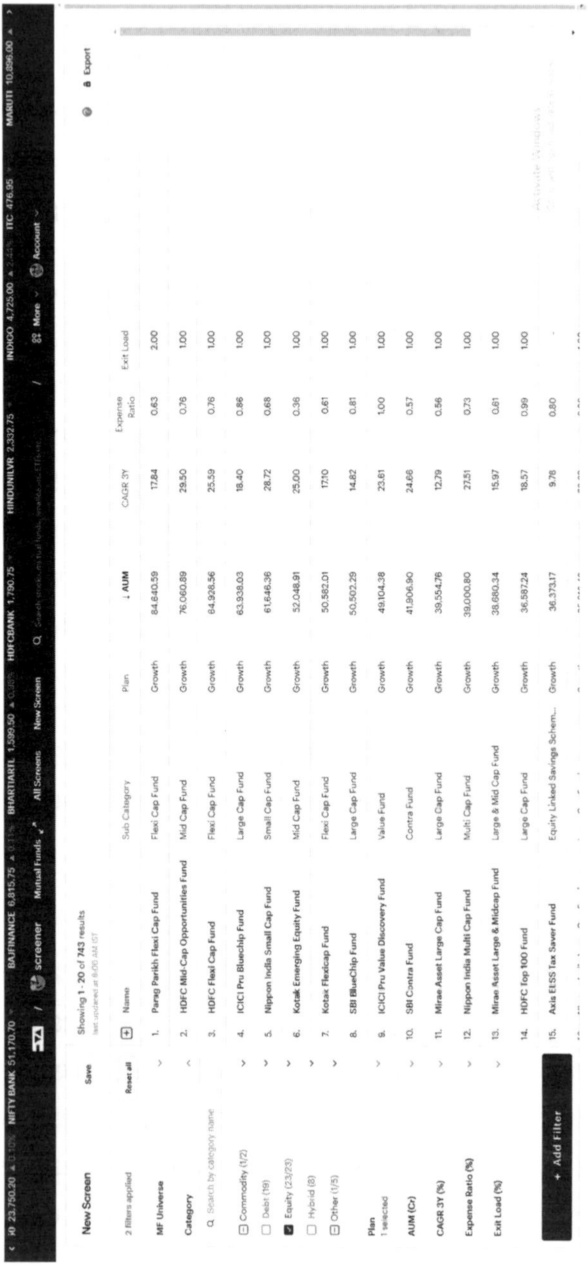

New Screen

Showing 1 - 20 of 743 results

	Name	Sub Category	Plan	↓ AUM	CAGR 3Y	Expense Ratio	Exit Load
1.	Parag Parikh Flexi Cap Fund	Flexi Cap Fund	Growth	84,640.59	17.84	0.63	2.00
2.	HDFC Mid-Cap Opportunities Fund	Mid Cap Fund	Growth	76,060.89	29.50	0.76	1.00
3.	HDFC Flexi Cap Fund	Flexi Cap Fund	Growth	64,928.56	25.59	0.76	1.00
4.	ICICI Pru Bluechip Fund	Large Cap Fund	Growth	63,938.03	18.40	0.86	1.00
5.	Nippon India Small Cap Fund	Small Cap Fund	Growth	61,646.36	28.72	0.68	1.00
6.	Kotak Emerging Equity Fund	Mid Cap Fund	Growth	52,048.91	25.00	0.36	1.00
7.	Kotak Flexicap Fund	Flexi Cap Fund	Growth	50,582.01	17.10	0.61	1.00
8.	SBI BlueChip Fund	Large Cap Fund	Growth	50,502.29	14.82	0.81	1.00
9.	ICICI Pru Value Discovery Fund	Value Fund	Growth	49,104.38	23.61	1.00	1.00
10.	SBI Contra Fund	Contra Fund	Growth	41,906.90	24.66	0.57	1.00
11.	Mirae Asset Large Cap Fund	Large Cap Fund	Growth	39,554.76	12.79	0.56	1.00
12.	Nippon India Multi Cap Fund	Multi Cap Fund	Growth	39,000.80	27.51	0.73	1.00
13.	Mirae Asset Large & Midcap Fund	Large & Mid Cap Fund	Growth	38,680.34	15.97	0.61	1.00
14.	HDFC Top 100 Fund	Large Cap Fund	Growth	36,587.24	18.57	0.99	1.00
15.	Axis ELSS Tax Saver Fund	Equity Linked Savings Schem...	Growth	36,373.17	9.78	0.80	-

We have covered many aspects related to mutual funds so far, lets delve deeper for better understanding!

Step 1) Open a screener software.

Step 2) Try different categories of funds, eg. equity, debt, commodities.

Step 3) Trace specific companies and their markers.

If we take the example of Kotak Equity Opp Fund, we can analyze its CAGR (Compound Annual Growth Rate) which measures the rate of return of an investment over a specific period of time, usually several years. Typically, a higher CAGR is preferable as it indicates a higher rate of return on investment over time. However, a high CAGR may also come with higher risk and volatility. Therefore, it's important to evaluate the investment's historical performance, risk level, and market conditions to determine whether a particular CAGR is considered good or not.

We can also add filters to check for exit load.

When monitoring exit loads, it is noticeable that some companies provide low exit loads, but their expense ratios are comparatively higher. For instance, SBI Large & Midcap Fund imposes an exit load of 0.10 and an expense ratio of 1.09, which compensates for each other. However, Bank of India Risk Fund charges an exit load of 4.00 and an expense ratio of 1.28. That is why it is crucial to examine the indicators before making investments.

I am elaborating these concepts in detail because I believe it's important for you to take ownership of your investments and not solely rely on third parties to make decisions on your behalf.

HERE ARE SOME IMPORTANT QUESTIONS TO ASK YOURSELF BEFORE INVESTING IN A MUTUAL FUND:

What is your investment time horizon? The time frame of your investment is crucial, as time is a fundamental aspect of compounding. It can make or break your investment. Even if a person has no knowledge of mutual funds or investing, investing in any random fund for a longer period of time can still yield a profit. The lesson to learn from this is the value of time. While debt funds can make money in the short run, if your investment time horizon is less than 2 years, you should consider debt funds. Otherwise, equity should be your choice.

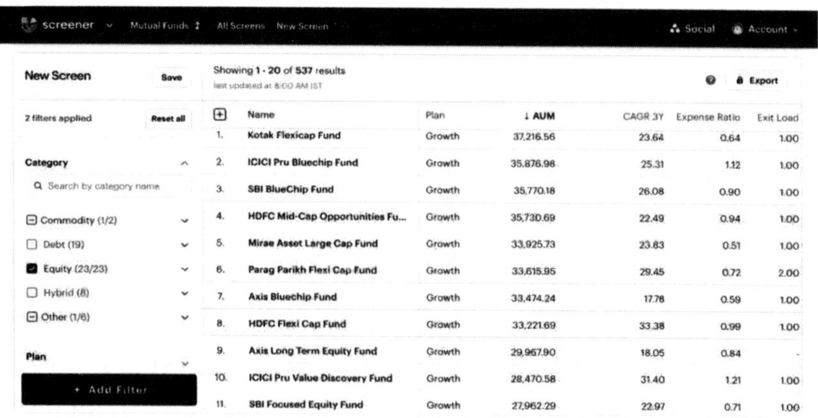

	Name	Plan	↓ AUM	CAGR 3Y	Expense Ratio	Exit Load
1.	Kotak Flexicap Fund	Growth	37,216.56	23.64	0.64	1.00
2.	ICICI Pru Bluechip Fund	Growth	35,876.98	25.31	1.12	1.00
3.	SBI BlueChip Fund	Growth	35,770.18	26.08	0.90	1.00
4.	HDFC Mid-Cap Opportunities Fu...	Growth	35,730.69	22.49	0.94	1.00
5.	Mirae Asset Large Cap Fund	Growth	33,925.73	23.83	0.51	1.00
6.	Parag Parikh Flexi Cap Fund	Growth	33,615.95	29.45	0.72	2.00
7.	Axis Bluechip Fund	Growth	33,474.24	17.78	0.59	1.00
8.	HDFC Flexi Cap Fund	Growth	33,221.69	33.38	0.99	1.00
9.	Axis Long Term Equity Fund	Growth	29,967.90	18.05	0.84	-
10.	ICICI Pru Value Discovery Fund	Growth	28,470.58	31.40	1.21	1.00
11.	SBI Focused Equity Fund	Growth	27,962.29	22.97	0.71	1.00

RETURN

One way to determine the yield on your investment is

to calculate the CAGR. Using any online platform, you can compare different markers and track these funds before making an investment decision.

RISK

The amount of risk you can take in your investments depends on how much time you have. Risk and time have an inverse relationship. If your time horizon is more than five years, you can consider taking calculated risks and invest in small, multi, and flexi cap mutual funds. On the other hand, if your time horizon is less than five years, large cap and mid cap mutual funds may be better suited for you.

For instance, the Kota flexicap fund is a flexi fund that can generate short-term profits. In the past 3 years, it has given a CAGR of 13.76, and in the past 5 years, it has given a CAGR of 7.61.

Likewise, if you consider the Quant Flexi Fund, you will observe that it has yielded returns of 38.50% in 3 years and 19.00% in 5 years. Additionally, you can also verify its expense ratio and exit load.

MANAGEMENT

Mutual funds can be classified into two types based on their management - active and passive. Active funds are managed by experts and come with a higher expense ratio. These funds aim to make profits by investing in profitable companies of the present or future through calculated investment decisions made by the fund manager.

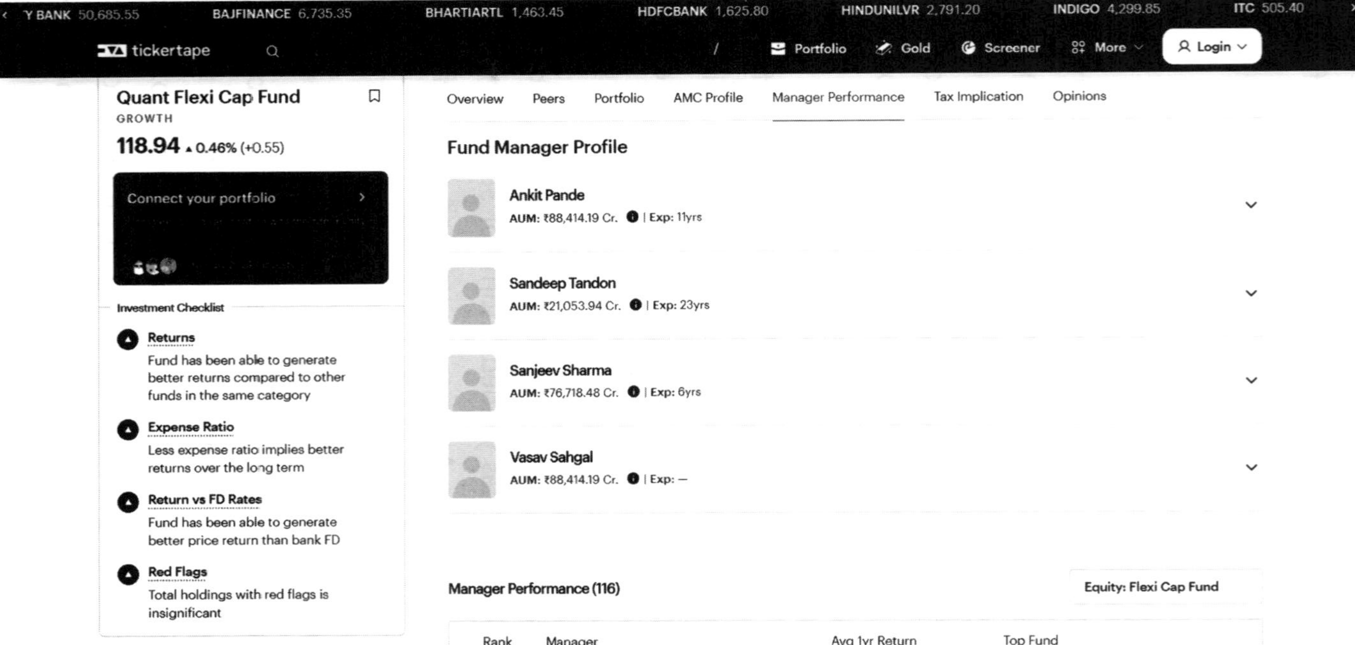
Y BANK 50,685.55
BAJFINANCE 6,735.35
BHARTIARTL 1,463.45
HDFCBANK 1,625.80
HINDUNILVR 2,791.20
INDIGO 4,299.85
ITC 505.40
tickertape
Portfolio
Gold
Screener
More
Login
Quant Flexi Cap Fund
GROWTH
118.94 ▲ 0.46% (+0.55)
Connect your portfolio
Investment Checklist
Returns
Fund has been able to generate better returns compared to other funds in the same category
Expense Ratio
Less expense ratio implies better returns over the long term
Return vs FD Rates
Fund has been able to generate better price return than bank FD
Red Flags
Total holdings with red flags is insignificant
Overview
Peers
Portfolio
AMC Profile
Manager Performance
Tax Implication
Opinions
Fund Manager Profile
Ankit Pande
AUM: ₹88,414.19 Cr. | Exp: 11yrs
Sandeep Tandon
AUM: ₹21,053.94 Cr. | Exp: 23yrs
Sanjeev Sharma
AUM: ₹76,718.48 Cr. | Exp: 6yrs
Vasav Sahgal
AUM: ₹88,414.19 Cr. | Exp: –
Manager Performance (116)
Equity: Flexi Cap Fund
Rank
Manager
Avg 1yr Return
Top Fund

Passive funds, on the other hand, do not require active management and track a specific stock index. Index funds are an example of passive funds that aim to replicate the performance of stock indexes. In 2007, Warren Buffett famously bet that the S&P 500 index would outperform a portfolio of hedge funds over a 10-year period. When the bet ended in 2017, it was clear that Buffett had won. The S&P 500 index generated a total return of 125.8%, while the five hedge funds selected by Protégé had an average return of only 36% over the same period. Buffett has always recommended investing in low-cost index funds, and the bet proved the effectiveness of this strategy.

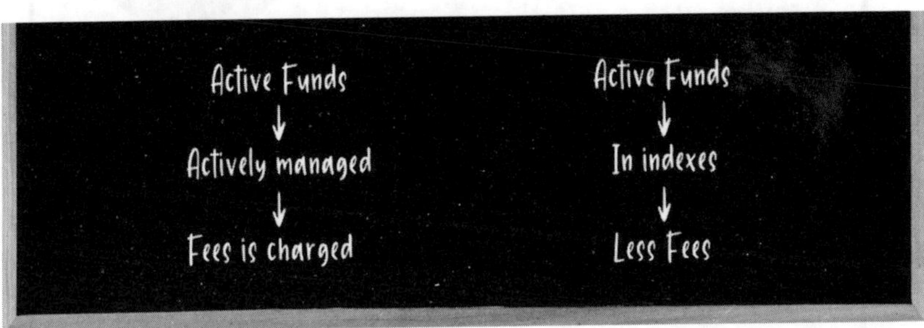

My personal recommendation is to invest in index funds instead of large cap securities, as index funds invest your money in top companies with a lower expense ratio. Additionally, it's important to check for markers such as fund managers and to conduct peer comparisons.

SIP VS LUMP SUM

Lump sum investment strategy involves investing a large amount of money in one go, while SIP (Systematic Investment Plan) involves investing a fixed amount at regular intervals over a period of time. Lump sum investment can be advantageous when you want to take advantage of potential market gains that are expected in a bearish market.

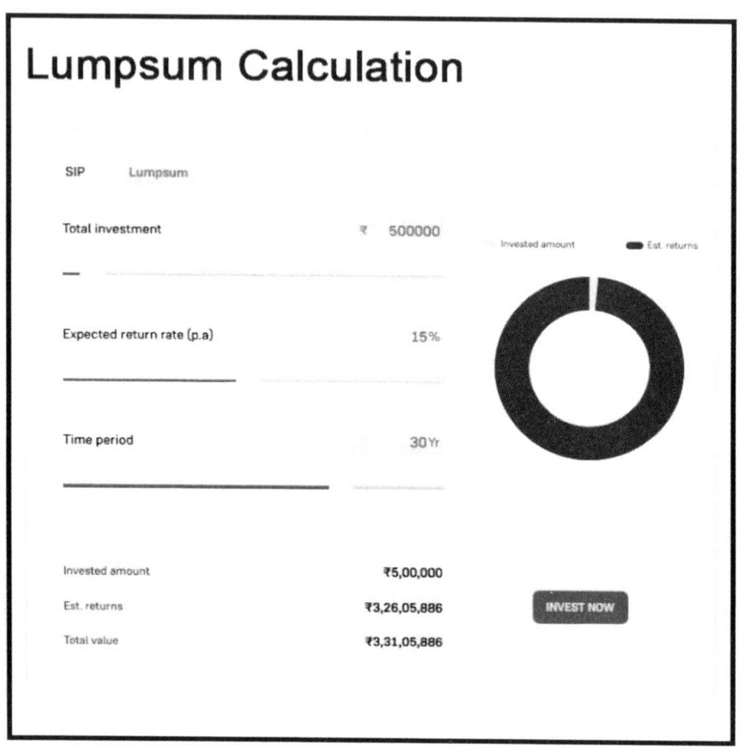

Suppose someone invested Rs. 5 lakh in the stock market and left it there for thirty years. In that period, at a return on investment (ROI) of 15%, the initial investment would grow to over Rs. 3 crores.

S.I.P
VS
LUMP SUM
PROTECTED FROM VOLATILITY
WHEN MARKET IS EXTREMELY DOWN
IN 5 YEARS

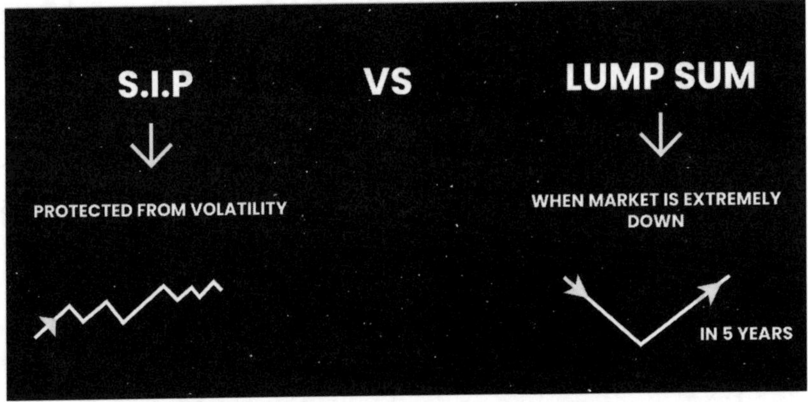

SIP Calculator

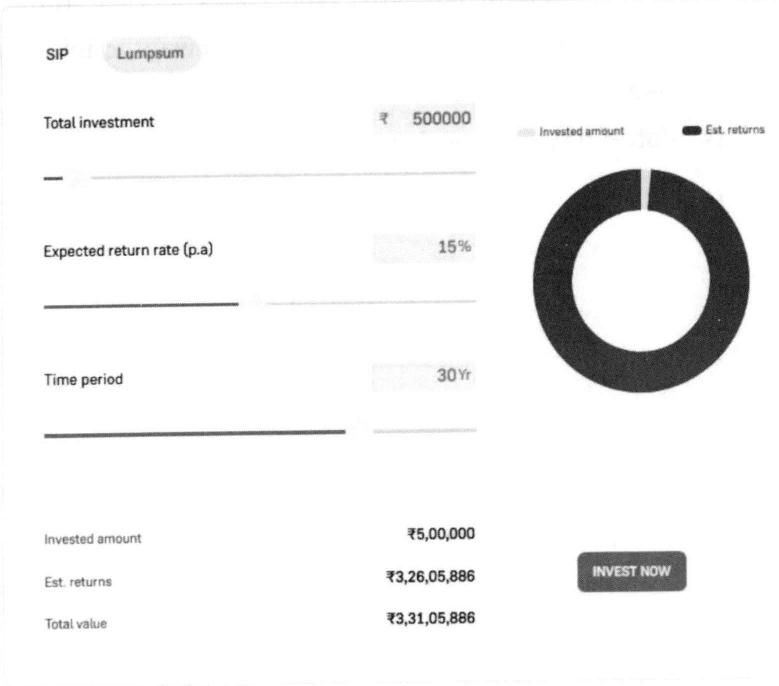

SIP
Lumpsum
Total investment
₹ 500000
Expected return rate (p.a)
15%
Time period
30 Yr
Invested amount
Est. returns
Invested amount
₹5,00,000
Est. returns
₹3,26,05,886
Total value
₹3,31,05,886
INVEST NOW

If you increase the ROI by just 1%, the total amount will become more than Rs. 4 crores, and this is the magic of compounding at work in lump sum investments as well.

If you have a steady monthly income, you can begin investing with any amount you desire, be it big or small. Just choose the appropriate mutual fund and management type, set a time frame, and let the numbers work in your favor. Remember, the earlier you start investing, the more profits you can make, and the longer you delay, the more you lose out on potential gains.

HOW CAN YOU INVEST IN A MUTUAL FUND?

Investing in mutual funds can be done through a demat account, once you have opened a demat account using any of the various trading platforms, you can select the mutual fund option and choose the type of fund you want to invest in. Using these platforms, you can easily track markers and price charts related to your investment too.

Chapter 6

To Open Free Demat Account, Just Scan the QR Code

ETF INVESTMENT STRATEGY

Believe it or not, this strategy only requires one minute of your time each day. If you're willing to dedicate one minute per day, you can earn profits. Although it may seem implausible, this simple strategy can work wonders for you. However, please note that this strategy is only applicable to ETF investments and not to stocks.

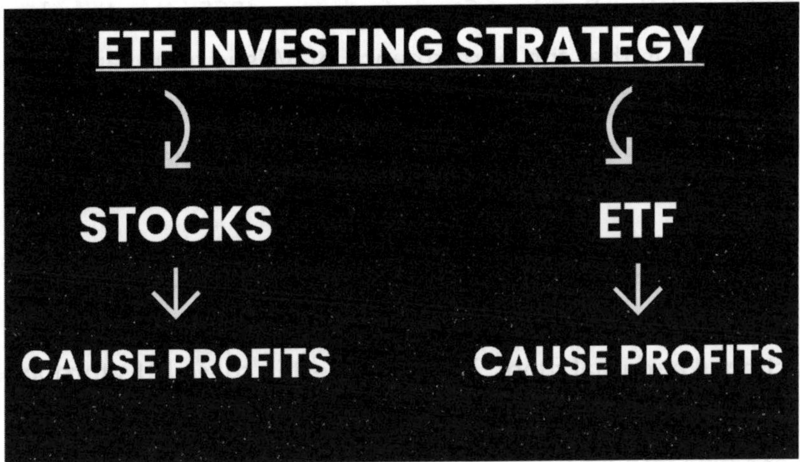

We previously discussed stock investing and fundamental analysis, as well as mutual funds. In addition to these categories, there is another type of fund known as ETFs or Exchange-Traded Funds.

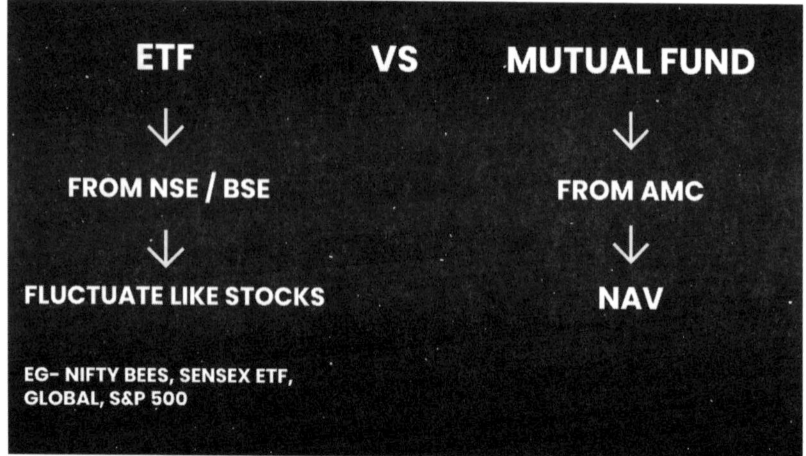

There are several differences between MFs and ETFs, the primary one being that mutual funds are purchased from an Asset Management Company (AMC), whereas ETFs are traded on Exchange platforms like the National Stock Exchange (NSE) and the Bombay Stock Exchange (BSE). Another key difference is that the performance of MFs is represented by Net Asset Value (NAV), which remains constant throughout the day, while the value of ETFs fluctuates in a manner similar to stocks.

Therefore, investing in ETFs can be described as 'stock investing of mutual funds,' functioning like stock investing but acting like mutual funds. You can invest in these ETFs through your demat account, similar to how you invest in other stocks. Let's dive into how you can do so!

An example of a popular ETF is Nifty Bees, which stands for Benchmark Exchange Traded Scheme. Lets breakdown what it means!

When we talk about benchmarks, we typically think of Nifty and Sensex. Nifty is an index of the top 50 companies on the National Stock Exchange (NSE), while Sensex represents the top 30 companies on the Bombay Stock Exchange (BSE). While you cannot directly invest in Nifty or Sensex, you can invest in mutual funds that track these indices, also known as Index Points. Alternatively, you can buy ETFs that track these indices.

When you invest in an ETF, it will appear in your Demat account. The profits will appear when the index (e.g., Nifty or S&P-500) goes up. It's worth noting that ETFs aren't limited to Nifty and Sensex; there are also ETFs for gold and the S&P-500, which is an index of the top 500 companies in the US. No matter where you live, you can invest in these foreign indices through mutual funds or ETFs.

Unlike India, fractional investing is allowed in the US market, which means that even if you have a small amount of money, you can still invest in stocks and ETFs. For instance, if one ETF costs $380, but you only have the capacity to invest Rs. 500, you can still invest that amount. Another reason why investing in US ETFs is beneficial is the appreciation of the dollar.

In recent years, we have seen a significant difference in the value of the Rupee compared to the Dollar, with the dollar's value increasing from Rs. 75 to Rs. 83 in a short period of time. By investing in US ETFs, you not only benefit from ETF appreciation but also take advantage of the difference in currency values when you invest in entities like S&P-500 or

Nasdaq. Additionally, investing in these ETFs offers portfolio diversification benefits.

ADVANTAGES OF INVESTING IN ETF

- Diversification is a key benefit of investing in ETFs. When we invest in a single stock, we run the risk of it losing all its value. However, ETFs are comprised of multiple stocks, which reduces the risk of any one stock plummeting to zero. Even if the value of one or more stocks in the ETF declines, the value of all the stocks combined will not fall to zero. This makes investing in ETFs like Nifty and Sensex much less risky than investing in individual stocks.

- ETFs are professionally managed by experts, just like stocks. The funds are issued by companies that are traded on the exchange, which means that investors benefit from professional management.

- When compared to mutual funds, ETFs have significantly lower costs associated with them. Mutual funds tend to charge fees that can eat into the profits of an investor, while ETFs have comparatively lower costs

- Before delving into any investment strategy, it's important to understand some general principles. The first and foremost principle is to invest at least 10% of your income. As time passes, your investments should surpass your expenses. It's important to allocate a small fraction of your money towards your personal expenses and spend the rest of it in investing as much as possible.

THE ETF STRATEGY

Assuming you earn Rs. 50,000 per month, allocating 10% of your income would amount to Rs. 5,000. As the stock market is closed on weekends, you could utilize the weekdays to engage in fractional investing, investing Rs. 250 each day in the chosen index (such as Nifty, Sensex, S&P-500, etc). To check whether there has been a decline or increase in the index, you can easily check through your demat account or Google in less than a minute. In case of a decline, that would be the entry window for investing, as per the strategy. However, the rule to be followed is to invest only when the index has declined. For instance, if you invested Rs. 250 on Day 1 upon observing a decline, but the market was up on Day 2, you would refrain from investing. On Day 3, if the index declines, you could invest the leftover Rs. 250 from Day 2 and the Rs. 250 intended for Day 3 together.

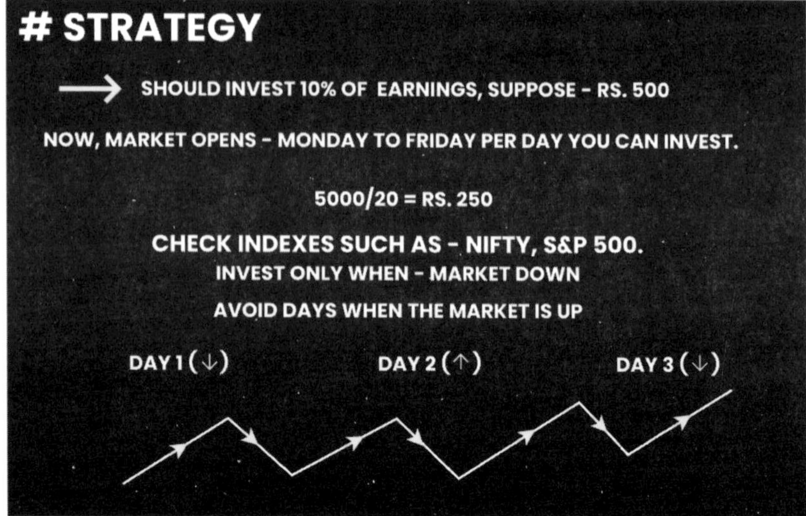

Assuming the index did not decline until the 8th day, you would have invested Rs. 250 each day by then. The logic behind this strategy is to invest a fraction of your income in a disciplined manner, with the aim of generating long- term returns. By investing in dips or declines, you could potentially benefit from market volatility, and with time, your investments could surpass your expenditures. It is important to remember to invest a portion of your income regularly and spend within your means.

In this strategy, you invest a particular amount every time the index goes negative, while refraining from investing on the days when the market rallies. It's better to invest in an index instead of a single company because the top companies in the index are bound to grow, and the chances of incurring a heavy loss are almost zero. For example, if you are willing to invest Rs. 2500 per day, and the market rallies for 10 days, you pool your Rs. 25,000 together and invest it all at once on the day of decline. As the market catches its pace, you can see profits in your portfolio. It's important to note that investing is a long game and such strategies can reward you with amazing returns.

Having learned about various aspects of the stock market such as types of analysis, funds, and when and how to invest and trade, if you continue to follow a disciplined approach, it will be hard to stop you from achieving your investment goals.

Chapter 7

To Open Free Demat Account, Just Scan the QR Code

SUPPORT AND RESISTANCE TRADING IN THE STOCK MARKET

By the end of this chapter, you will have a comprehensive understanding of support and resistance, and be able to guide others as well. In the most basic sense, support refers to the zones or levels where buyers are willing to purchase an asset, leading to an increase in demand and subsequently driving the price upwards. For instance, if the price of gold drops from Rs. 50,000 to Rs. 25,000 in a single day, there will likely be a surge in potential buyers looking to purchase gold, resulting in an increase in demand and a decrease in supply. As a result, the price of gold will begin to rise, with the particular zone where buyers are willing to buy acting as a support mechanism that determines the future price trend. As prices continue to rise, buyers will start to book profits and sell their assets. For example, if the price of gold rises to Rs. 70,000, sellers will come into the market, increasing the supply of gold and decreasing the demand, resulting in a price drop. This phase is known as the "resistance phase" since buyers are hesitant to buy while sellers are eager to sell. In order to attract buyers, the prices will have to decrease.

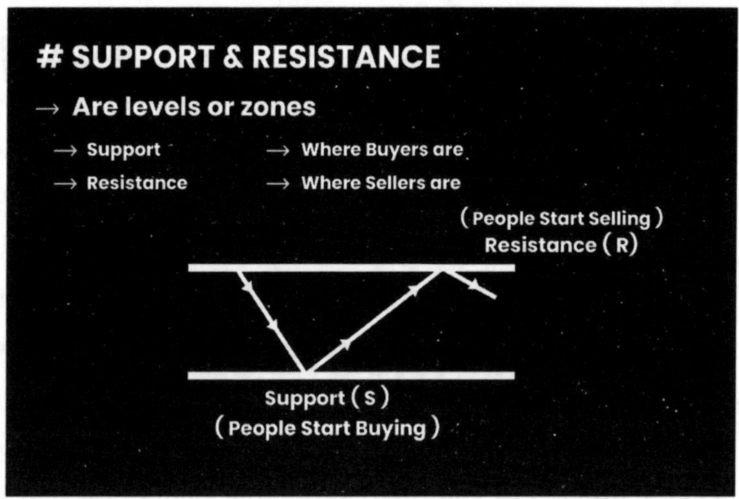

To further understand this phenomenon, let's consider a scenario where everyone in a particular area is looking to sell their property. You and your neighbor both own a property worth Rs. 1 crore each and want to sell. You put your property on the market for Rs. 1 crore, while your neighbor offers the same property for only Rs. 80 lakhs. As soon as potential buyers learn of the lower price, they will be inclined to purchase your neighbor's property instead. Consequently, you may decide to sell your property at a lower price as well, and other sellers in the area may follow suit. This resistance to a further rise in price will lead to a continuous decline in prices.

The Support and Resistance phenomenon is applicable in almost all markets including the stock market. To understand this phenomenon in detail, let's delve deeper into it.

When does the price break through the resistance? This occurs when the price reaches a level low enough to attract buyers. As the number of buyers increases, sellers regain the power to increase the price. In the earlier example, the price of gold hits Rs. 70,000 and then dipped, leading sellers to sell at lower prices. However, if buyers continued to buy at Rs. 70,000, the price would have broken through that level of resistance and kept increasing to Rs. 80,000. But once the price hits a ceiling of Rs. 80,000, buyers back off due to the high price, and sellers start selling at lower prices to attract them. Thus, the price starts declining again, resisting any increase due to the lack of buyers. As the prices fall, they reach a zone of support where buyers are willing to purchase the gold. Suppose the sellers are looking to exit the market and willing to sell at any price. Hence, the price falls further to another level of support, where buyers come in again, trying to increase the price. To put it simply, resistance is a period when sellers decline to raise the price because they want to sell, whereas support is a stage where buyers rush to purchase a particular stock, prompting sellers to eventually increase the price.

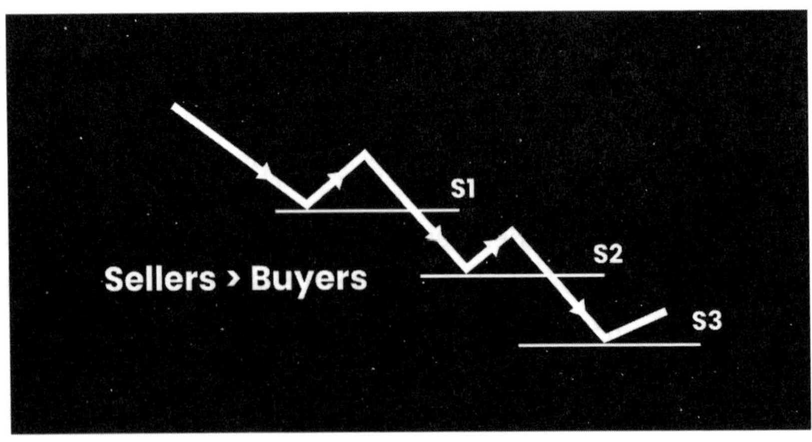

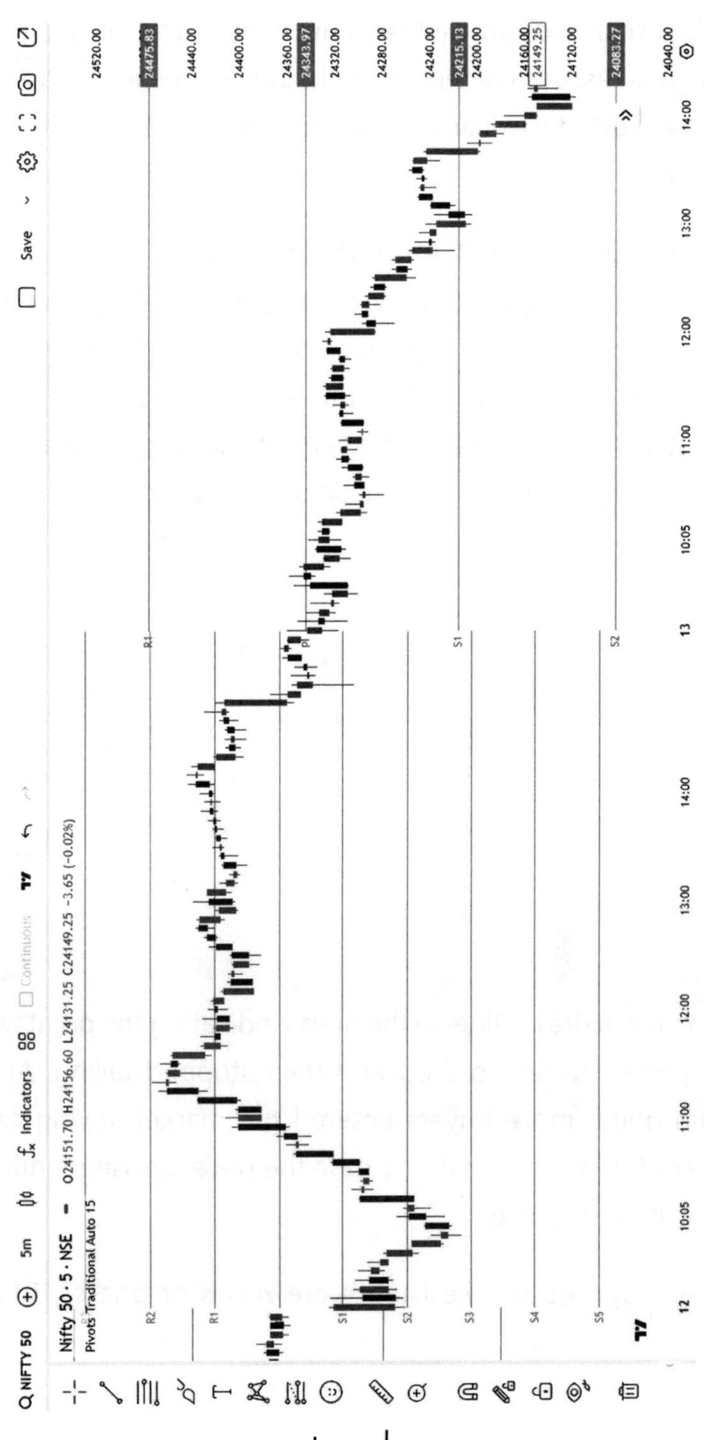
NIFTY 50
5m
Indicators
Save
Nifty 50 · 5 · NSE
O24151.70 H24156.60 L24131.25 C24149.25 −3.65 (−0.02%)
Pivots Traditional Auto 15
24520.00
24475.83
24440.00
24400.00
24360.00
24343.97
24320.00
24280.00
24240.00
24215.13
24200.00
24160.00
24149.25
24120.00
24083.27
24040.00
R2
R1
S1
S2
S3
S4
S5
P
12
10:05
11:00
12:00
13:00
14:00
13
14:00

Drawing support and resistance lines or axes on a price graph can assist in determining the price direction. These lines can be plotted manually or obtained automatically with just a few clicks.

DRAWING SUPPORT ANG RESISTANCE LINES

After creating a demat account, you can easily access the price action graph of any company you wish to invest in. To plot lines on the graph depicting the status of Nifty 50, you can utilize various tools such as Line or Rectangle. Please refer to the image below for a visual demonstration.

You can draw a line on the graph indicating the point where the prices started to drop and then stopped falling. At that same point, more buyers entered the market, giving sellers the confidence to slowly increase the price. Consequently, the price started to rise.

As Support and Resistance are zones or phases, I find it helpful to use the rectangular tool to analyze these areas. In the image below, the lower rectangle denotes the support phase, while the upper rectangle represents the resistance zone.

As can be observed from the graph, the price initially increased, then moved sideways, and eventually decreased. When the price reached the support zone marked by the lower rectangle, buyers pushed the trades again, causing the price to rise towards the resistance zone marked by the upper rectangle.

If the price falls, it will hit the first support zone shown in the picture. If it continues to fluctuate between the two marked zones, it will be referred to as a sideways trend, as explained in the earlier chapters of the book. You can identify and mark support zones similar to the ones shown in the picture, where prices tend to trend upwards. When prices fall to these support zones, there is a likelihood of an upward trend.

An additional tool that can assist you in identifying trends related to support and resistance is the Pivot Point Standard indicator. Once you select this indicator, you will notice lines labeled as 'P' (resistance) and support lines automatically appearing on the graph. When the price tries to move up from its support, it will aim to reach the first resistance level. If the price breaks the first resistance, it will aim for the next resistance level. Similarly, if the price falls, it will come down to its first support level, and from there the price can either move up or down depending on the buyer's demands.

Unlike other indicators that follow the price, the Pivot Point indicator relies on data from previous patterns. This makes it a crucial tool for identifying support and resistance levels, and thereby aids in making trading decisions.

Chapter 8

To Open Free Demat Account, Just Scan the QR Code

PRICE ACTION

Price action refers to the movement of an asset's price, whether it be a stock, currency pair, or commodity, over a period of time. This movement is indicative of the buying and selling activity of traders in the market, and can be utilized by traders to inform their trading decisions. Essentially, price action analysis involves examining an asset's patterns, trends, and price levels in order to anticipate its future movement. Traders who rely on this type of analysis believe that price is the most reliable indicator of future market movements, and that by scrutinizing price patterns, they can identify potential trading opportunities. In the market, buyers and sellers are the two major components, and their interaction can be likened to a game of tug of war. These two sides pull in opposite directions until one emerges victorious over the other.

Price movements can help you comprehend the psychology of buyers and sellers, which can aid in predicting whether the market will become bullish or bearish. To understand things at a fundamental level, one needs to grasp four essential markers: trends, charts, support and resistance, and charts. Charles Dow was a pioneering researcher who proposed a theory on the correlation between the market and trend. The Dow Theory is a technique for comprehending and assessing stock market trends based on the concept that history tends to repeat itself, and that patterns in the stock market can be employed to anticipate future movements.

Further study into price action requires understanding four major characteristics:

- Trend analysis
- Support and Resistance analysis
- Candlesticks
- Chart pattern

These four indicators do not operate independently but function together to produce price movements and reflect price action. Therefore, rather than explaining each one individually, I will provide examples that demonstrate their collective use.

Candlesticks are captivating and visually striking depictions of price movements. Each candlestick on the chart depicts the price action during a specific time period, such as a day or an hour. A candle comprises a body and a shadow (or wick) that extends from the top and bottom of the body.

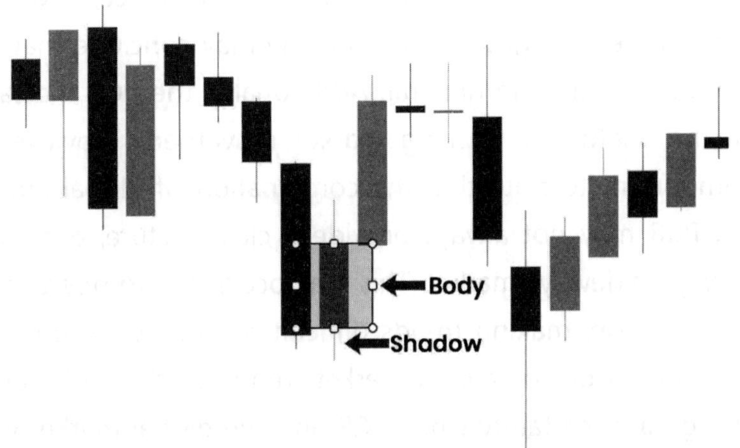

A candlestick that is green in color opens at the bottom and closes at the top, while a red candlestick opens at the top and closes at the bottom. The color of the body can also provide crucial information. A green or white body in a bullish candlestick represents a price increase, while a red or black body in a bearish candlestick represents a price decrease.

To interpret a candlestick, you need to first identify the time period represented by the candlestick. After that, you should examine the body and the wicks to determine the opening and closing prices, as well as the highest and lowest prices during that time period.

In order to gain insights into future price movements, it is important to look for patterns or trends. However, different investors may have opposing views of the market, even when analyzing it in the same time frame. To expand one's scope of vision, it is recommended to take a broader view of the market, such as by analyzing global market indices. This can provide context for the Indian market. For instance, if Nasdaq and other exchanges are bearish, one may conclude that the market is bearish in general. Additionally, the PCR indicator can be useful for tracking market movement. However, it is important to note that the combination of global indices and PCR may not always provide a clear picture, especially during a sideways market. This may occur due to operational manipulation, making trends difficult to deploy. Overall, the goal should be to catch a market trend, which can be done with greater certainty when PCR and the global market view point in the same direction.

The Anatomy of a Candlestick

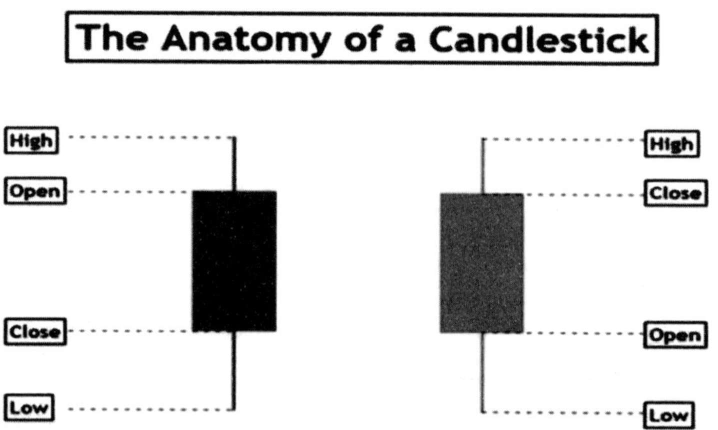

Candlesticks, in these cases become of great help as it is a database of bigger market movements over a longer period of time.

Here are some steps to follow when conducting trend analysis:

- **Identify the time frame:** First, determine the time frame of the candlestick chart you are analyzing. Typically, this will range from minutes to months or even years.
- **Identify the trend:** Look for a series of candlesticks that are moving in the same direction, either up (bullish) or down (bearish). This will indicate the trend direction. A trend line can be drawn connecting the highs or lows of the candlesticks to further help identify the trend.

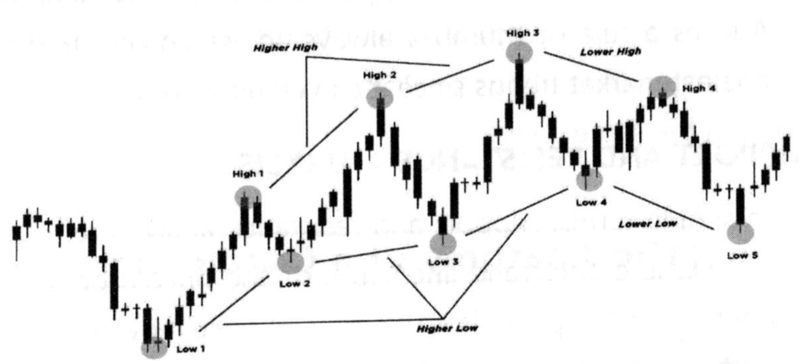

- **Confirm the trend:** Look for confirmation of the trend direction by analyzing other technical indicators such as moving averages or momentum indicators.
- **Look for patterns:** Identify any candlestick patterns that occur within the trend. For example, a bullish trend may have a series of white or green candlesticks with long bodies and short wicks. A bearish trend may have a series of black or red candlesticks with long bodies and short wicks.

- **Watch for reversals:** Keep an eye out for changes in the trend direction. A reversal pattern, may indicate that the trend is about to change. Market always seeks support from its trend line, prices always tend to return to their base trend line but sometimes there may occur a break which is called trend reversal. Analyzing trends through a candlestick chart can provide valuable information about the market's general direction and potential trade entry and exit points. Nevertheless, it's essential to keep in mind that a comprehensive understanding of the market requires the use of multiple indicators and analytical techniques. That's why we'll now focus on support and resistance analysis. And as a rule of thumb, I always advise against trading against market trends since it can result in losses.

SUPPORT AND RESISTANCE ANALYSIS

In simple terms, support and resistance analysis refers to the area where one trend line supports the price drop, while another resists the price rise. This zone of price movement can be better understood by using a rectangle. The support line is where buyers sit, and the resistance line is where sellers sit. By analyzing support and resistance levels on a candlestick chart, you can identify key levels where the price is likely to find support or resistance. Even if the price breaks through one support or resistance level, the analysis can help you locate the next support and resistance level. Trading is based on direct price action and not on indicators. Additionally, a hammer or pin can be used as another marker while using this analysis.

NIFTY 50
5m
Indicators
Continuous
Save
Nifty 50 · 5 · NSE
O24781.70 H24787.95 L24775.00 C24781.90 −0.35 (−0.00%)
24790.00
24781.90
24770.00
24760.00
24750.00
24740.00
24730.00
24720.00
24710.00
24700.00
24690.00
24680.00
24670.00
24660.00
24650.00
10:30
11:00
11:30
12:00
12:30
13:00
13:30
14:00
14:30
15:00
22

A hammer or a pin point is observed when the shadow of a candle is longer than its body, indicating a sharp rise after a dip in the prices. This point can be used as a stop loss marker while trading.

The double top pattern is an important analysis technique used in trading. It occurs when an asset, such as a stock, rises in price, falls back, and then rises again to the same level as the first peak, forming a pattern with two peaks and a trough in between, known as the neckline. The neckline is generally seen as a good point to buy, as it can lead to a profit equivalent to the difference between the neckline and the double tops. However, sometimes prices may hover around the zone but not touch the trend lines, indicating low volume trade. Breakouts in such cases usually occur only when the trading volume increases. This pattern helps to identify the repetitive behavior of price movement and can assist in making informed trading decisions, such as entering or exiting trades at these levels, and predicting potential future price movements.

Choosing the right instrument and protecting your capital from losses are crucial factors to consider when trading. It's important to avoid becoming stubborn after incurring a loss and trying to make up for it immediately, as well as using the wrong instruments despite continuous losses. Such behavior often leads to significant losses. Therefore, I recommend trading only when there is a genuine opportunity.

To summarize, it's essential to trace the trend before making a purchase, understand the figures, avoid trading against the trend, and use indicators to confirm your market view. You can use various online platforms to use such indicators or tools.

Chapter 9

To Open Free Demat Account, Just Scan the QR Code

BREAKOUT AND BREAKDOWN

TRADING

Studying any subject in a stepwise manner has the biggest advantage of retaining the learned concepts in a sequence, leading to a strong foundation for advanced topics. In this chapter, I will explain the emergence of breakouts and breakdowns and how to trade during these situations in a simple manner, building on the topic of support and resistance. When the price moves between the support and resistance levels, without surpassing them, it is referred to as sideways movement. If the price consistently breaks through the support levels, it is a downtrend. Conversely, if the price starts breaking through the resistance level, it indicates an uptrend. This price breakthrough is known as a breakout. However, determining whether it will continue as an uptrend requires considering the role of volumes. The straight line of candles beneath the price graph in the image below represents volume data. A significant increase in volume indicates a substantive breakout of the price above its resistance. In the absence of volumes, the price may rise briefly and then decline.

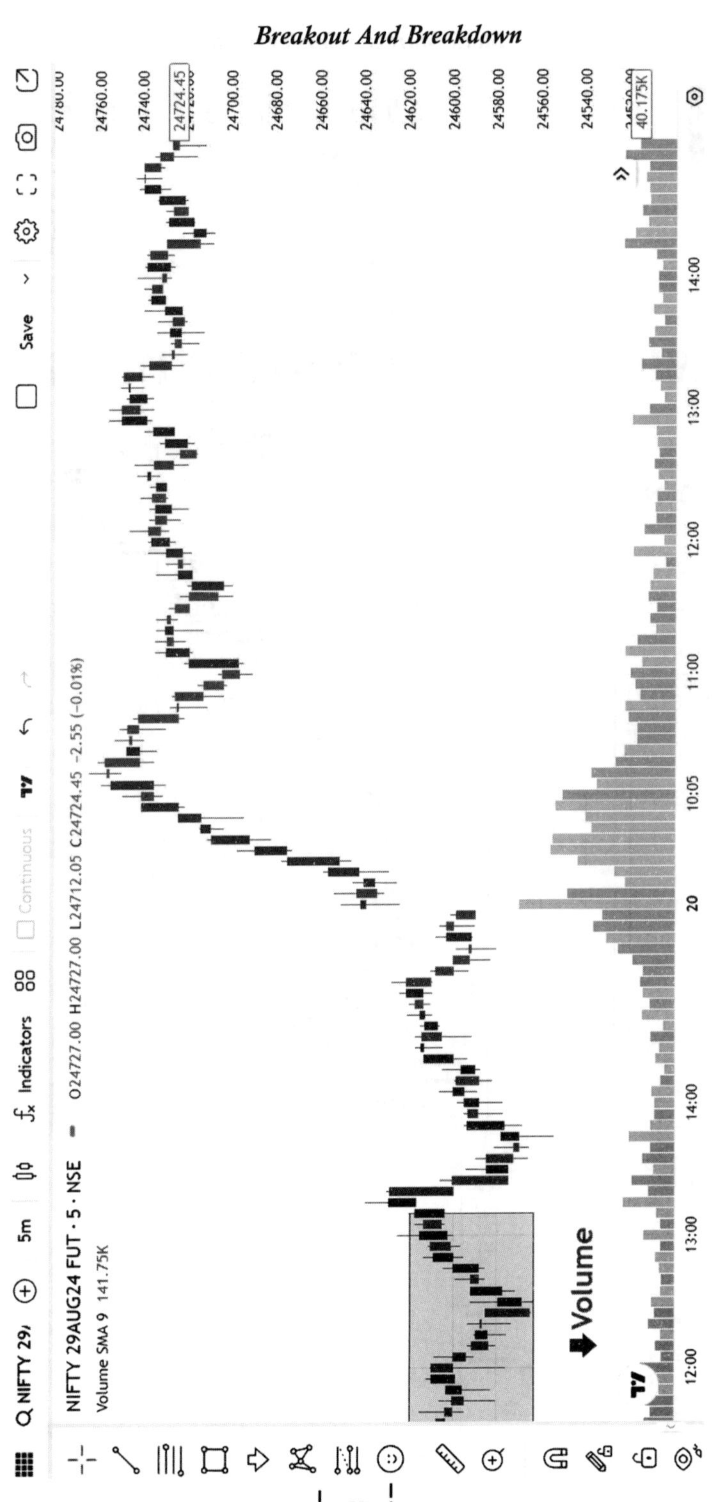
NIFTY 29AUG24 FUT · 5 · NSE
O24727.00 H24727.00 L24712.05 C24724.45 −2.55 (−0.01%)
Volume SMA 9 141.75K
Indicators
Save
5m
Volume
24760.00
24740.00
24724.45
24700.00
24680.00
24660.00
24640.00
24620.00
24600.00
24580.00
24560.00
24540.00
40.175K
12:00
13:00
14:00
20
10:05
11:00
12:00
13:00
14:00

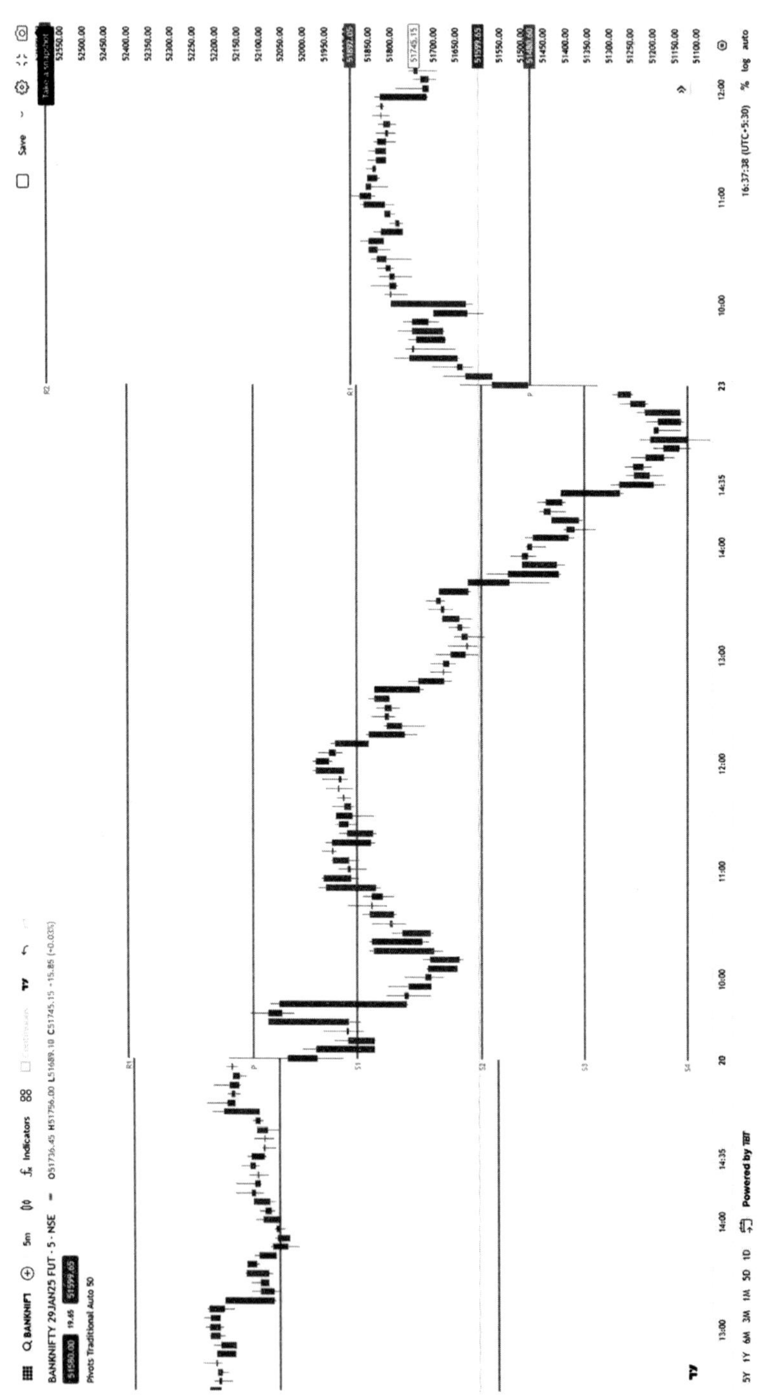
BANKNIFTY 29JAN25 FUT · 5 · NSE
Pivots Traditional Auto 50
Indicators
Save
Powered by TBT

Once a price breaks through the resistance line and tries to reach the next level, the previous resistance line becomes its support line. This is clearly visible in the image below, where the price action crossed R1 and tried to reach R2, but fell back to R1, which was used as a support and began to rise again. With an increase in volume, the chances of the price breaking through R2 become higher. Therefore, this can be a good entry point for trading.

WHAT HAPPENS IN A BREAKDOWN?

Once a price breaks through a resistance level and moves towards another, if it experiences a breakdown, it will fall back to the prior resistance level and attempt to use it as a support. If the price subsequently breaks through this support level, it may be a good time to enter the market as the volume appears to be increasing.

To trade during breakdowns, it is crucial to trail your stop loss intelligently with every candle formed during a live market. This technique helps in safeguarding your capital with minimal losses. Once you observe a green candle, you can then book your profits.

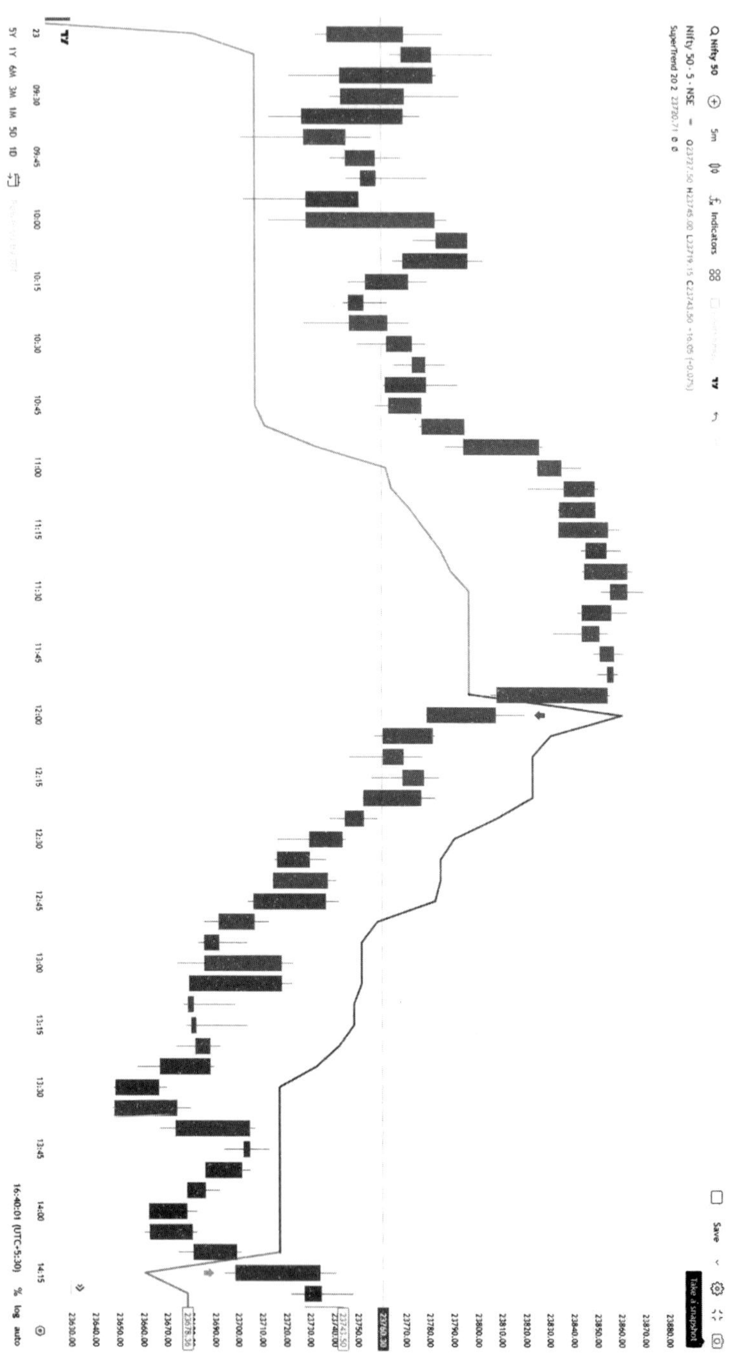
Nifty 50
5m
Indicators
Nifty 50 · 5 · NSE
Save
Take a snapshot
09:30
09:45
10:00
10:15
10:30
10:45
11:00
11:15
11:30
11:45
12:00
12:15
12:30
12:45
13:00
13:15
13:30
13:45
14:00
14:15
5Y 1Y 6M 3M 1M 5D 1D
16:40:01 (UTC+5:30)
% log auto

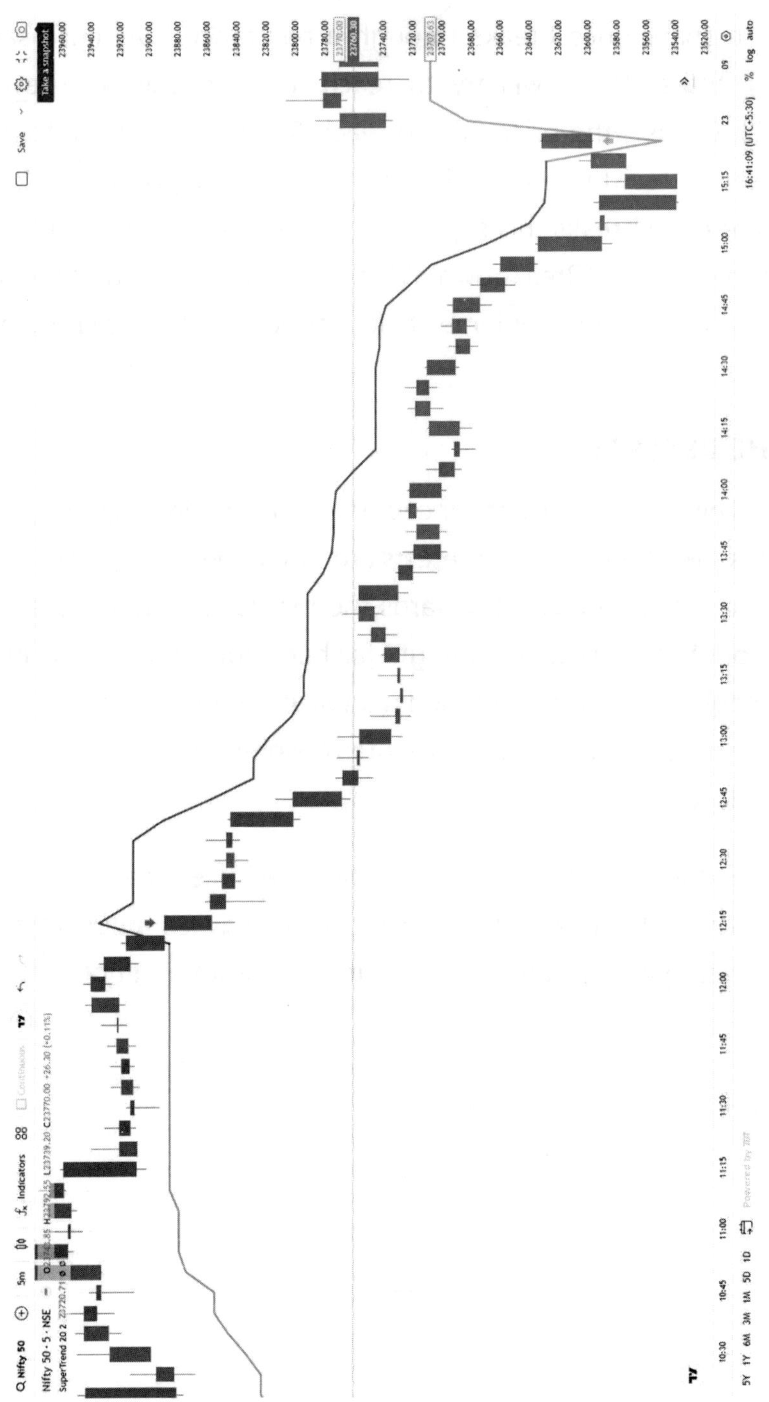
Nifty 50
5m
Indicators
Save
Take a snapshot
Nifty 50 · 5 · NSE
SuperTrend 20 2
23960.00
23940.00
23920.00
23900.00
23880.00
23860.00
23840.00
23820.00
23800.00
23780.00
23770.00
23760.30
23740.00
23720.00
23707.63
23700.00
23680.00
23660.00
23640.00
23620.00
23600.00
23580.00
23560.00
23540.00
23520.00
10:30
10:45
11:00
11:15
11:30
11:45
12:00
12:15
12:30
12:45
13:00
13:15
13:30
13:45
14:00
14:15
14:30
14:45
15:00
15:15
23
09
5Y 1Y 6M 3M 1M 5D 1D
16:41:09 (UTC+5:30)
% log auto

If share price breaks through a resistance level (let's say R1), thereafter, it will try to reach its next resistance level (R2). In case, the price fails to reach R2, it will fall back to its previous resistance level (R1) and use it as a support now. But if the price breaks this support and goes further below, it will be known as a "Breakdown". This point can be a good time to make a entry if the volumes below appear to be increasing as well.

THE RETESTS

This is an important concept that you should keep in mind. Let's take a look at what retests are - imagine that you see the price moving upwards towards the resistance. After it breaks through the resistance, it might fall back down for a retest, but it could also go back up again, indicating an uptrend. In this situation, you can always re-enter despite having a stop loss in place.

In the case of a downtrend, when the price breaks through its support line and rises to retest, it may continue to fall further, giving you the opportunity to re-enter multiple times.

Chapter 10

TOP 5 INDICATORS FOR INTRADAY TRADING

This chapter entails top 5 indicators that have made it to my favourite list, because of their assistance in increasing the trading accuracy. These indicators have certainly worked out for me and I'm sure they will work out for the readers as well. As we have already learned of price section, which is also one of the leading indicator, whereas, most indicators are focused on price only. Often the beginner's begin with a wrong 'view' that leads to missing out on a big opportunity or incurring a loss. This where role of indicators come in they help in rectifying your view and enhancing it to a certain extent.

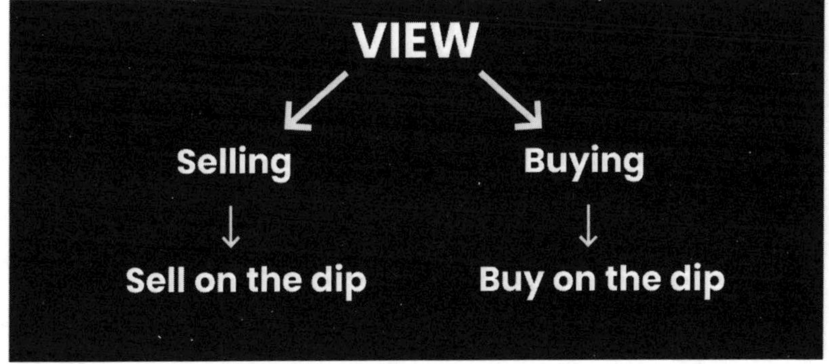

Reviewing through the previous graph for understanding weak and observe how the price dropped to the pivot point and took support from there it went on to reach it's next resistance.

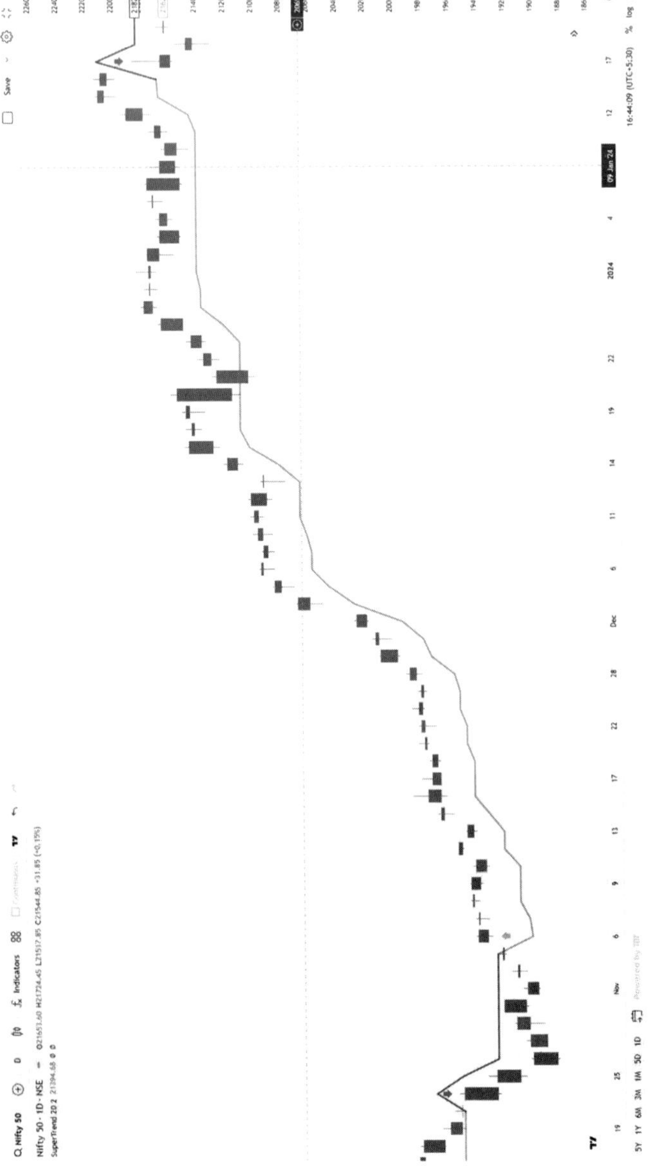

1st INDICATOR: SUPERTREND

Now, in order to understand the price action better, we'll use the indicator known as SUPERTREND. For better clarity, you can change the setting of the super trend; length to 20 and factor = 2. This will increase the efficiency of this indicator. When we use supertrend with default settings (length =10 and factor 3), the supertrend line tends to be distant from the price, but as soon as the setting are changed (length = 20 and factor=2), the supertrend line starts trailing the price closely and more accurately. This change in setting makes the supertrend faster, and also provides you with more trades. Other than that, with the changed settings, the stoploss automatically shrinks, which leads to more profits or we can say; whenever there is a big move, the probability of a loss reduces due to this shrinked stop loss. Like most trends, supertrend follows the price and it's probable. In a matter of seconds, this indicator shows the trend that is going on.

Let see how can you trade with supertrend, keeping in mind one of the important rules: trend is your friend. The supertrend clearly indicate a uptrend when the graph is making higher highs, vice versa, representing a down trend when the graph is making lower lows. Now, on this particular candle; the supertrend indicates a sharp down trend. Where can you enter the market? In the next candle.

Note – whenever you're using supertrend, it is important to check the volumes before entering in a trade. When the volumes are high and supertrend is also indicating a buy or sell signal, it means the price can go up or down with a strong momentum. Also, in your trading account, the volumes don't appear in charts of spot, but if you will open the futures chart of Nifty or Bank Nifty, the volumes will automatically appear and you can analyze the same below to be sure.

Once you have confirmed that it is the perfect time to enter, next step is to define your stop loss. Once you hit your stop loss it is time to get out without re-thinking to hold on. Your stop loss in itself becomes an indicator of the direction that the prices is taking. The trick to break through profit is to follow a particular concept with diligence. The only situation where you cannot make money using super trend is when the market goes sideways.

Also time frame plays an important role in using supertrend. While using a smaller time frame can lead to a loss. If change the time frame from 5 minutes to 1 minute. In this time frame, graph seems to almost sideways, not giving any significant ups or downs.

The more your time frame is, the more accurate and easy the super trend becomes to use. Shifting the time frame from 1 minute to 15 minutes - the graph drastically changes.

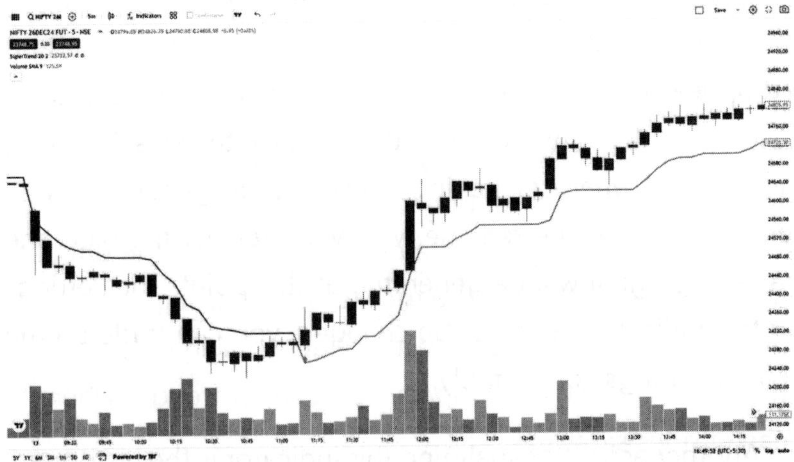

In this above image you can clearly absorb the better trends then the previous one and when you move according to these trends, you hold the potential to make profits. When it comes to Intraday trading, it is better to use the time frame of 5 minutes and later 15 minutes time frame for higher accuracy.

The another way of approaching the market is through observing the upward movement using the supertrend feature. In the below image - you can observe the super trend is indicating an up trend at this particular candle, this is where you enter. These after you can observe the graph keeps on increases until it changes the trend again. But is observing the super trend is enough? No, there are many more indicators to be used to increase accuracy. This chapter will take you through each and every indicator, after which you can combine them all and curate strategies of your own.

2nd INDICATOR - MOVING AVERAGE : CONVERGENCE / DIVERGENCE (MACD)

Through this indicator, we can observe moving averages. The moment this indicator is selected, two lines - blue and red appear on the graph. This concept behind this indicator is very simple. Wherever the Blue lines intersects Red line, this point is where or buying signal will be generated. Vice versa - wherever the red line will over intersect the blue one - a selling signal will be generated at this point. The settings for this indicator need not be changed, you can trade on the default settings comfortably.

Another aspect of analyzing this indicator is the histogram. The green erect volumes are a good sign of an uptrend. Whereas, the red inverted volumes signify a decline in price or a downtrend. You can observe the divergence of the volumes. As the volume decreases of the red scales, the chances of decrease in price gets lower too and the price can rise. Vice versa, if the green volumes increase, the price may rise up, if the green volumes decrease - the price may go down accordingly.

Similar to the previous indicator, the bigger time frame you use, the better. You can analyse. Instead of using a 5 minute time frame, if I change it to 15 minutes - we can observe a cross over blue line intersects the red one from above - hence the price can be seen declining.

Another important aspect of analyzing this indicator is the placement of crossover - here, the blue line has crossed over. The crossover takes place above the base line. If the same was taking place below the baseline, the selling signal would have been stronger. Vice versa, if the same takes place above the baseline, this would generate a stronger buying signal.

3rd INDICATOR - VWAP

This is one of the important indicators that I prefer using a lot - elaborated as Volume Weighted Average Price. This indicator appears as a blue line on the graph, around which the price revolves around. This indicator appears based on the average that the price is trying to reach - based on volumes .

As you read earlier, the price tries to reach its average. In the below image you can observe the price has gone above the average line, hence, it'll go down towards the VWAP line, it'll try to come up again to reach the VWAP line but it'll try its best to reach back to it again.

In case the price has gone far down from the VWAP and selling is still being done, still I'll resist entering the market because the price could bounce back, even though it comes back down, it is a possibility that an operator is trying to trap the trader. Since the price has come down far from VWAP, I wouldn't sell. I'd only consider selling if the price was ranging near or above the VWAP.

It is imperative to understand that each indicator has its own importance and particular use. These guidelines are only applicable to VWAP. VWAP resists the traders in understanding when to sell. The movement price goes way above the VWAP, the chances of it falling down increases.

Let's add the super trend to the mix and see what we can observe, in a graph of time frame of 5 minutes. As we can observe, there was a downtrend going on, until the trend changes, we cannot enter even though VWAP is above the price - because its riskier to trade against the trend. If the trend is clearly changing, and we can see the VWAP is above, then the chances of increase in price are much higher, it'll try to reach the VWAP.

If the price has gone beyond the VWAP, then we must analyse what are the chances of the price going higher. At that point you can avoid buying, since it could be a possible trap. Hence, VWAP helps us to avoid such traps.

If the price is way lower than the VWAP, you can buy. Vice Versa, if the price is way above the VWAP, then you can sell. This entire process is to be done with following other indicators too. If a trend is running amuck, it's also a possibility that it won't bother reaching the VWAP. Generally, the price comes around a VWAP during a trend reversal.

For example, in the image below, we can see the price is slightly above the VWAP and shifts from a downtrend to an uptrend. If a trend is strong, it is possible that the price won't try to reach the VWAP at all the entire day.

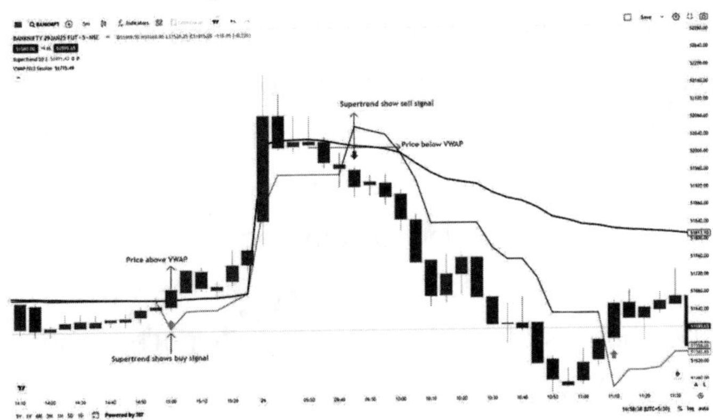

It is imperative to understand here that - if there was a possible trade in the above example, I would have expected the price to come down towards the VWAP. Trading in this scenario would mean trading against the trend which one should generally avoid. If the trend is going on strong, it may stray far from its VWAP.

The same can observed in the image below. A major trend is going on, hence, the price has gone farther away from its VWAP. It all depends upon the strength of buyers and sellers. But despite all, eventually the price will come back to the VWAP anyhow.

4th INDICATOR: ADX (AVERAGE DIRECTIONAL INDEX)

The first thing to note while using this indicator is that it must be above the value of 25. If the ADX is above 25, it means the trend has certain strength to maintain itself and go further. As the ADX rises, the strength of the ADX also increases.

As we can observe in the image below, a downtrend started as indicated by the supertrend. The ADX keeps increasing too, as it crosses the value of 25, the trend changes.

The fluctuation in ADX does not determine where the price will go, but only the strength of the ongoing trend can be deduced. This is an added confirmation. If you're willing to enter the market, you would want to know how strong is the trend that you wish to make the profits off.

Often, during a continuing trend, the people panic if they see a red candle. This is where the ADX steps in to tell you that there is still strength in the trend and you can continue to stay put.

Let's take the example of Bank Nifty futures. Before initiating your trades, you must check the PCR and VWAP. The data appearing on the platform is benign data that can help you to gain clarity over the market situations. PCR and VWAP gives signal of buying or selling. If both appear to be giving the signal of buying, then you should refrain from selling at this point. You can get trapped. The reason behind viewing the PCR first thing before trading is that your view becomes clear.

Intraday Data — 5 mins | 15 mins

Time	Call	Put	Diff	PCR	Option Signal	VWAP	Price	VWAP Signal
1530	16019450	27745050	11725600	1.73	BUY	18046.00	18113	BUY
1525	16265350	27605450	11340100	1.70	BUY	18044.00	18117	BUY
1520	17912500	28018000	10105500	1.56	BUY	18041.00	18122	BUY
1515	18317300	28345500	10028200	1.55	BUY	18037.00	18117	BUY
1510	20075300	26358800	6283500	1.31	BUY	18032.00	18112	BUY
1505	22828950	26965200	4136250	1.18	BUY	18029.00	18095	BUY
1500	22535400	27452550	4917150	1.22	BUY	18027.00	18060	BUY
1455	23471250	26579250	3108000	1.13	BUY	18026.00	18071	BUY
1450	24002850	25919850	1917000	1.08	BUY	18025.00	18066	BUY
1445	25368900	25568700	199800	1.01	BUY	18024.00	18062	BUY

Whenever we begin with trading, we come with a certain view, either to sell or to buy and accordingly we employ a certain approach. Instead of coming with an already decided view, you can check what's the atmosphere of the market, whether it is 'sell on the rise' market or 'buy during the dip' market.

There are two possibilities; two views. If you come with the view of selling, you come with the intention & approach of selling. What if you sell and the price goes down only to shoot back up again? You missed an opportunity to sell higher, because of your mistaken view. Similarly, if you approach the market with the view to buy, you employ the strategy of 'buying during the dip'.

Once a trader approaches the market with a fixed view, they tend to ignore the signs of the market. Viewing the market must be objective and flexible - to be based on benign data such as PCR. Put call ratio displayed on the online platforms, is derived on the bases of real time market activities and the money being invested. If the PCR is above 1.5 or 2, its better not to do any selling. In case the PCR is lesser than 0.5, thereafter, selling can be carried out.

EXAMPLE

Points to keep in mind:

- Never trade against the supertrend.
- In the image above, we can observe that the MACD has given a crossover, indicating a possible decline in price. The price did come down a little, but the trend did not change, until the trend does not change, I wouldn't advise you to trade against it. Hence, I emphasize more on supertrend than MACD.
- ADX can observed in the above image to be increasing, denoting strength of the trend.
- As we can see, the price is trailing way above the VWAP, but keep in mind, if it goes too far, it'll surely come down towards VWAP again.
- Until the trend changes, you can keep trailing your stop loss and make profits accordingly.
- PCR helps you to correct your view in terms of what is going to happen today in the market, hence, you should check it once before beginning to trade.

Chapter 11

CANDLESTICK CHART PATTERNS

This chapter entails various candlestick chart patterns that will immensely help you in your trading career. Single, double, as well as triple candlestick patterns have been encapsulated in this chapter, so read thoroughly, there's a lot to learn!

The topic contains the word 'pattern', which also reminds me of a cliché phrase; History repeats itself. So what does 'pattern' really means in the world of the stock market? How often do patterns occur? How can we identify and use them to our advantage? I intend to resolve all your doubts.

In simple words, patterns refer to any activity that occurs often from time to time; if studied closely, we can discern the probability of further events. The stock market is not for its stability or being extremely predictable. This is exactly why we study numerous patterns in order to discern the probability of a particular future event and gain a sense of confidence in using such probability to our advantage.

With diligent studying of such patterns over time, one can increase their accuracy and efficiency, as well as decrease their losses. An important thing to understand about the price pattern is that it is interdependent on the volume. If the volume does not align with the change in trend, therefore the trend is not powerful enough. Hence, the accuracy of patterns decreases.

Vice Versa, if the volume increases while the price indicates a change in trend, it implies that the trend is strong and the probability of its path or pattern becomes higher.

TYPES OF CANDLES

When we observe a price chart or a graph, it is made up of green and red vertical rectangles, generally called candles. These candles are of two types, green and red, which differ in their nature. Both types have 3 things in common as shown in the below image; upper shadow, body and lower shadow.

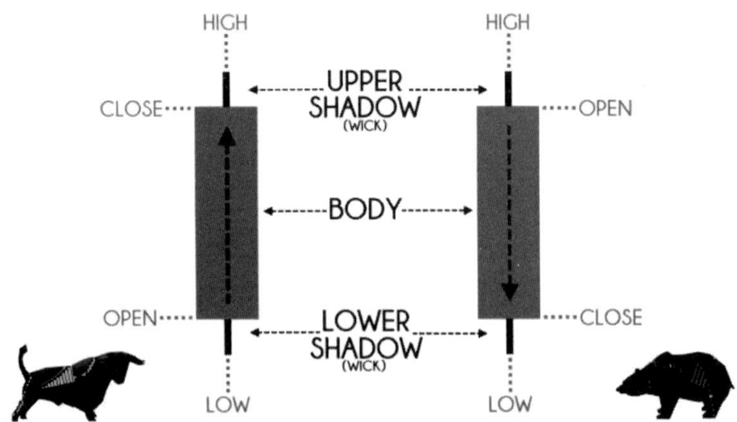

1. **Green Candle** - These candles represent a rise in price, hence, they start or begin from below; from a point called open. The top of a green candle is known as close.

2. **Red Candle** - These candles represent a decline in price, hence they begin or open from the top and get closed at the bottom.
3. In order to understand shadow, let's suppose; the price at the open of red candle was Rs. 100 and it came down to a close of Rs. 90. But 90 was not the lowest low the price had reached, it was Rs. 85 at the shadow. Similarly, the open price of Rs. 100 was not the highest, the highest was Rs. 105 at the upper shadow.

Therefore, we can say that the candles impart four important values: high, close, open, and low.

SINGLE CANDLESTICK PATTERNS

Beginning with single candlestick patterns, we are going to read about some important patterns under this topic that will be easier for you to spot while beginning to trade.

1. **HAMMER & HANGING MAN** - Beginning with understanding the patterns, we can see two illustrations in the below image. The green pattern is known as the Hammer, which is bullish in nature; because it pushes the price upwards. Whereas, the red pattern is marked here as the Hanging man is bearish in nature because it pushes the price down.

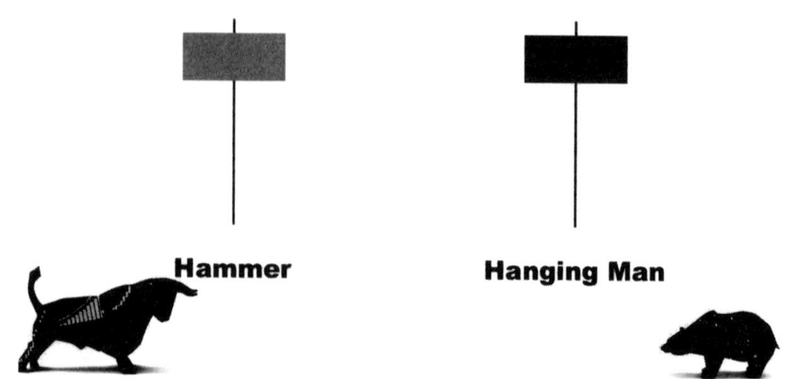

- **Hammer**

It is also called Pinbar (Pin/). One thing to keep in mind is that the Hammer always forms at the bottom of the chart, and from that particular point of its formation; the price shoots up. In case the Hammer forms on top of the chart, it becomes bearish in nature; therefore, the price shall decline from thereon.

A bearish pattern forms on the top and the price goes down. Bullish patterns form in the bottom and the price shoots up.

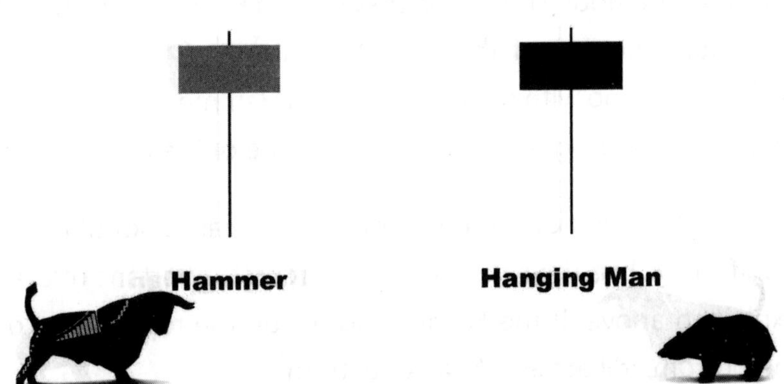

How does the market react when a Hammer forms?

As we know, the Hammer comprises of a high, open, close, and a low. Now, let's suppose, Rs. 100 was the opening price. The sellers try to sell at lower prices, causing the price to decline to a low of Rs. 80. But turns out there were stronger buyers in the market, which caused the price to rise to a high of Rs. 105 and managed to close it at Rs. 104. The upper and lower wick of the Hammer represents the psychology and strength of the buyers and the sellers.

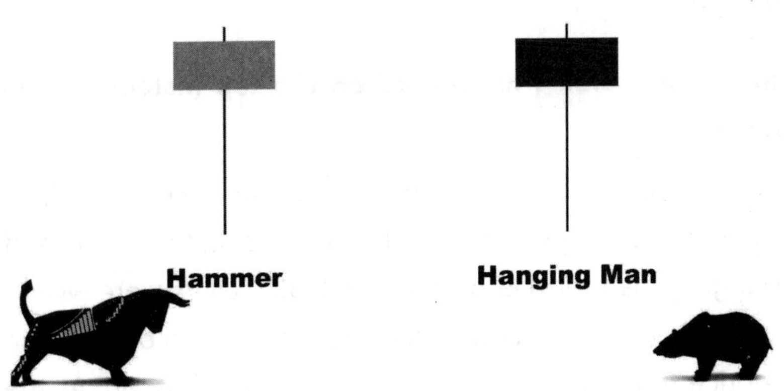

Whenever you see a Hammer form, the size of the lower wick and the body should be checked. The lower wick should be at least double of the size of the body of the Hammer. Moreover, along with the formation of a Hammer, the volumes must be increasing too; in order to be sure of the rise in price.

Also, the color of Hammer or Hanging-man is not of much significance but their nature plays a more important role as explained above. If the Hammer forms on the top instead of the bottom, it'll act as a bearish pattern.

Whereas, when we speak of Hanging-Man; it is known to be bearish in nature but if it forms at the bottom of the chart instead of the top, it'll work opposite to its nature and cause a rise in price. Let's suppose, the open price was Rs. 100 that came to its highest low of Rs. 80. It reached a maximum high of Rs. 105 but finally got closed at Rs. 95. Though there is not much difference in the open and closing price, what matters is that strong buyers managed to bring the price up from Rs. 80 to Rs. 105 and close at Rs. 95. The lower wick or shadow is double the body, Hence, we can say that the buyers still have more strength.

What if the same was formed on the top instead of the bottom?

In this scenario, we would assume the price to decline. Let's suppose, the price had kept on increasing for a while and a Hanging-man formed on the top. Now, sellers were willing to sell at lower prices and hence, they manage to bring down the price from opening of Rs. 100 to a low of Rs. 80. At the same time, the buyers tried to push the prices up but only managed to bring the price to a close of Rs. 95. Here, buyers couldn't make a significant push against the lowering prices. Hence, from here on the probability of the price going down significantly increases.

How to attain confirmation on a HAMMER?

In the below chart, we can see a Hammer formed quite below. The color remains irrelevant. As soon as this Hammer is formed, we wait for the confirmation; which is the next candle.

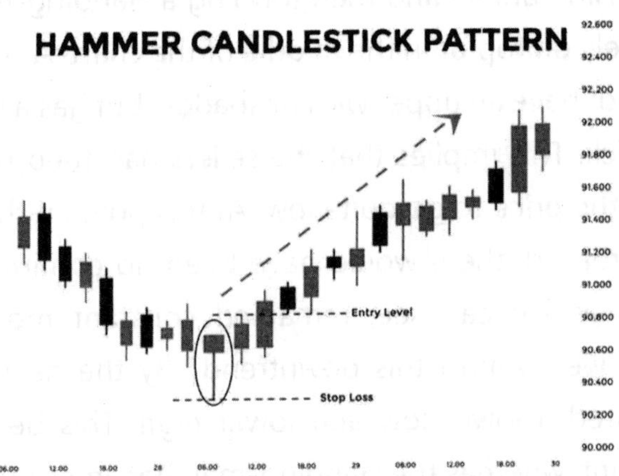

In all patterns, the next candle after the Hammer or Hanging-man plays a crucial role in the confirmation of the trend. In the example image above, all we need for confirmation is for the next candle to break the hammer's high. As soon as a new higher high has formed along with a simultaneous increase in volume - this becomes a good opportunity to mark your entry. Hereafter, you can mark the stop loss that you must respect. Keeping your risk-to-reward ratio in mind which can be 1:2 or 1:3. Suppose your stop loss is of 40 points then you must attain a reward of at least 80 points in order to stay in profit.

Another point to keep in mind; trail your stop loss when you clearly see a trend forming. Let's assume you remarked your stop loss three candles after the entry point. Even in case the price goes further up and declines back, you will hit your stop loss but still exit with a profit. One can choose to stay on their position and keep trailing the stop loss until the trend changes. The advantage of trailing the stop loss is evident.

- **Hanging-Man**

In the image above, we can observe that the price had started rising above and then forming a Hanging-man, which is relatively on top or in the middle of the chart. As we can see, it does not have an upper wick or shadow but has a longer tail/ lower wick. This implies that the sellers had tried hard to sell causing the price to go quite low. At this point, if the volumes had decreased, there would have been no confirmation, but volumes as we can see; remained constant more or less. How do we confirm this downtrend? By the next candle. It has created a lower low and lower high. This becomes our entry point, whereas the Hanging-man becomes our stop loss - despite this small stop loss, you could exit with a good profit. Trailing increases your chances of profits, keeping in mind the reward ratio of at least 1:2.

With that, you've learned the basics of candlestick chart patterns. Let's delve into these patterns further.

INVERTED HAMMER & SHOOTING STAR

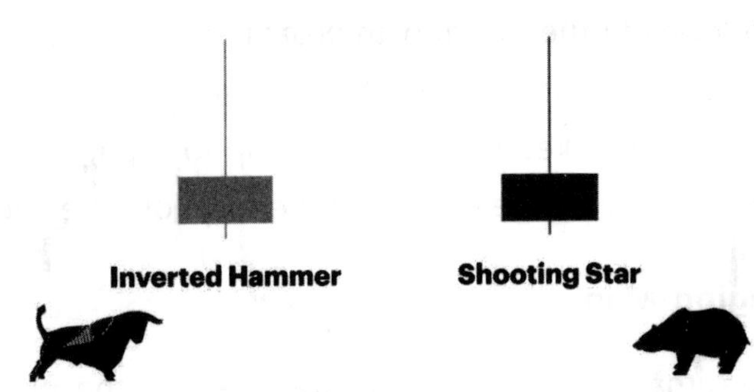

- **Inverted Hammer**

The Inverted Hammer has the following: close, open, high, and low - marked as shown in the below image. Now, if this inverted hammer is formed at the bottom of the chart, it is bullish in nature. Whereas, if it forms somewhere on top, then it becomes bearish in nature, to be called a Shooting Star.

Let's suppose, the opening price was Rs. 100 and declined to a low of Rs. 95 but then attained a high of Rs. 120 and eventually got closed at Rs. 110. We can conclude; because of strong buyers, the price had reached a good high but somehow sellers still managed to lower the prices. Despite everything, the closing was done at Rs. 110, which was higher than the open price. Since this pattern appears at the bottom, it becomes our inverted Hammer, a significant hint at a possible uptrend.

In the below image, we can see the price decline to the bottom and form a candle with a small body and long shadow. This inverted hammer is also referred to as a Pin, irrespective of the color. For confirmation, we look at the second candle and take the entry as soon as it breaks the high of the pin. Now, we can mark the pin as our stop loss and keep trailing it until it's a good time to exit with profits.

- **Shooting Star**

In the image below, as we see the price moving upwards, a pin or shooting star occurs. We know it's a shooting star, because it forms on the top, with a small body and long tail upwards. Now, we wait for the confirmation of the second candle as well the volumes. As the second candle breaks the low of the pin, we take this candle as the entry point, and also, marking the high of the pin as the stop loss.

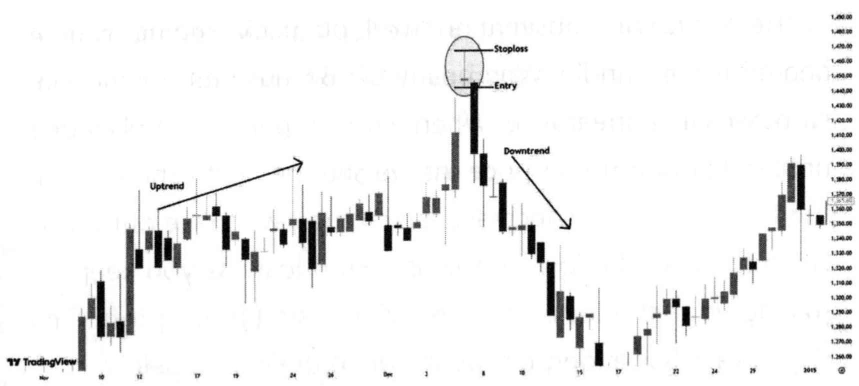

1. DRAGONFLY DOJI AND GRAVESTONE DOJI

These candles mostly appear to be black because the price closes at the same value on which it opened. If it slightly moved higher, it would begin to appear green. If the price would have slightly declined, it would begin to appear red, as shown in the image below.

- **Dragonfly Doji**

Similar to the previous bullish patterns, this one too forms at the bottom of the graph. let's take an example with help of an image below.

Here, we can observe a small pullback ending with a beautiful doji candle. Why beautiful? Because its significance surpasses its appearance. When a doji appears, it implies of a probability of a rise in price. As we see the next candle break the high of doji with increase in volumes, we make our entry, while marking the low of doji as a stop loss. As you keep on trailing your stoploss, you'll exit with a significant profit. The doji always has a long tail, as shown in the image below.

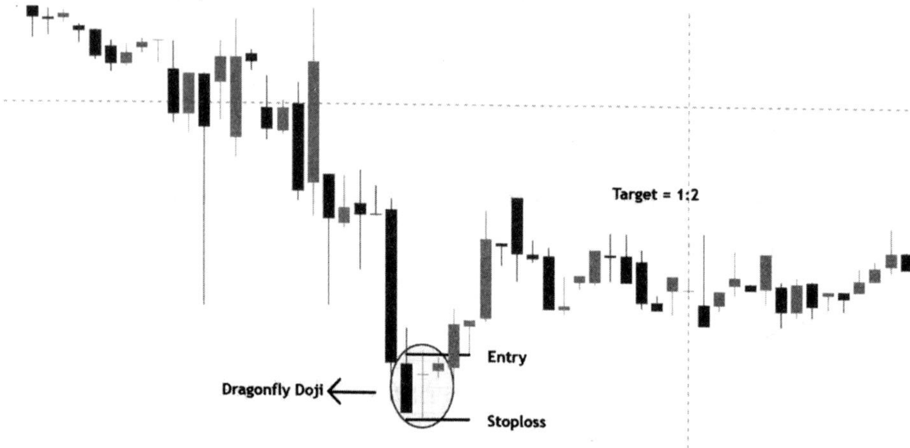

- **Gravestone Doji**

You must be wondering why is it named so! Because, from here the price is going to take a deathly dip, its time to exit as soon as you can. If you trade in options, this will help you to minimize your losses while gathering good profits. Let's see what's this one all about.

In the image below, you can see, the price was fluctuating upwards until a gravestone doji appeared with a long tail above. As you see the next candle breaking doji's low, it's your time to enter, while marking the doji's high as the stop loss.

Keep trailing your stop loss and you're all set.

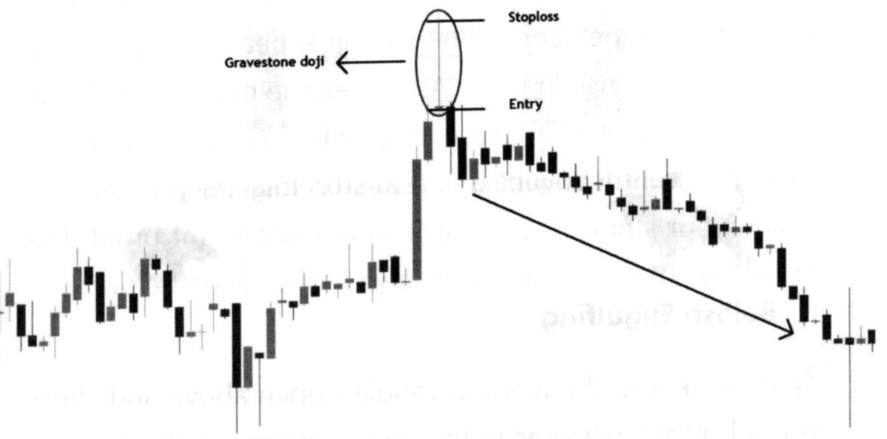

DOUBLE CANDLESTICK PATTERNS

1. BULLISH ENGULFING & BEARISH ENGULFING PATTERNS

These patterns appear in a pair, where one the second candle is a dominant one, that crosses all the points of the previous candle; in a way engulfing or overpowering it, hence, they are named so. Moreover, similar to the previous ones, if the bullish engulfing pair appears at the bottom; it implies high probability of price shooting up. Whereas, if the bearish one appears at the top, it implies a very high probability of price shooting down.

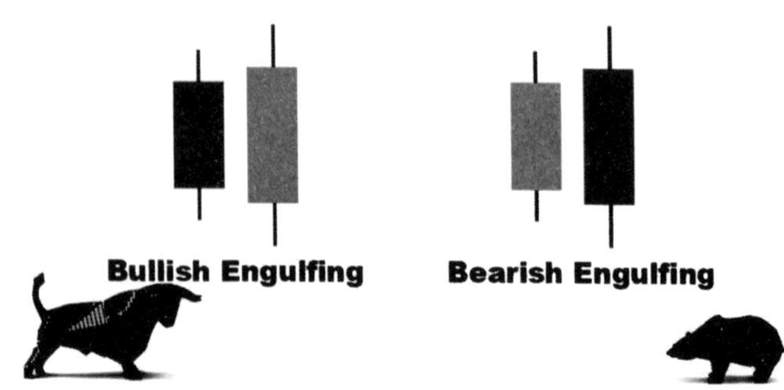

- **Bullish Engulfing**

As we know, the first red candle's open above and closes at the bottom, whereas in the second green candle; it opens below but due to strength of buyers, they are able to push the prices above and higher and make the price finally close above. In the second green candle, the price did come down till its shadow but finally got closed higher than the previous candle. Therefore, the second green candle has its significance because it was able to close the price way higher than the previous red candle.

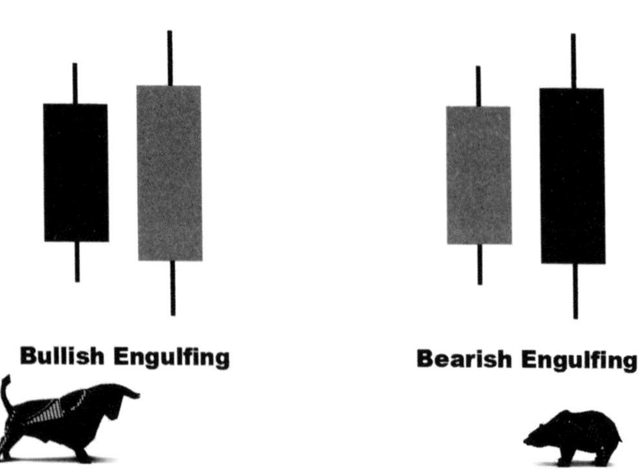

- **Bearish Engulfing**

In this patterns we can see how the second red candle is stronger than the previous green one, and therefore, engulfs all its efforts to push the price up. Here, in the first green candle the price opens at the bottom and closes above, while attaining some lower or higher value at the upper and lower shadows. In the next red candle, the price does open higher but the sellers dawn heavy upon the price and push it downwards; making it close at the bottom, lower than the previous candle. This patterns indicates that price may go downwards from here.

EXAMPLE

In the image below we can see the bullish engulfing pattern forming at the middle. The lower the placement of this pattern on the graph, the better it is. We see a small red candle below which is engulfed by the next green candle. When you see this pattern forming, you can wait for the confirmation. When the next candle after this pattern breaks the high of the pattern, you can enter the market. The stop loss can be marked on the low of the previous pattern candle as shown below.

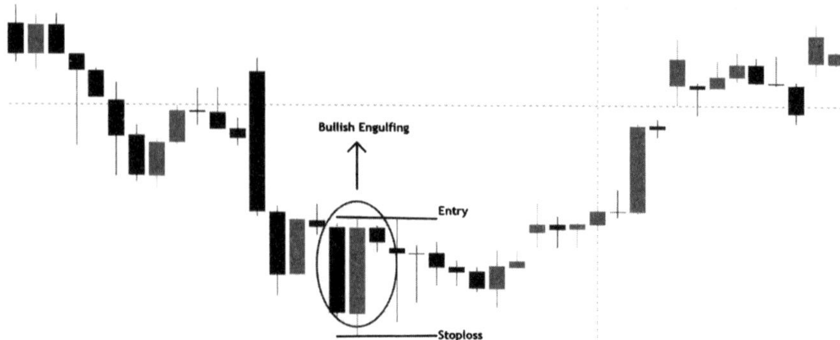

After the entry, the price goes up only to go downwards thereafter. In case this happens, you can simply take note of any other patterns forming in the graph. The fourth red candle had engulfed the previous green one, forming a bearish engulfing pattern. This indicates that you better take your exit despite whatever amount of profit you may not or may have made.

But wait, the game is not over yet. You can surf this trend too. The moment you see bearish engulfing pattern, wait for the confirmation of the next candle, is it breaks the low - its your time to enter once again and make use of the downtrend. After entry, you will mark your stop loss the high of the engulfing candle as shown below. Now you are all set to keep trailing the stop loss and make profits until the this trend changes.

The key to profitably surfing any trend is; to know when to enter, when to exit and understand what are the indicators trying to tell you.

2. BULLISH & BEARISH HARAMI

These patterns are opposite to the engulfing patterns. The previous candle is always the bigger one and it is known as the mother candle, whereas the second smaller candle is known as the baby candle. Similar to the previous patterns, the bullish harami becomes significant if it forms somewhere below in the chart. The bearish harami becomes significant when it forms somewhere up in the graph.

- **Bullish Harami**

The first big red candle opens from above and closes the price at the bottom. Thereafter, the price opens slightly above at the green candle and the buyers manage to push the price a little further and it closes at the top of the baby candle. One important thing that people often forget about this patterns is that the baby candle should always close above the half of the previous mother candle as shown below. If the baby candle doesn't not close above the half of the mother, it means it not a strong bullish harami.

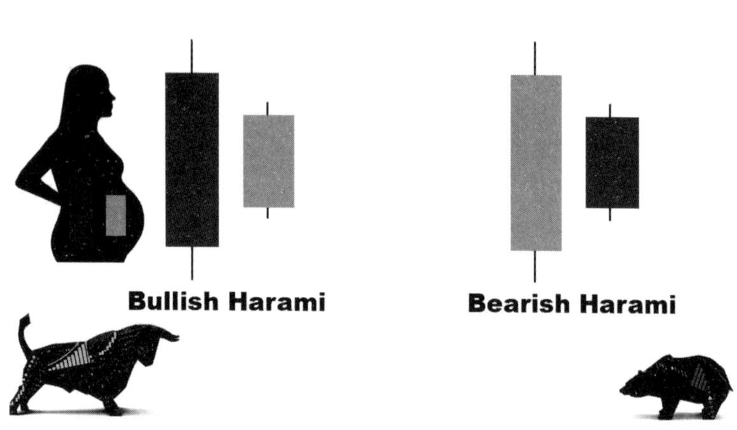

- **Bearish Harami**

The green mother candles forms before a red baby candle. In the green candle, the price opens from below and closes quite above, making a quite a big candle. Thereafter, the red baby candle forms, in which the price opens little below, sellers try to bring the price down, but only manage to push it so far that the price closes at the end of the baby candle, lower than the half of the mother candle as shown below. This shows that the sellers managed to push the price down from the closing price of the mother candle.

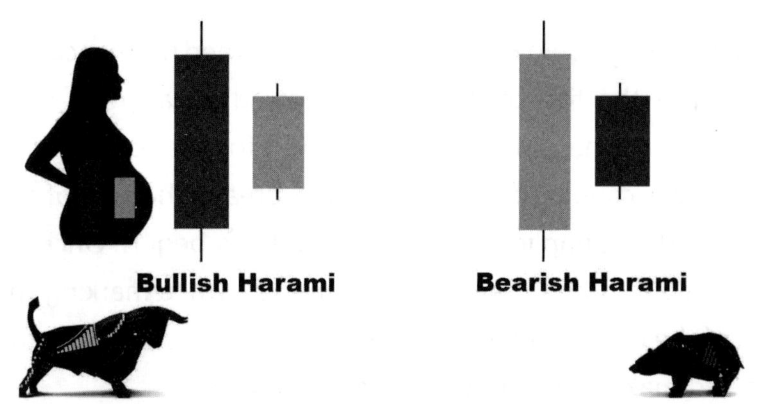

EXAMPLE: Bullish Harami

In the chart below, we can see the pattern forming quite below, implying that it could be a trend changer. We can see a red mother candle being followed by a green baby candle. Thereafter, we wait for the confirmation. As the soon as the next candle breaks the high of the baby candle, we can enter the market, while marking the lower shadow of the baby candle as the stop loss. After entering, you can keep trailing your stop loss and exit when the trend changes.

EXAMPLE: Bearish Harami

In the image below, you can observe a green mother candle forming at the top of the chart, followed by a green baby candle. Once, this pattern forms, we wait for the confirmation of the next candle. If the next candle breaks the low of the baby candle, it implies that a new trend has begun. Once we get the confirmation, we enter the market, while marking the high of the baby candle as our stop loss. Keep trailing the stop loss and make profits until the trend changes.

In the same chart, we can see engulfing patterns form, refer to the image below. As the price keeps moving below, the bullish engulfing pattern emerges and takes the price above. Soon after a bearish engulfing pattern forms and the trend drastically changes. Therefore, we have keep note of the such patterns forming. Along with noticing these patterns, one must simultaneously note the volumes as well, in order to check the strength of these trend changing patterns. Once you begin to understand and timely catch such patterns, your trading accuracy will significantly increase with time.

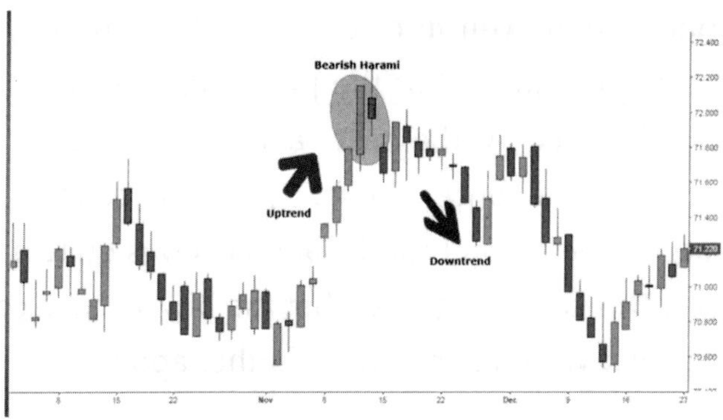

THREE CANDLESTICK PATTERNS

1. MORNING STAR AND EVENING STAR

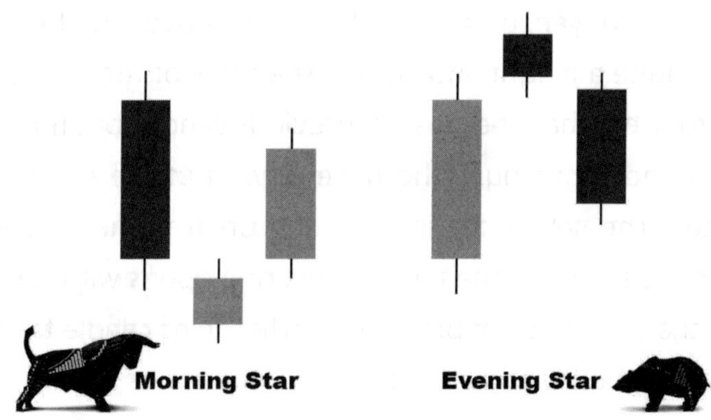

These patterns comprise of three candles, wherein the third candle plays the most important role. The morning star becomes significant when it appears at the bottom of the chart, whereas, the evening star becomes significant when it appears at the top. Let's see what these ones are all about!

- **Morning Star**

As we can see in the image below, the price open above with the red candle and sellers managed to push the price further below, achieving its close at the bottom. The next candle opens with even a lower price. Here, the buyers try to push the price above but the price closes lower than the previous red candle. At the next candle, the buyers try even harder to take the price above. The third candles opens slightly above the second candle and achieves quite a height and closes. This candle signifies that the buyers have come to the market and will take the prices further above.

- **Evening Star**

In this pattern the price opens at the bottom of the green candle. The buyers try to push the price above and the candle attains quite a height and closes. The price of the next candle begins higher than the close of previous candle, but the sellers step in and try to push the price down but the price hardly declines. The sellers try to push the price farther ahead. As third candles enters the picture, this one opens with the price lower than the close of previous candle. Third candle takes the price quite below and closes.

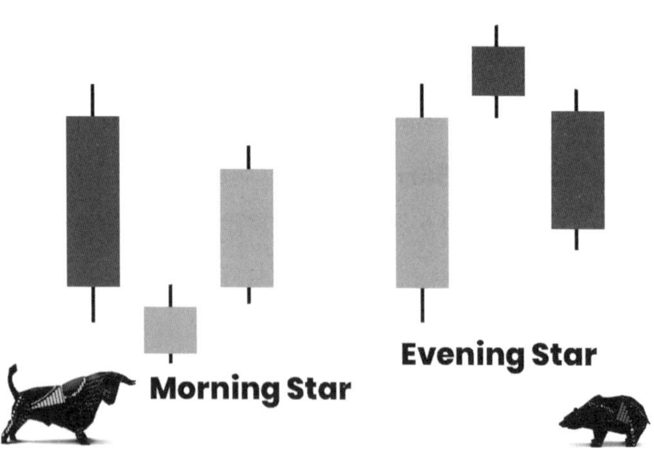

EXAMPLE: Morning Star

Suppose you're trading in intraday, taking the time frame of five minutes. As soon as we change the time frame to 15 minutes, one candle will be enough to deduce the significant change its going to bring. Now, we'll draw a fourth candle. We'll take the maximum high and maximum low the pattern achieved. As we take the open of the first candle and close of the third candle, the body of the new candle will be formed and rest will be marked as the shadow, as shown below. This fourth candle looks like a candle, but what is the colour? Since it opens from above and closes below, it is a red candle. If this pattern is forming at the below of the chart, it implies that the price will shoot up thereafter.

At the time frame of 5 minutes, we observed a morning star, but at the time frame of 15 minutes, a fourth candle appears to be a hammer. As soon as the high of this fourth candle is broken by the fifth candle, we can take our entry and mark the lower shadow of the fourth one as our stop loss. If the volumes are increasing simultaneously, the price is definitely going upwards.

EXAMPLE: Evening Star

In the same chart, we'll draw the fourth candle taking the highest and lowest point achieved by the pattern. Thereafter, we'll take open of the first green candle and close of the third candle and create the body, whereas, the rest will be marked as a shadow. Since the open is below and the close is above, it'll appear to be a green shooting star. Within 15 minutes, a single candle can tell where the trend will go. The next candle and volumes will become your confirmation. This pattern becomes significant when it emerges at the top.

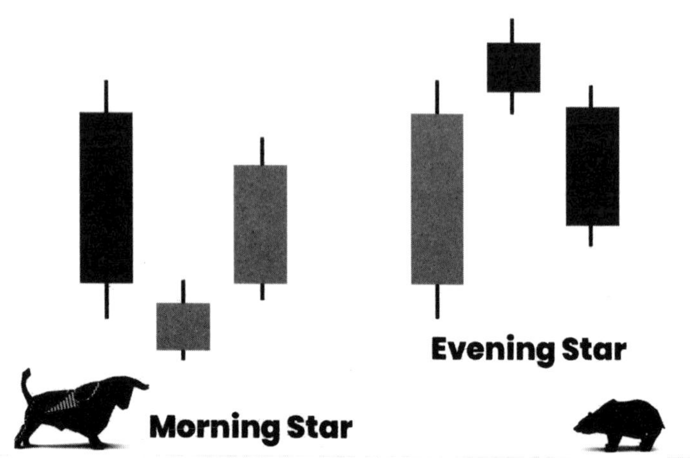

1. **BULLISH ABANDONED BABY AND BEARISH ABANDONED BABY**

People often confuse this one with the previous patterns. Lets see how this pattern differs from all the others.

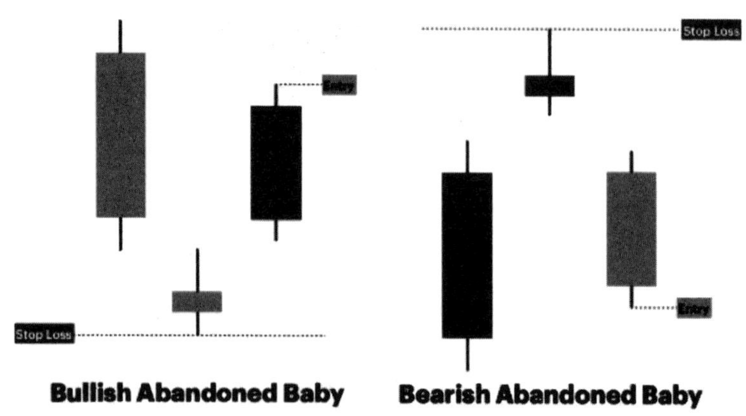

- **Bullish Abandoned Baby**

This pattern begins with the a green candle and after a huge gap, another green candle begins. The third candle begins with a huge gap with the previous one. Now, we'll create our fourth candle following the same technique. We'll take the highest and lowest point achieved. Now we'll take the open of the first candle and close of the third one. This will end up creating the pattern called doji. If this whole pattern emerges at the bottom after changing the time frame from 5 to 15 minutes, it implies that the price will shoot up from here.

- **Bearish Abandoned Baby**

In this pattern, the price opens from the top of the first red candle, with huge gaps in between, two candles emerge further. Now, we'll create our fourth candle taking highest and lowest points achieved. We'll draw the body taking open of the first candle and close of the third one. This fourth candle with emerge as a doji. When you see this fourth candle forming, you can enter the market and mark your stop loss at the high of the previous candle.

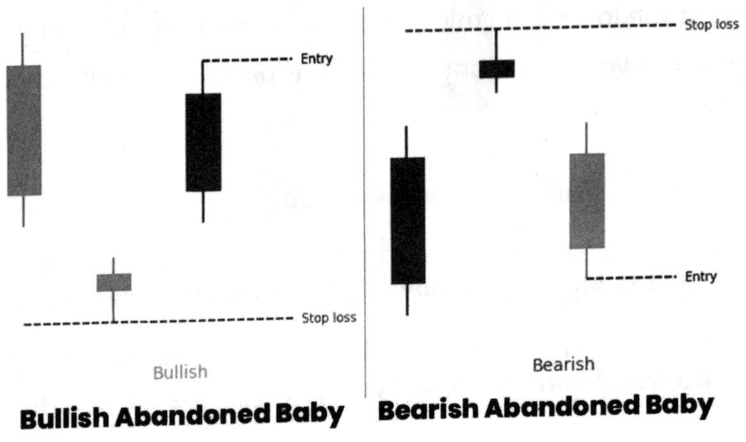

Bullish Abandoned Baby **Bearish Abandoned Baby**

EXAMPLE

In the image below, you can the morning star pattern emerging at the bottom of the chart. As soon as the fourth candle breaks the high of the previous red candle, you can take your entry and mark the high of the red candle as your stop loss. Thereafter, you can trail your stop loss and gain profit until the trend changes.

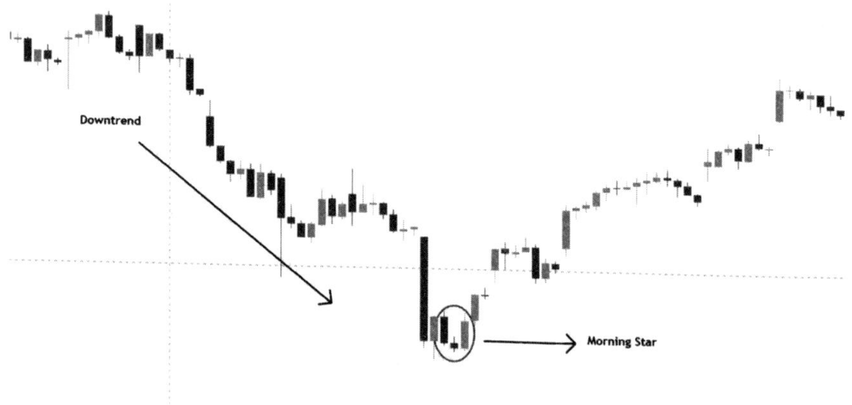

In the same example, we can see another morning star emerge at the bottom. As soon the fourth candle breaks the high of the pattern, you can take your entry and mark the stop loss at the low of the middle candle of the pattern. Keeping in mind the volumes along with these patterns, you'll be good to go.

EXAMPLE: Bullish Abandoned Baby

In this example, this pattern emerges at the bottom, as shown in the below image. At the middle candle, we can say the bulls or buyers become active and try to push the price above. As soon the seventh candle breaks the high of the first candle of the pattern, we'll take our entry and mark the low of the sixth candle as the stop loss. Thereafter, we can trail your stop loss and book profits accordingly.

EXAMPLE: Bearish Abandoned Baby

In the below image, you can see a green candle forming, after a huge gap another small candle forms in the middle, ending with the third long red candle. As soon as the fourth candle breaks the low of the third candle, you can take your entry and mark your stop loss at the high of the middle candle of the pattern. Thereafter, you can see big profits.

There are many more candle patterns, but I assure you we have covered the most important ones. Lets see more examples and how can we implement these patterns.

In the image below, we are observing the Nifty chart on the time frame of 5 minutes. As you can see there was a drastic dip in the price beginning from this particular candle with a long tail above. This candle is a shooting star. Suppose you entered the market as soon as you saw the next candle broke the low of the shooting star, at the same time marking the stoploss at the high of the shooting star. When this trend changing pattern emerges, you can check the volumes rising too, this implies that this trend has quite a strength. Till the trend changes again, you can trail your stop loss and earn big profits.

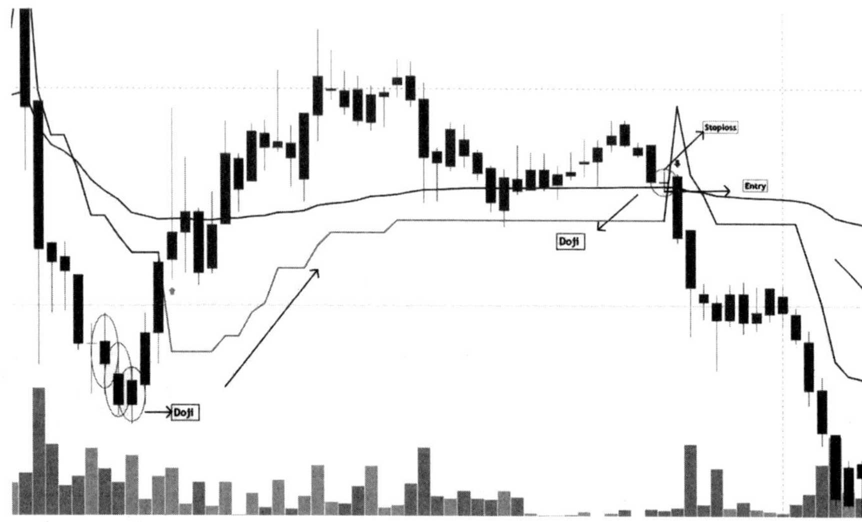

In the same example, you can also observe a doji appear at the bottom which took the price above, as shown in below image. This implies that such patterns do have a significant impact on the graph. If they are decoded correctly, one's trading accuracy can increase immensely.

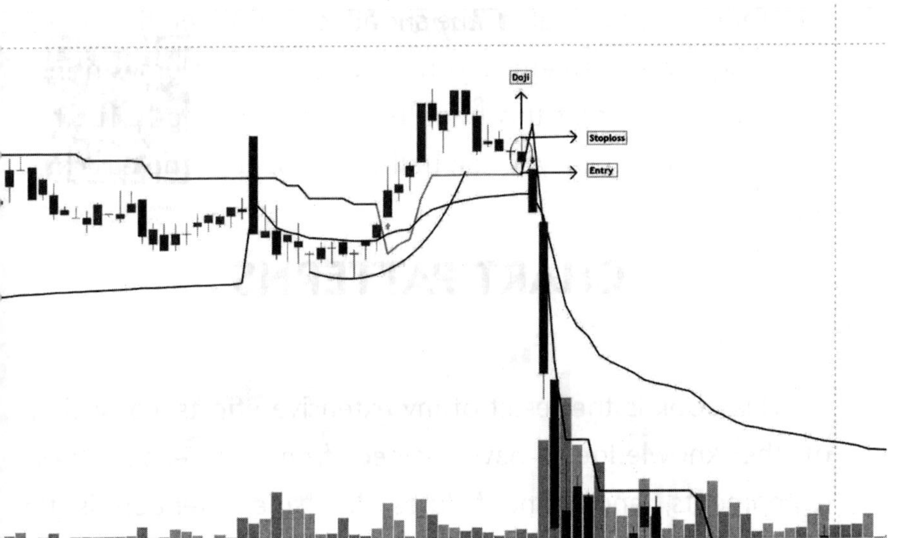
Doji
Stoploss
Entry

Chapter 12

CHART PATTERNS

This book is the result of my extensive efforts, consisting of the knowledge I have gained from my experiences, experiments, and some failures. My sole intention is to provide you with quality information in one place and through one medium. This chapter focuses on Chart patterns. We aim to master price action to enhance our understanding of investments. The stock market charts reflect patterns that can be analyzed under three categories. These charts show three significant patterns.

1. Reversal
2. Continuation
3. Neural Patterns

REVERSAL PATTERNS

It signals the reversal of a price trend.

1. **Double Top pattern:**

This is one of the most elegant chart patterns that you can frequently spot in the stock market movements. Typically, chart patterns encompass multiple candlesticks for study, unlike the analysis of a segment of candlesticks so far. To study a chart pattern, the time segment can zoomed out to a larger scale to reveal the patterns. The double top pattern is a bearish chart pattern characterized by two peaks with a moderate trough in between. The second peak is followed by a sharp downtrend, indicating a reversal.

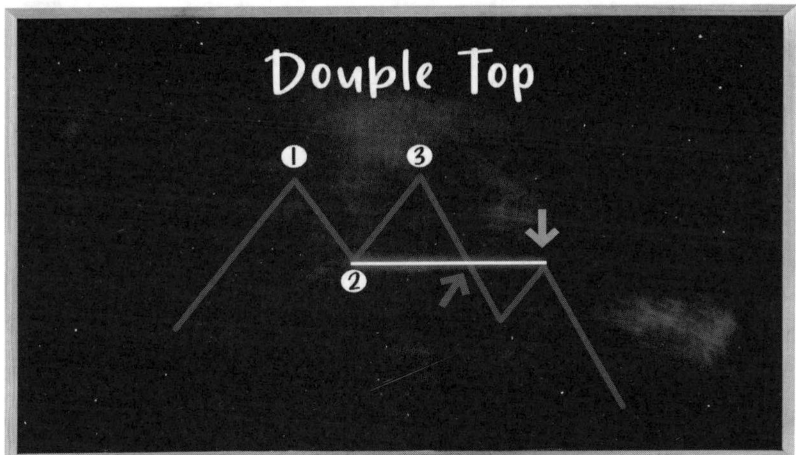

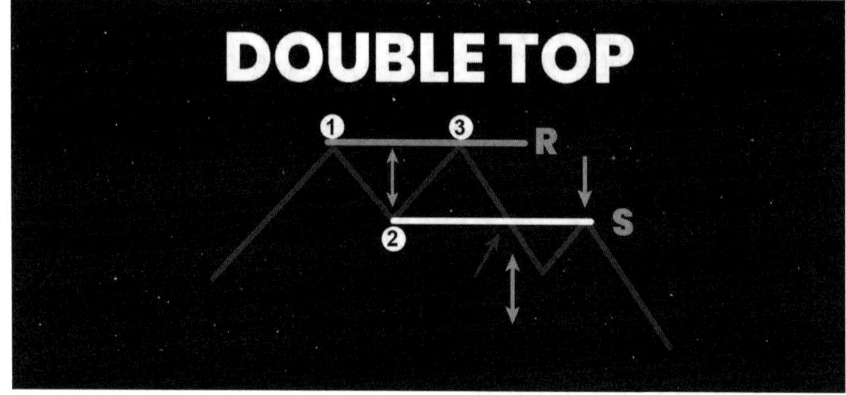

Unlike the analysis of a segment of candlesticks, chart patterns usually involve studying multiple candlesticks. By zooming out to a larger time segment, chart patterns can be easily identified. The double top pattern is a bearish chart pattern that features two peaks with a moderate trough in between. A sharp downtrend typically follows the second peak, indicating a reversal.

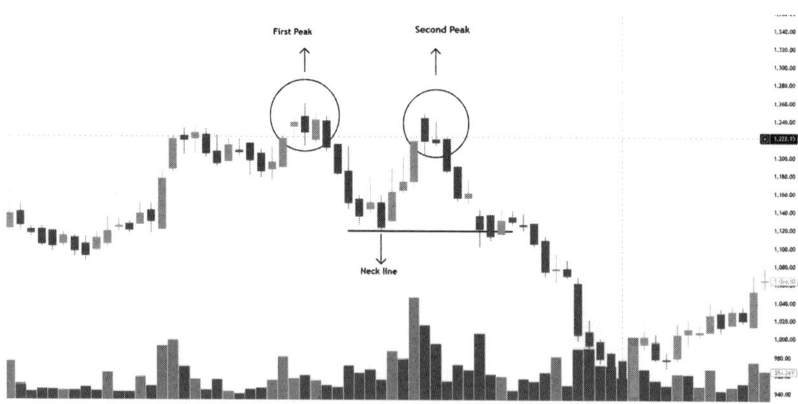

Once an asset price breaks out or declines from a support level, there is a chance that the price may rise back up to the support level and then decline again, as the support level now becomes the new resistance for the price. This often occurs when people attempt to retest the market, although it is not guaranteed to happen.

When the volume during the first top is greater than the second top, it adds further confirmation to a double top pattern. The difference between the support and resistance levels can be considered as the expected target from the breakout point of the price.

1. **Double Bottom:**

This chart pattern is the opposite of the double top and is a bullish pattern. It begins with the price falling and reaching a support level, then rising to a resistance level, followed by a drop back to the support level. Subsequently, the price starts rising again and breaks through the resistance level. When the market breaks through the resistance level, it is a good opportunity for traders to buy. After the breakout, there is a possibility that the price might retest the resistance level and then rise again. This retesting of the price by the market may or may not occur.

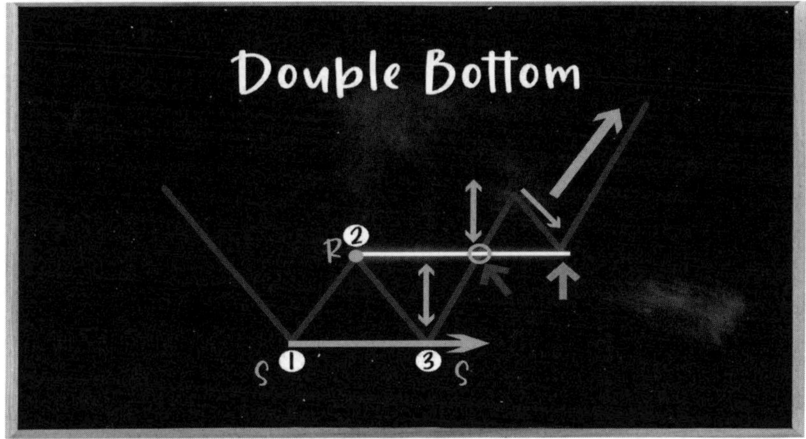

Before making a trading decision, it is important to check the volume during the breakout time. Additionally, the difference between the prices of the support and resistance levels can serve as an expected target from the breakout point of the price.

1. **Head & Shoulder pattern:**

This pattern is observed when the price is initially in an uptrend and reaches a resistance level. Then, the price falls to the support level forming the left shoulder of the pattern. The price then rises again from the support level and breaks the resistance level of the left shoulder.

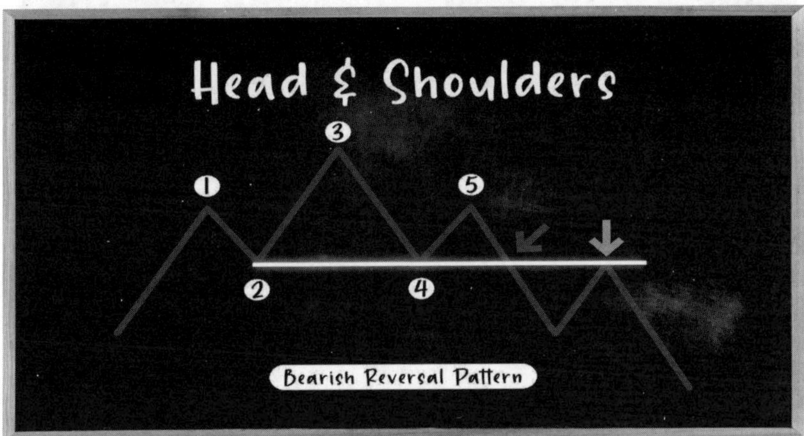

However, it faces resistance again at a higher level and falls back to the support level forming the head of the pattern. Subsequently, the price pulls back and rises again from the support level, but only reaches the resistance level of the left shoulder before falling back to the support level forming the right shoulder.

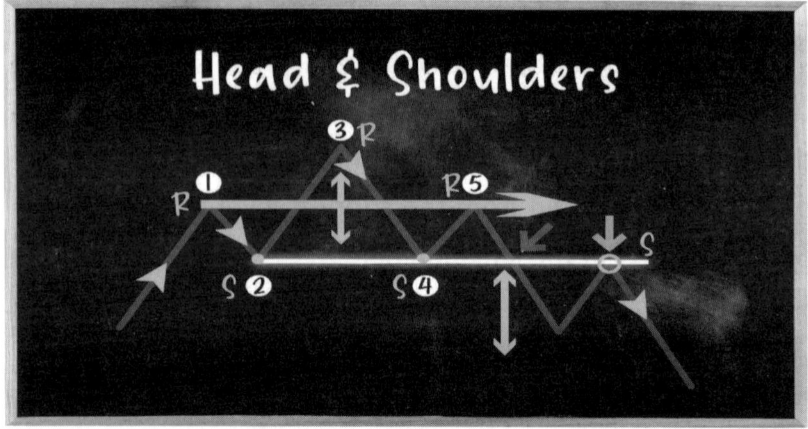

Finally, the price breaks below the support level, indicating a bearish signal for the traders to sell or take other bearish positions. The fall in price from the support level is typically the difference between the resistance point of the head or top of the head and the support point.

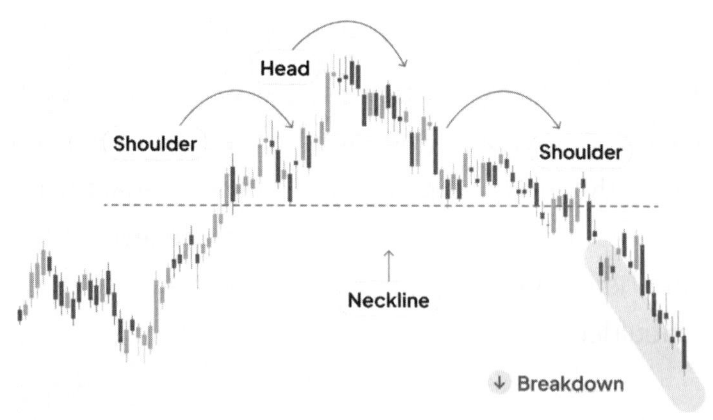

1. **Reverse Head & Shoulder pattern:**

This pattern is the complete opposite of the head and shoulder pattern. Initially, the price of an asset is in a downward trend, and then it starts to rise, forming the first support point.

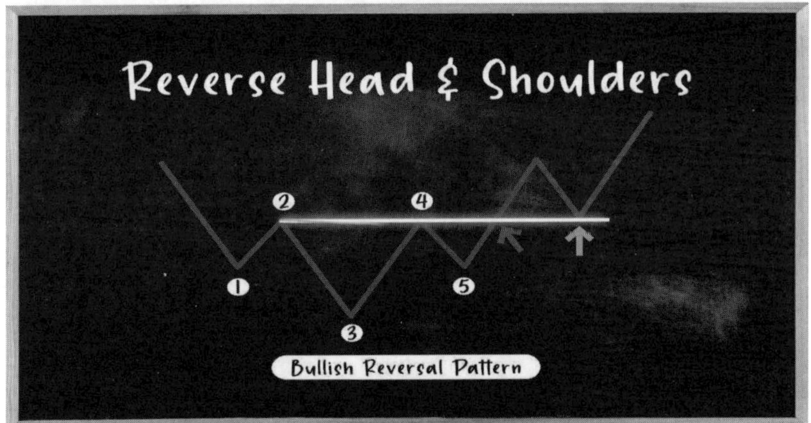

After that, the price reaches a resistance point, followed by a fall and a break of the initial support point, forming a second support point. Then, the price starts to rise again and reaches the resistance point again, but this time it only falls back to the first support point.

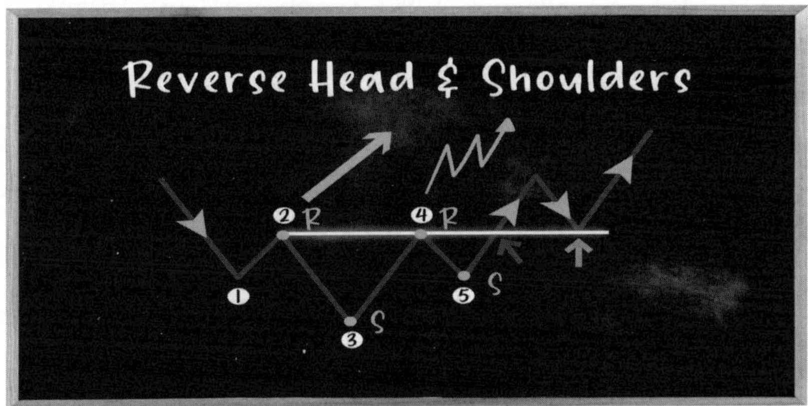

Eventually, the asset price starts increasing again, breaking the resistance point and going higher. This breakout above the resistance point is a good point for traders to enter the market.

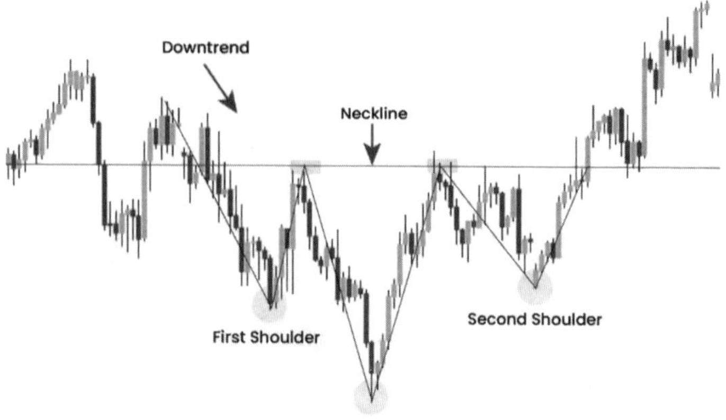

CONTINUATION PATTERNS

1. Bullish Rectangle:

In the financial market, there are three main trends that are observed: upward, downward, and sideways. In a sideways trend, the price is confined within a narrow range of support and resistance.

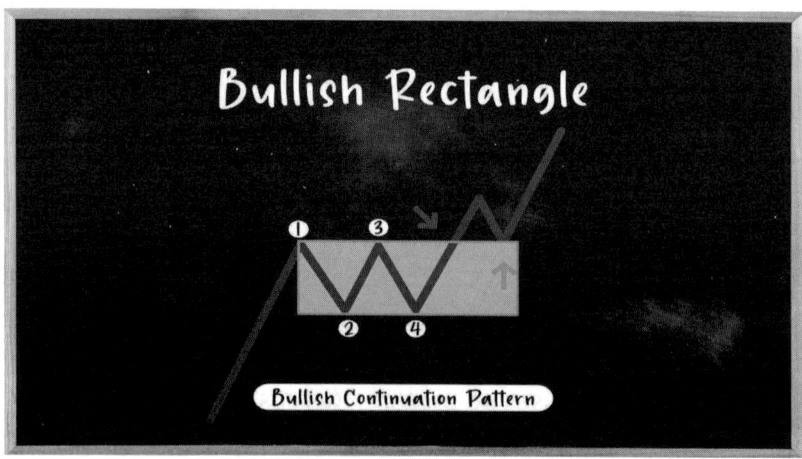

false

Initially, the asset price moves upward, but then enters a sideways trend for a period of time before resuming an upward trend. During an uptrend, the asset price increases and forms a resistance level. Then, it moves up to a certain level, drops down to a lower level, and rises again to create a rectangular pattern.

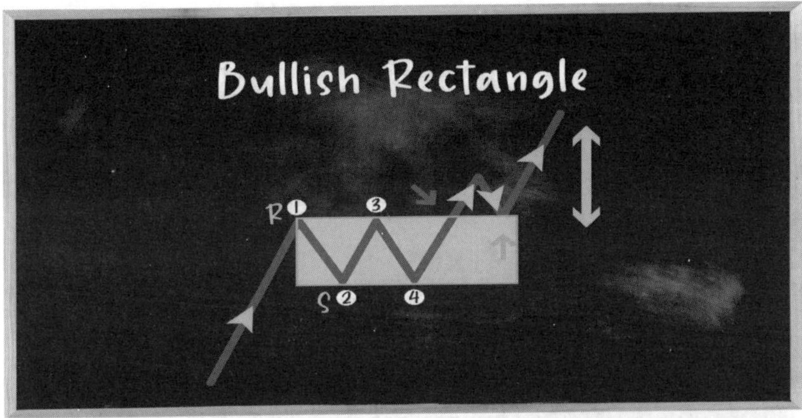

Eventually, the asset price breaks out of the rectangular pattern and resumes its upward trend. The formation of the rectangle is considered a good opportunity to enter the market as it signals an upcoming upward trend.

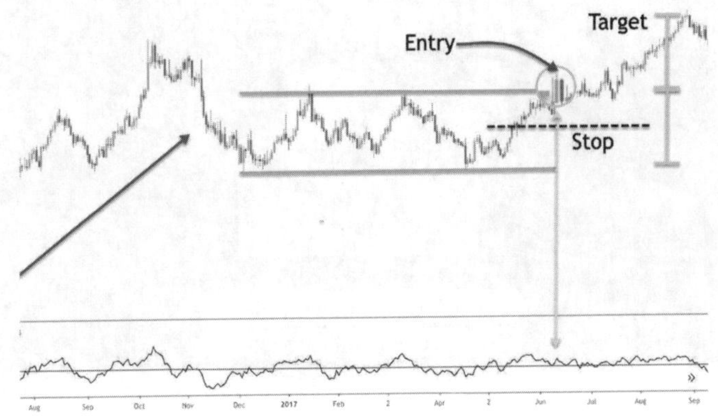

Traders typically target the price difference between the support and resistance points of the rectangle.

1. **Bearish Rectangle:**

During a bearish rectangle formation, the price initially experiences a downward trend, followed by a period of sideways movement, and then resumes the downward trend.

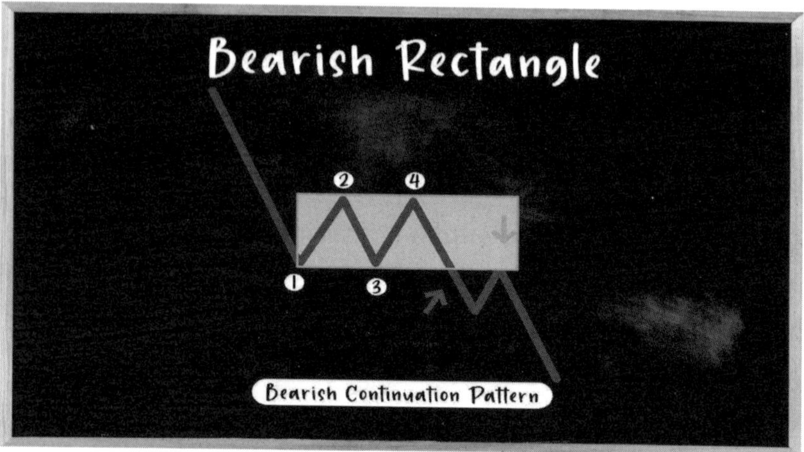

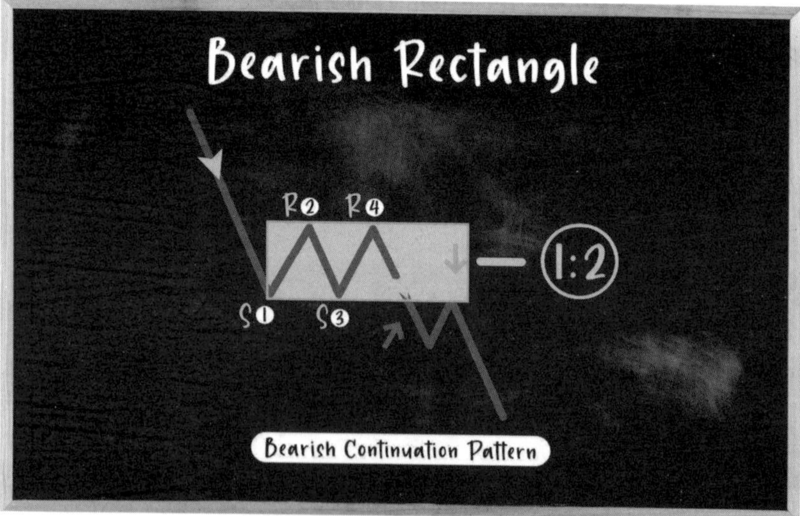

The price drops to a support point, after which it moves up to a certain level, drops to a lower level, and rises again, creating a rectangular pattern. Eventually, the price breaks out of the rectangular pattern and resumes its downward trend.

Traders can take advantage of this breakout point to enter the market. The target price is typically the difference between the support and resistance points of the rectangle.

NEUTRAL PATTERNS

1. **Symmetrical Contracting Triangle pattern:**

This pattern in the financial market is characterized by price being trapped within a range at the end. During this pattern, the resistance continually tries to decrease the price, while the support pushes the price up.

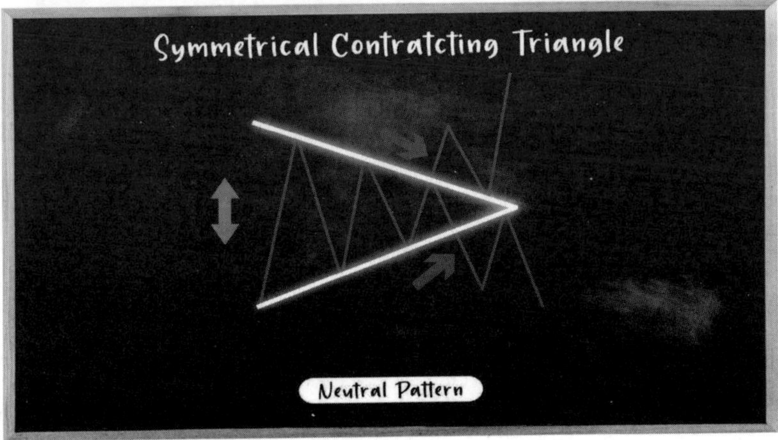

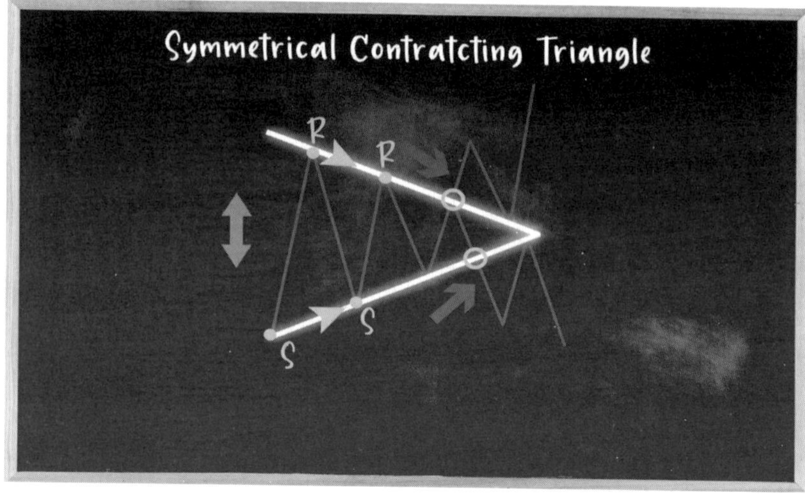

By plotting lines at the resistance and support points, traders can observe that the distance between the two lines contracts, and the price approaches an intersection point, forming a "symmetrical contracting triangle." The volume of trades also decreases during this pattern. Once the pattern reaches its intersection point, the breakout point is reached, and the volume of trades starts to increase again.

The breakout from the pattern is a potential signal for traders to buy or sell the asset, depending on the direction of the breakout. A breakout occurs when the price moves beyond one of the trend lines with significant volume and momentum.

1. **Symmetrical Expanding Triangle pattern:**

This pattern in the financial market is characterized by the range between the resistance line and the support line increasing. During this pattern, the resistance continually increases, while the support decreases until reaching a breakout point.

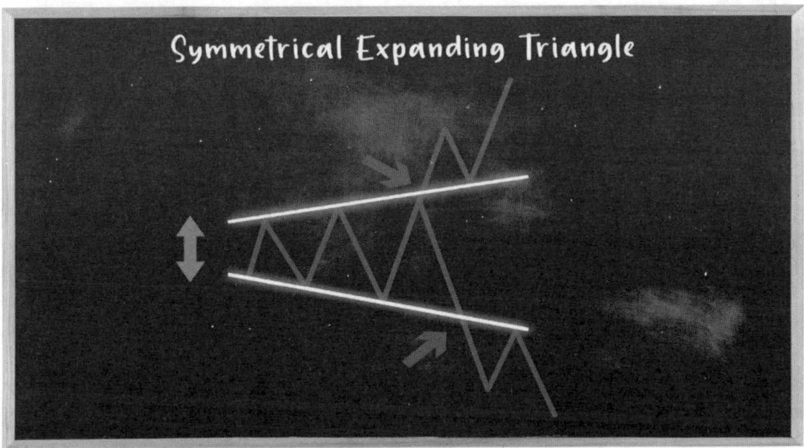

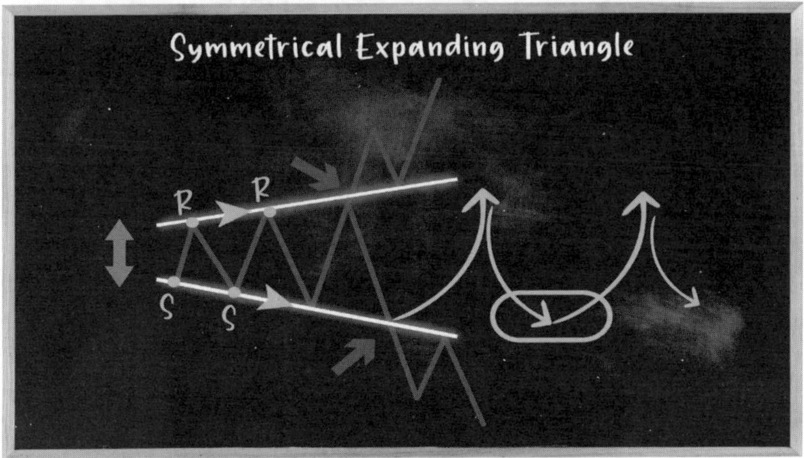

By plotting lines at the resistance and support points, traders can observe that the distance between the lines starts to increase or "expand," forming a "symmetrical expanding triangle." Traders can take advantage of this pattern not only after the breakout, but also during the pattern occurrence as the range keeps increasing, providing a good point difference to trade.

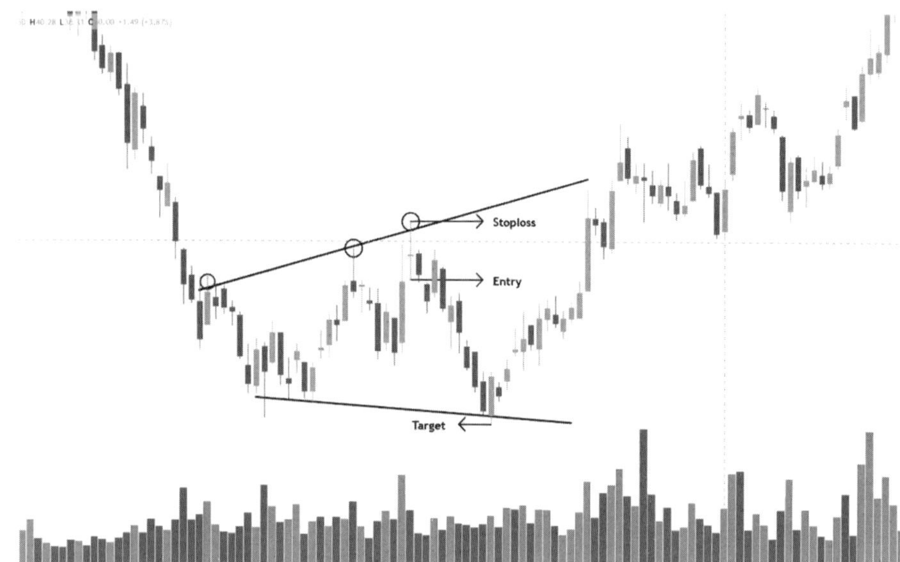

Chapter 13

FIBONACCI RETRACEMENT TRADING STRATEGY IN THE SHARE MARKET

Simplifying a complex concept can be challenging, while making it seem more complicated than it actually is can be easy. The title of this chapter might make the concept sound difficult, but it can actually be understood in just a few minutes. Unlike various other books and experts that bring a lot of history to this concept, I curated it in a very crisp and clear manner, down to business as fast as we can!

Fibonacci retracement is based on the Fibonacci Ratio, which comes from the work of an Italian mathematician known as Fibonacci. This ratio is found throughout nature and has applications in finance too. Fibonacci retracement is a tool that helps traders identify potential patterns and trends during live trading. When used in conjunction with support and resistance, it can provide investors with a clearer understanding of price movements.

FIBONACCI RETRACEMENT HAS TWO MAIN PURPOSES :

1. To assist in regard to price action and its probable movement between support and resistance points.
2. Retracement of the high and low fluctuations during an uptrend or downtrend.

As you have likely grasped by now, during an uptrend, prices do not move straight upward but instead experience fluctuations or highs and lows. In an uptrend, prices reach a higher high and then retract to a higher low, which is called a retracement. Similarly, in a downtrend, prices are decreasing but occasionally attempt to rise, resulting in fluctuations called lower highs, which are referred to as retracements too.

LET'S SEE HOW YOU CAN PUT THIS TOOL TO USE:

Suppose you missed buying a stock earlier, but now it's showing an uptrend and the prices are rising. As the price moves up, it will eventually retrace to a higher low, which presents an opportunity for you to buy the stock and sell it later when the price increases. The price will continue to fluctuate upward until it reaches a resistance level.

Similarly, you can use the retracement technique during a downtrend. You can select the 'Fib Retracement' option from the toolbox menu for live trading. To study a downtrend, drag the tool down from the highest high point to the lowest low. The Fibonacci rectangle on the side displays levels with ratios and percentages representing Fibonacci ratios, such as 23.6%, 38.2%, 61.8%, and 78.6%. Additionally, the number 50% is also used as an exception to Fibonacci numbers.

The image below demonstrates the price moving between Fibonacci levels. As it is a downtrend chart, you can observe the price breaking the support or Fibonacci levels and reaching a new lower low. Therefore, this tool can aid you in identifying an entry point in the market as well as exit points.

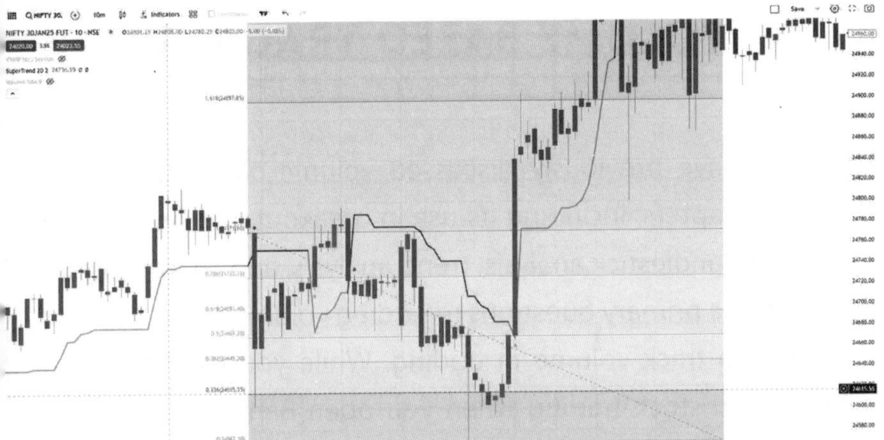

Let's examine how this tool operates when analyzing an uptrend. In this scenario, the Fibonacci tool is moved from the lowest high to the highest high of the desired observation period. As in the case of a downtrend, the price fluctuates and responds when it touches or crosses the Fibonacci levels. This approach makes it easier to identify critical support levels, which in turn helps you determine when to sell.

You can utilize online platforms to check the current Put Call Ratio (PCR) of any stock. The PCR is a measure of the number of put options compared to the number of call options. If the ratio is less than 1, it indicates a higher probability of a further price decline. Conversely, if the PCR ratio increases above 1, it suggests the possibility of an uptrend.

Chapter 14

To Open Free Demat Account, Just Scan the QR Code

VOLUME BASED TRADING

We have previously discussed volume-based trading in earlier chapters, including its use in breakout and breakdown trading, candlestick analysis, trend analysis, and chart analysis. One of the primary questions regarding volume-based trading is how to track volume in trading. While you can easily see volume in stock trading when you open Bank NIFTY's chart, it's not as straightforward to find volume information for index trading on a trading platform. To access volume information for index trading, you will need to open futures and options, where you can find volume charts.

When analyzing a chart, it's important to pay attention to the volume and look for trade vehicles with higher volumes. However, this raises the question: higher volumes than what exactly?

To clarify this point, let's use the example of Virat Kohli. Suppose his average score is 30 runs. If he scores 60 runs on a particular day, we would say that he performed better than the previous day, and if he gets outrun, we would compare his performance with the previous day as well. Similarly, when analyzing trading volume, we need to compare it to previous volumes to determine whether it's higher or lower.

When it comes to volume-based trading, a similar approach is taken. We establish an average reference point and then track the volume relative to that point.

It's a common assumption that rising stock prices indicate buyers are dominating, while falling prices indicate sellers are dominating. However, this assumption is not entirely accurate. The stock trading space operates as a market, which by definition is a place where buying and selling occur simultaneously.

When stock prices rise, there is indeed a lot of buying taking place, but at the same time, there is also a supply that meets the demands. The same goes for when stock prices fall; a large amount of selling is supplemented by an equal amount of buying. As previously discussed, two individuals can interpret a stock differently, which creates buyers and sellers. For instance, suppose a larger player purchased D1 lakh shares and then sold them, with ten different people buying 10,000 shares each. If the share price continues to fall, there will be subsequent selling and buying because these two groups of people perceive the same event differently. A seller may sell their shares out of fear of loss, while a buyer may purchase shares with the prospect of a profit. These individuals invest with varying psychologies and mindsets.

Trade volume reflects the level of interest of buyers and sellers in a particular stock. To illustrate this, imagine a sweet shop that sells sweets every day, but one day he has a lot of business because many people are buying from his shop and he sells more to meet the increased demand. This surge in demand signifies a generated interest. In the same way, when we refer to trade volume, we are essentially referring to the level of interest of buyers and sellers.

During volume analysis, there is always a correlation between price and volume. If the price rises above its moving average, it signals an increase in trade volume, and if it falls below its moving average, it signals a decrease in trade volume. It is important to remember that volume reflects the level of buyer-seller interest. Low trade volumes can result in false breakouts, while high trade volumes often result in genuine breakouts.

Price ↑ Volume ↑ = Bullish (Strong)

Price ↓ Volume ↓ = Bearish (Strong)

Price ↑ Volume ↑ = Sign of Reversal (Weak trend)

Price ↓ Volume ↓ = Sign of Reverssal (Weak)

- This is the first case, Consider the scenario where you're trading using support-resistance analysis and the price and volume are within a range in the support-resistance zone. Now, if there is a breakout, you should promptly check the volume of the trade for that segment. If the volume is close to or higher than its average line, it signifies a genuine breakout, otherwise, it suggests a false breakout. This is a situation of high volume and high price that creates a robust trend and a bullish market.

- The second scenario is when the volume stays at or above the average line, but the price drops to its support level. This leads to a strong trend and a bearish market.

- In the third scenario, if the price is moving towards its pivot/resistance line but the volume is decreasing, it is an initial indication of a reversal under a weak trend. This weak trend is due to decreased interest of both buyers and sellers, which is reflected in the low volume.

- In the fourth scenario, both the price and volume experience a decline, indicating a weak trend and a potential reversal. This decline in buyer-seller interest (volume) is accompanied by a decrease in price.

The first and second cases, where the volume is above its average line, give rise to price trends. These trends need to be comprehended through strategies and analysis, which is covered in the upcoming chapters.

Chapter 15

To Open Free Demat Account, Just Scan the QR Code

SWING TRADING STRATEGY

Swing trading is a popular trading system that has gained traction over the years, even though its name suggests high risks and swift returns. In simple terms, swing trading mainly involves buying stocks. Unlike intraday trading, futures, and options, which involve both buying and selling, swing trading is limited to buying. Investing is done over long periods of time, while trading takes place within days. In contrast, swing trading ranges from a few days to a few months with the goal of earning decent profits.

One of the most common mistakes people make in swing trading is not respecting their stoploss. Since this type of trading is a combination of investing and trading, it requires a balanced approach. The entry and exit points in swing trading are predefined, and the targets are clear.

When it comes to investing, people usually have a five-year horizon. They invest in SIPs, ETFs, Mutual Funds, etc., with a long-term goal. As a result, they may remain ignorant of any short-term market fluctuations. However, when it comes to trading, quick profits are necessary while minimizing losses. Since swing trading ranges from days to months, one can choose to sell as soon as the trend changes or hold positions for an extended period. Although the chances of incurring losses in swing trading are low, people may still incur losses. Why? Because they only invest in penny stocks and feel good about being called an investor, but they are merely speculators.

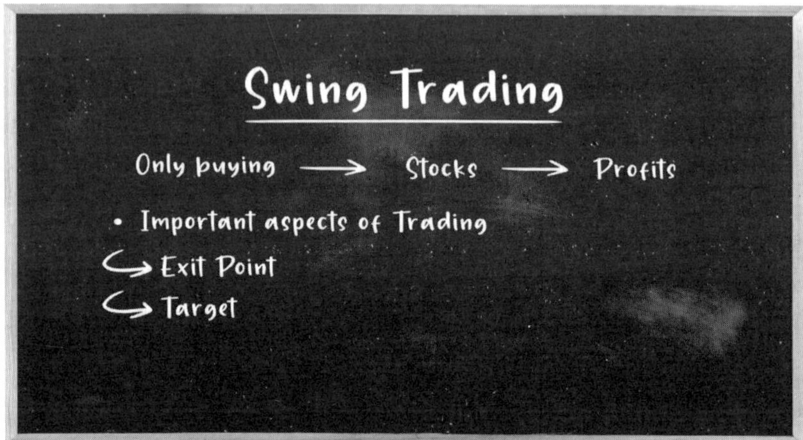

If you wish to follow swing trading, the first thing to do is to check the Nifty 100, which comprises the top 100 companies in India. These 100 companies are the best options for swing trading since they steadily grow and earn profits over time. They make it to this list based on their performance, so the risk of investing in them is lower than investing in companies outside this index. Before proceeding with swing trading, one must check whether the company they wish to invest in is a part of the Nifty or Sensex index.

Now the question arises, which company to invest in among these top 100? The answer lies in the strategy and analysis we learned in earlier chapters. As we discussed earlier, fundamental analysis involves carefully selecting good stocks for value investing. Technical analysis involves using technical tools like support and resistance, indicators, etc. Quantitative analysis requires analyzing certain data to help you with your swing trading strategy.

Often, people who participate in swing trading only look at charts and graphs, ignoring delivery data that must be analyzed. So, what is this delivery data? Let's find out.

By now you have already understood the concept of volume, which depends on the amount of buying or selling being done by buyers and sellers. Delivery refers to the settlement of trades that are carried forward to the next trading day. In trading, a specific margin is required, whereas in delivery, the capital deployed is higher.

For instance, let's say you want to buy a share of Reliance, which costs Rs. 2500. In intraday trading, you may trade 100 shares of Reliance by providing a margin. If you make a good profit, you can square off the margin within the same trading day.

However, if you anticipate that a positive trend will continue, you may carry your position to the next day for delivery. In intraday trading, a margin of 15% to 20% is typically required, but in delivery trading, the capital deployed is calculated as the share price multiplied by the number of shares carried forward. This is the foremost difference between swing trading and other types of trading; swing trading requires the deployment of capital, while intraday trading requires only minimal margins.

Suppose you traded 100 shares, of which you squared off 50% during intraday due to limited capital, and carried forward the remaining 50% for delivery. if you have shares worth Rs. 10 crore and carry forward Rs. 2 crore worth of shares for delivery, the delivery percentage would be 20%. Similarly, if you carry forward Rs. 5 crore worth of shares for delivery, the delivery percentage would be 50%. This is the concept of delivery and delivery percentage.

The third concept that is essential to understand is the difference between trading stocks and investment stocks. The names themselves suggest what activities take place within those stocks. To recognize which stocks should be traded instead of being invested in for the long term, analyzing delivery data is crucial. When going through the delivery volumes, you will come across various stocks that have an average delivery market percentage of 50-60%. This implies that delivery shares are carried forward more often.

Here, delivery refers to the deployment of capital, whereas a decrease in delivery indicates that trading volumes are increasing, where margin deployment is higher. For example, you will find many shares where, if the volume is 1 crore shares, the delivery percentage is only 10%-20%. These stocks are classified as trading stocks. Stocks that have a delivery percentage of 50%-60% are categorized as investment stocks. You can check the delivery percentage of any company in which you wish to invest. Now that you understand these concepts, let's see how they can help us implement trading strategies and much more.

DELIVERY DATA

With help of online platforms, you can easily view delivery data, PCR data, option chain data, and more with just a few clicks. The charts below show data for Nifty derivatives. You can use the delivery data and the delivery average scanner to analyze the data.

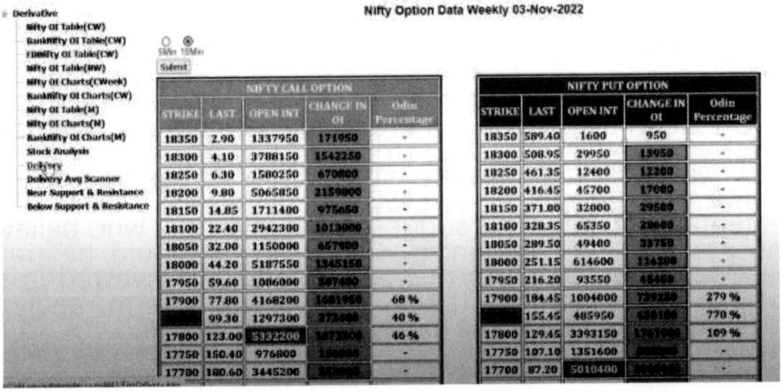

Derivative
- Nifty OI Table(CW)
- BankNifty OI Table(CW)
- FINNifty OI Table(CW)
- Nifty OI Table(NW)
- Nifty OI Charts(CWeek)
- BankNifty OI Charts(CW)
- Nifty OI Table(M)
- Nifty OI Charts(M)
- BankNifty OI Charts(M)
- Stock Analysis
- Delivery
- Delivery Avg Scanner
- Near Support & Resistance
- Below Support & Resistance

5Min 15Min

Submit

Nifty Option Data Weekly 03-Nov-2022

NIFTY CALL OPTION				
STRIKE	LAST	OPEN INT	CHANGE IN OI	Odin Percentage
18350	2.90	1337950	171950	-
18300	4.10	3788150	1542250	-
18250	6.30	1580250	670800	-
18200	9.80	5065850	2159000	-
18150	14.85	1711400	975650	-
18100	22.40	2942300	1013000	-
18050	32.00	1150000	657900	-
18000	44.20	5187550	1345150	-
17950	59.60	1086000	387400	-
17900	77.80	4168200	[illegible]	68 %
	99.30	1297300	[illegible]	40 %
17800	123.00	5332200	[illegible]	46 %
17750	150.40	976800	[illegible]	-
17700	180.60	3445200	[illegible]	-

NIFTY PUT OPTION				
STRIKE	LAST	OPEN INT	CHANGE IN OI	Odin Percentage
18350	589.40	1600	950	-
18300	508.95	29950	13950	-
18250	461.35	12400	12200	-
18200	416.45	45700	17000	-
18150	371.00	32000	29500	-
18100	328.35	65350	[illegible]	-
18050	289.50	49400	33750	-
18000	251.15	614600	[illegible]	-
17950	216.20	93550	[illegible]	-
17900	184.45	1004000	[illegible]	279 %
	155.45	485950	[illegible]	770 %
17800	129.45	3393150	[illegible]	109 %
17750	107.10	1351600	[illegible]	-
17700	87.20	5010400	[illegible]	-

Let's take an example of Maruti, which had cuaght a good momentum, and the stock went from Rs. 9000 to Rs.9500. Was there something in the delivery data that we could've caught earlier and gained profit?

MARUTI							
Scrips	Open	High	Low	Close	Volume	Delivery	Delivery(%)
Average (30days)	8904.72	9008.54	8791.78	8898.29	624590	269911	44
28-OCT-2022	9095.00	9549.95	9051.00	9492.55	1873029	407777	22
27-OCT-2022	9050.00	9076.95	8902.00	9041.95	849108	521220	61
25-OCT-2022	8820.00	9017.00	8797.40	9005.00	727441	389605	54
24-OCT-2022	8788.80	8788.80	8745.85	8765.45	30052	9272	31
21-OCT-2022	8730.00	8794.00	8641.00	8703.30	356203	203216	57
20-OCT-2022	8700.00	8739.20	8611.00	8707.40	328270	171538	52
19-OCT-2022	8851.40	8855.00	8695.00	8719.35	385416	209668	54
18-OCT-2022	8765.05	8888.25	8752.05	8807.35	369973	169480	46
17-OCT-2022	8610.00	8749.70	8567.05	8723.80	304671	128906	42
14-OCT-2022	8760.00	8766.60	8606.30	8617.30	274160	104772	38
13-OCT-2022	8665.00	8785.45	8592.00	8649.55	355605	151257	43
12-OCT-2022	8698.00	8720.00	8590.60	8686.60	380365	165187	43
11-OCT-2022	8811.00	8850.00	8665.00	8684.15	422610	191963	45
10-OCT-2022	8675.00	8876.45	8658.00	8862.40	411218	152899	37
07-OCT-2022	8750.00	8845.60	8711.00	8779.10	428616	126437	30
06-OCT-2022	8734.00	8825.00	8690.50	8703.00	474445	228413	48
04-OCT-2022	8699.00	8758.55	8630.00	8690.50	503140	193078	38

In the image above, we can see the last column, which is labeled as "Delivery." This column represents the average delivery percentage. For example, if we calculate the average delivery percentage of Maruti over the last 30 days, it would be 44%, as shown in the image. This means that out of every 100 shares bought or sold, 44 shares were carried forward for delivery, indicating an investment category. Any company with an average delivery above 40% is considered efficient for investment.

On October 27, 2022, the delivery percentage for Maruti stock was 61%, significantly higher than its average delivery percentage of 44%. This suggests that investors who believed that Maruti would perform well immediately invested in the stock, resulting in a surge in delivery percentage.

As we observe the data, we can see that after October 19, the price of the stock was around Rs. 8800, and delivery percentage rose to 54%, surpassing the average. The delivery percentage continued to increase, reaching 61% in just a few days. This trend indicated an accumulation of Maruti stock. The price rose from Rs. 8800 to around Rs. 9400.

Based on this data, we can check the chart to see how the trend took over the market.

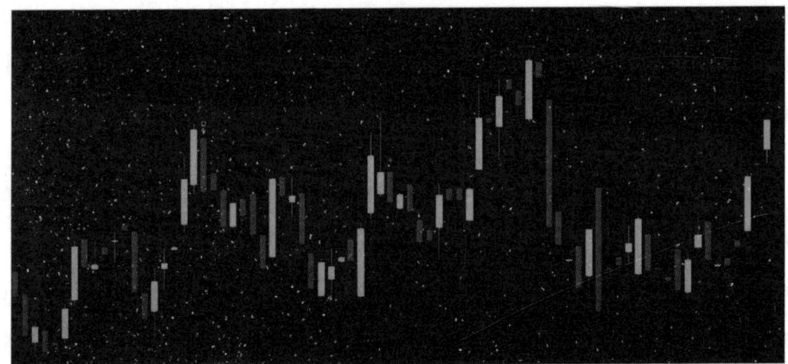

The price had taken a dip and continued in a sideways trend. As we can see, a doji formed at the bottom, and the price thereafter shot up. An increase in delivery percentage indicates a significant move in the market, but it can be positive or negative. Solely on this basis, it can only hint at the upcoming move unless other factors such as patterns and indicators are taken together for better confirmation.

An example of this can be studied in the chart below, wherein MGL's price went significantly downwards, but suddenly the price shot up in a matter of a day or two.

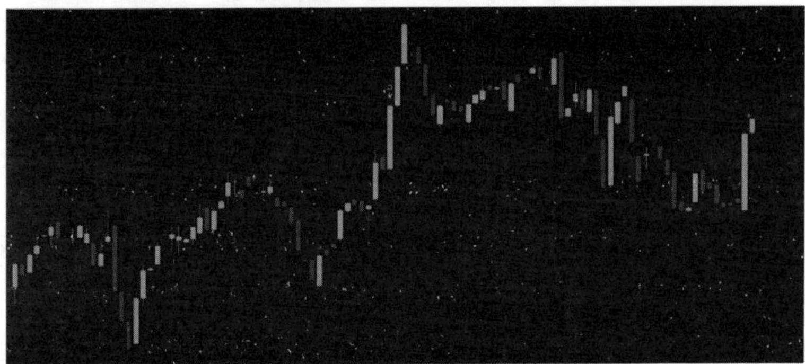

In the data below, we can see that the average delivery of Sunpharma is 37%, therefore, it is generally seen as a trading stock. As we see the delivery percentage rise in a stock, it implies that investment activities are being done in a trading stock. When such activities take place, it implies that there is going to be a significant move in its price.

On 25th October, due to investment activities, the delivery percentage had risen from 29% to 48%. This increase in delivery percentage was a hint that accumulation was going on in the Sunpharma stock. It was followed by a breakout on 27th October, after which the stock price started to rise. Within a few days, the stock price had increased from Rs. 900 to Rs. 1010, which was an increase of 10%.

Therefore, by analyzing the delivery data, we can anticipate the potential swing movements in the market and take advantage of them to earn significant profits.

SUNPHARMA							
Scrips	Open	High	Low	Close	Volume	Delivery	Delivery(%)
Average (30days)	942.22	953.22	934.14	944.04	3255139	1850879	57
28-OCT-2022	1002.00	1003.50	987.55	990.00	3934980	2480838	63
27-OCT-2022	999.00	1013.40	992.50	1011.65	4379157	2957465	68
25-OCT-2022	991.95	997.35	985.50	991.55	2119595	1325574	63
24-OCT-2022	986.00	989.95	982.10	987.00	191840	77757	41
21-OCT-2022	981.00	991.90	975.75	977.70	1791608	947703	53
20-OCT-2022	970.00	982.85	966.55	980.35	1669666	947422	57
19-OCT-2022	975.60	980.70	965.05	976.90	2424533	1366351	56
18-OCT-2022	983.75	985.00	972.75	978.35	2065146	1279595	62
17-OCT-2022	976.30	985.00	973.30	980.00	2647369	1599630	60
14-OCT-2022	976.00	979.90	964.00	976.30	3307000	2138516	65
13-OCT-2022	956.85	973.75	951.50	968.40	4498223	2569060	57
12-OCT-2022	946.00	960.00	941.05	955.55	2875040	1585714	55
11-OCT-2022	950.80	951.90	940.00	944.75	2426935	1652713	68
10-OCT-2022	945.95	954.25	935.25	946.05	1683827	867946	52
07-OCT-2022	953.00	961.55	946.20	955.15	1762328	884134	50
06-OCT-2022	954.70	962.00	947.55	953.90	3449485	2272188	66
04-OCT-2022	955.70	956.30	943.05	944.55	1856830	1032559	56

The average delivery percentage of Sunpharma is 57%, implying that it is a good investment stock. When we look at the data above, we can see that on October 11th, the delivery percentage rose from 52% to 68%. Thereafter, the rise in delivery remained consistent. As a result, the price had risen from Rs.950 to more than Rs.1000.

As you can observe in the Sunpharma chart below, there is a consistent uptrend. By checking the delivery data and the chart, you can identify where the big moves took place. It also gives you an idea of where to set your stop loss and how long to hold onto this swing.

The model of swing trading is such that it can provide the trader with significant profits in a matter of 3 to 5 days. Numerous stocks accumulate deliveries in sideways phases, and due to this, the price gets a push from the buyers and breaks out. The sustainability or strength of this breakout can be figured out from the delivery data. In option trading, after studying the data, if one can catch an upcoming move, they can make double the amount of profits. The analysis of delivery data is best for option trading as it provides a good idea of the move as well as the stop-loss.

DELIVERY AVERAGE SCANNER

Delivery Average Scanner								
Scrips	Open	High	Low	Close	Volume	Delivery	Average	Delivery(%)
HDFC	2383.70	2420.25	2379.30	2400.45	777 (Cr.)	2466963	62	76.27
HDFCAMC	2081.90	2098.00	2055.85	2069.30	48 (Cr.)	166248	46	72.27
ITC	347.55	348.60	345.10	345.80	453 (Cr.)	9445679	56	72.27
TCS	3150.00	3178.50	3145.00	3163.25	429 (Cr.)	988134	58	72.89

This tool allows you to filter out specific companies based on their delivery percentages. In the image above, by adjusting the settings, we can see all the companies that have a delivery percentage higher than 70%. These companies have delivery percentages significantly higher than their average, which implies that there may be a price breakout in the near future. By keeping an eye on these stocks and entering the market as soon as the price breaks out, you can trail the stop loss and earn profits accordingly

EXAMPLE

In the image above, we can observe the data of ITC too, where the current delivery percentage is 72%, higher than its average delivery percentage of 56%. The high is at 348 and the low is at 345. If the high gets broken, it implies that buyers are coming in and the price may go up. If the low gets broken, it implies that selling is being done and the price is coming down.

In the chart below, we can see that the price is moving sideways, with an emerging support level of 344 and a resistance level of 350. This implies that within this range, either accumulation or distribution will take place. After the last red candle, if the low gets broken, we can enter the market, while using the last candle of the graph as our stop loss.

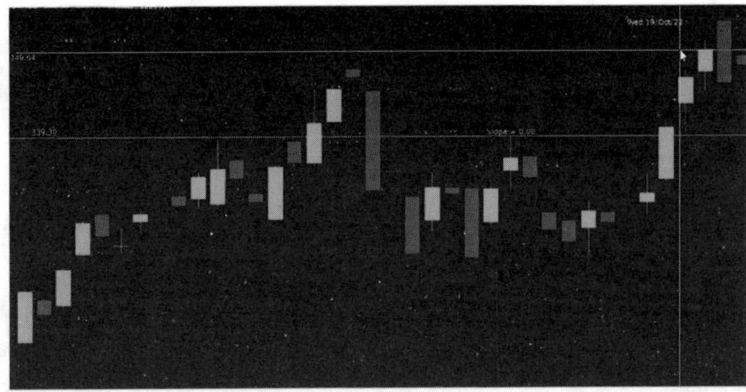

The usage of delivery data can also be made in Breakout and Breakdown trading.

EXAMPLE

In the data below of ACC, we can observe that the charts are near the support and slowly the price of stock is rising.

ACC							
Scrips	Open	High	Low	Close	Volume	Delivery	Delivery(%)
Average (30days)	2400.67	2432.14	2347.38	2384.60	1159492	260600	25
28-OCT-2022	2315.00	2330.00	2284.00	2324.45	650727	261718	40
27-OCT-2022	2275.00	2318.00	2250.40	2313.00	561435	166064	30
25-OCT-2022	2260.05	2278.90	2242.80	2247.50	383657	155896	41
24-OCT-2022	2265.25	2279.85	2252.30	2257.10	46329	13673	30
21-OCT-2022	2271.00	2300.00	2241.05	2256.55	389554	97496	25
20-OCT-2022	2230.00	2299.00	2227.95	2287.60	713402	292190	41
19-OCT-2022	2219.00	2258.40	2212.55	2246.45	724058	203685	28
18-OCT-2022	2259.00	2293.20	2216.00	2219.25	1189726	339975	29
17-OCT-2022	2232.00	2285.05	2205.30	2270.10	1512370	309012	20
14-OCT-2022	2272.00	2285.95	2237.05	2243.65	446497	103252	23
13-OCT-2022	2316.00	2318.00	2242.90	2253.90	528138	141453	27
12-OCT-2022	2318.00	2339.40	2282.10	2316.80	611941	133914	22
11-OCT-2022	2375.05	2376.75	2305.70	2311.65	380893	92002	24
10-OCT-2022	2350.00	2399.90	2350.00	2369.25	383666	51053	13
07-OCT-2022	2370.15	2400.00	2350.00	2384.75	567262	111532	20
06-OCT-2022	2371.45	2397.75	2344.00	2381.75	690259	180302	26
04-OCT-2022	2355.00	2373.30	2288.05	2359.65	714858	151688	21

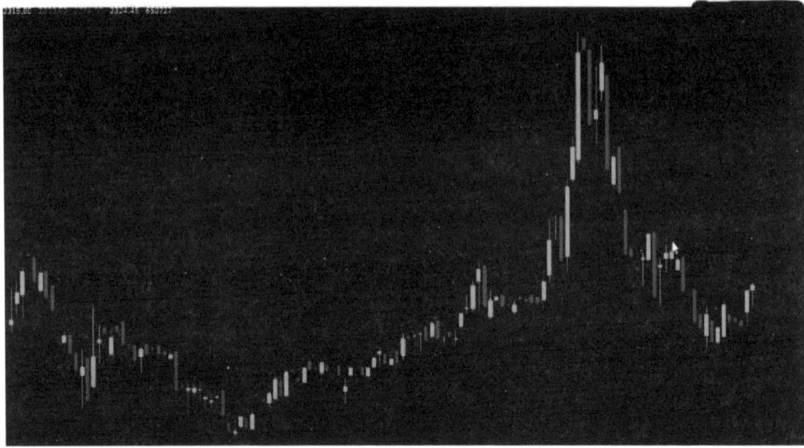

At the end of the chart, we can see the price rising above once again, but is there any strength in this trend? Let's find out from the data above. We can see the average delivery percentage is 25%, but the current delivery seems to be fluctuating significantly higher, being double the average. This implies that certain buying or selling is taking place which was not being done before. We can see a hint of upward momentum in the graph, with the price being at the verge of a breakout.

EXAMPLE

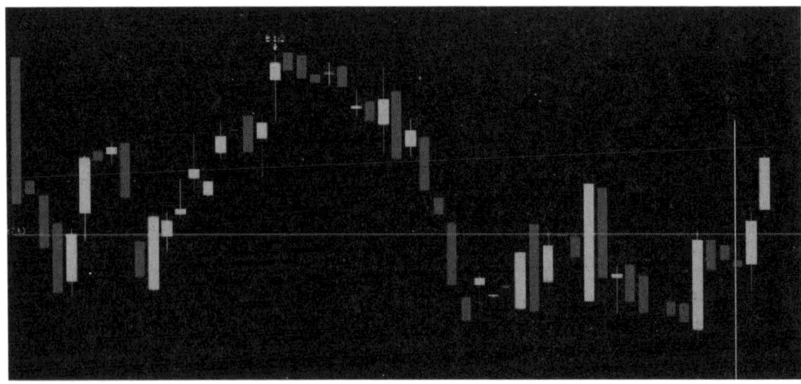

In the chart above of Gale, we can the price breaking out at the end.

GAIL Delivery

GAIL							
Scrips	Open	High	Low	Close	Volume	Delivery	Delivery(%)
Average (30days)	87.39	88.28	86.14	87.21	10885203	6007439	55
28-OCT-2022	88.40	90.25	87.85	90.05	20036187	12164194	61
27-OCT-2022	86.65	88.35	85.80	88.05	12203430	7739860	63
25-OCT-2022	86.80	87.55	85.90	86.55	7086629	4265650	60
24-OCT-2022	[illegible]	87.30	86.50	86.80	869107	606325	70
21-OCT-2022	87.45	88.10	86.25	86.45	7929074	3721821	47
20-OCT-2022	84.60	87.80	84.15	87.45	17120292	10056398	59
19-OCT-2022	85.45	85.80	84.50	84.80	7157063	3803473	53
18-OCT-2022	85.50	85.90	84.90	85.00	8035885	4592635	57
17-OCT-2022	85.10	85.65	84.35	85.05	9373705	5800132	62
14-OCT-2022	86.30	86.80	85.05	85.10	6931298	4084194	59
13-OCT-2022	86.65	87.20	85.25	85.45	6397554	3388329	53
12-OCT-2022	86.25	86.65	85.10	86.35	11033418	6110282	55
11-OCT-2022	89.10	89.10	86.00	86.20	13259938	7043551	53
10-OCT-2022	85.50	89.50	85.50	89.20	11158338	4731841	42
07-OCT-2022	87.55	87.65	86.05	86.85	12478992	8015144	64
06-OCT-2022	87.60	88.15	87.00	87.55	10663228	6816520	64

Below, we can observe that the delivery percentage rose up to 70% when the price was at Rs.87 and reached Rs. 90. This implies that the momentum is not yet strong. The average delivery percentage is 55%, whereas, 70% delivery took place on 24th October. If we track this delivery on the graph, we can see the graph rising up.

I hope that by now you have understood this valuable concept of delivery data. If you can implement this technique in conjunction with other indicators, your trading accuracy will be immensely higher.

Chapter 16

BEST INTRADAY STRATEGY

This is one of my most favourite strategies that I follow. The key behind this strategy is to follow the trend in order to make money, by using some particular indicators. Before delving deep into this strategy one has to understand two important aspects of the market.

1. Volatility
2. Stagnation or sideways

In the volatile phases of the market, the prices significantly go up or come down - both of these movements can be used to make profits. Hence, for this strategy, we need the market to be volatile.

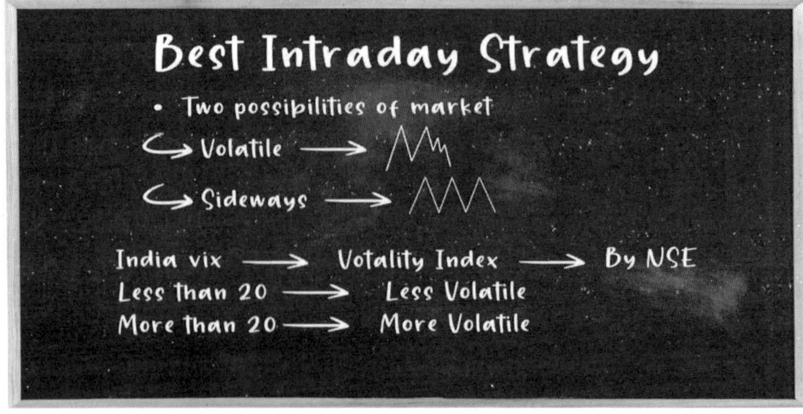

Whereas, in the Stagnation or Sideways phase, the prices slowly fluctuate within a close range and gets consolidated. The strategy is difficult to implement in this phase, but sometimes a particular situation can allow you to make profits nonetheless.

There is a popular index known as India Vix, which provides an idea of current volatility of the market. One can simply Google it in order to know of its current value. In the image below, the value appears to be 15.92 or almost 16. Now the question arises whether this value is good enough or not?

When India Vix remains under the value of 20, it implies the market is less volatile. Vice Versa, if the Vix value is above 20, the market tends to be more volatile. This index is produced by the NSE. It does so by calculating the premium of the options, and comes out with a value representing the market's volatility.

According to the above value, the market is less volatile, hence, the trades you'll get will be slow or of less value. Therefore, always get keep checking the current of value of Vix in order to get an idea about the market's volatility. This strategy is not limited to Nifty or Bank Nifty, but can be used on any type of stock because trend is the key. Wherever there is a price trend - this strategy can be implemented.

Let's begin with Bank Nifty. In the below image we can clearly observe a downtrend taking place as the price keeps making lower lows and lower highs.

There are three indicators to be used in this strategy. First being the SuperTrend, with its settings changed; Length =20 and Factor=2, to increase its efficiency. As soon as we implement the supertrend indicator on this graph, we can observe how quickly the market changed from sideways to a downtrend. Hence, the supertrend should not be used alone, but in combination with other indicators. Trading on the basis of Price Action is good but usage of several indicators help you confirm a trend to a good degree.

In the below image, the Supetrend has given us the first confirmation: at this particular candle the price is going to attain a downtrend.

Once the above downtrend is confirmed through Supertrend, we'll implement another indicator known as MACD, which we read about in the 10th chapter. In the below image, the blue line has intersected the red one from above, hence, the MACD is also implying that the price will fall.

We're not going to trade yet, we need a third confirmation

for which we'll use the indicator known as VWAP. As soon as we implement this indicator, we see a blue line emerge above the supertrend line.

Now, where the supertrend and MACD has given their indications of downtrend, at the same the point the price should be near the VWAP line. If the price is way above the VWAP, it indicates more chances of a downward moment, because as soon as the price goes away from the VWAP line, it tries to reach its average again.

In the below image, the VWAP is also seen following the price, as the price goes down, relatively, the VWAP slightly comes down too.

As we can observe that the price has gown way below the VWAP, nonetheless, at a particular point the price will start going back to reach this average or VWAP line.

Observe the below image, the price is near the VWAP and the it begins to move below, implying that a downtrend has started.

If the VWAP would have been already below the price, then again the price would try to reach it, again confirming the start of a downtrend.

When the price is near the VWAP, you can take your entry into the market. As the price will again try to reach its VWAP after going down, your stop loss will lessen.

Let's suppose, we enter the market on this particular point as shown in the below image. We can see the MACD is still below, supertrend is showing a downtrend and the price has continued going down. But now, your stoploss has more room, because, if the price tries to move towards the VWAP now, it'll lead to a loss. Hence, its more advantageous to take the entry where the price is near the VWAP.

Suppose we enter at this point where price is near the VWAP. This is the triple confirmation, wherein, the supertrend and MACD has both indicated the change in trend.

Now as we enter, we'll need to define our stop loss. We'll take a horizontal line, and mark the stop loss 3 candles before the entry point, as shown in the image below. Now if the price, moves up again after going down and your stop loss gets hit; you'll immediately get out. Because this would imply a change in the trend.

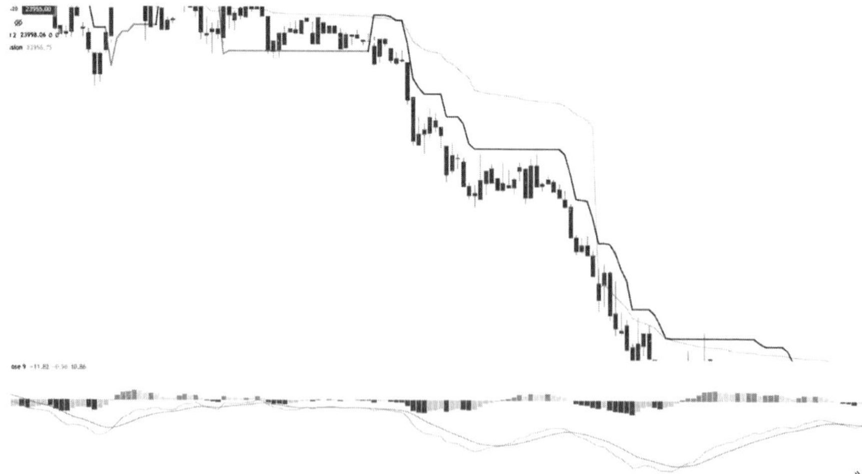

If the trend has changed, we should immediately get out. What would be our target? This point in the below picture, where we will exit. Although, if you wish to take lesser risk, then you can take note of the MACD; the blue line will intersect the red one from below, from here an early sign is generated that the price is likely to go up. Therefore, you can book your profits here if you wish to or you can keep trailing your stop loss. You can stay put till the time the trend is maintained.

Till now, we've been reading charts based on time frame of 5 minutes; for better confirmation, we can also read charts of 15 minute time frame as well, in order to increase our accuracy. I often refer to this strategy as the Brahmastra, because whenever it forms - it ends up generating good profits.

USE OF THIS STRATEGY IN UPTREND

In the below image, at this particular candle we can observe the supertrend and MACD indicating an uptrend. The price too is near its VWAP line. This candle becomes your entry point, whereas the previous 3rd candle becomes your stop loss as shown in the images below.

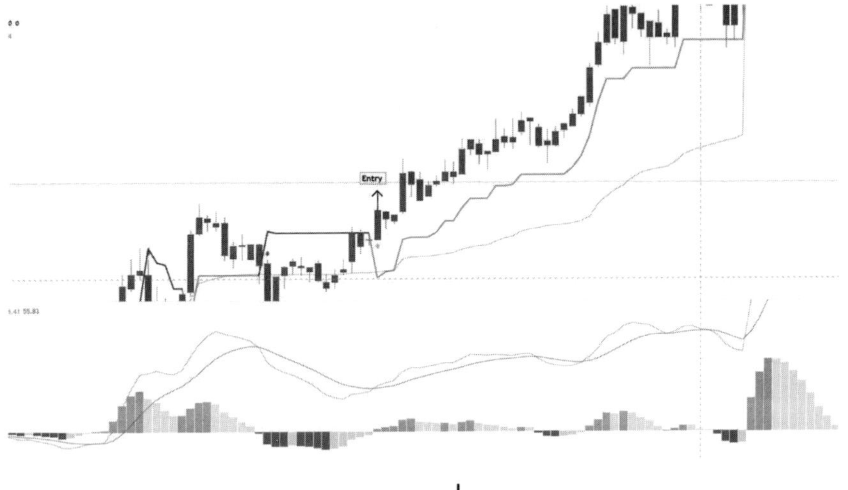

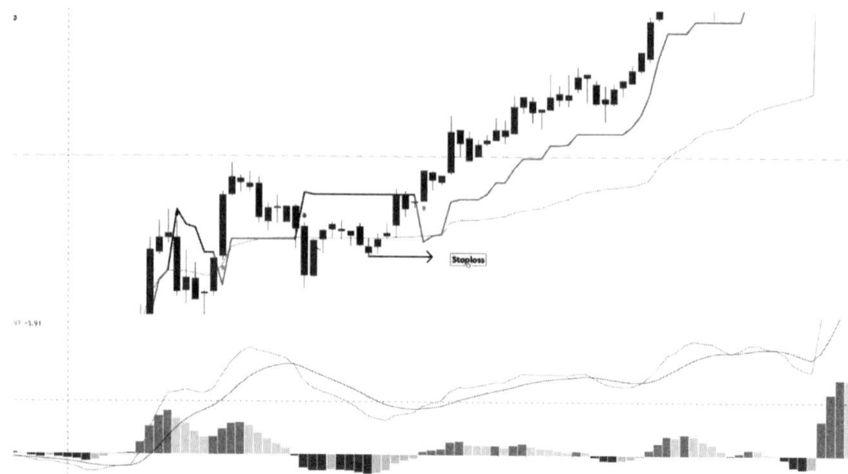

From here on, we simply wait. Till the time the trend continues, we will generate profits. In between you can observe the MACD crossover, where you can book your profits too or hold the position.

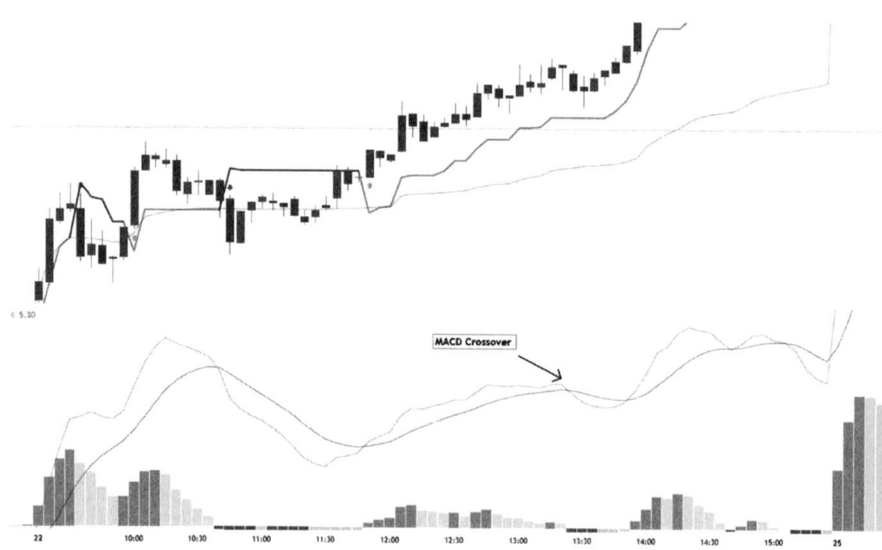

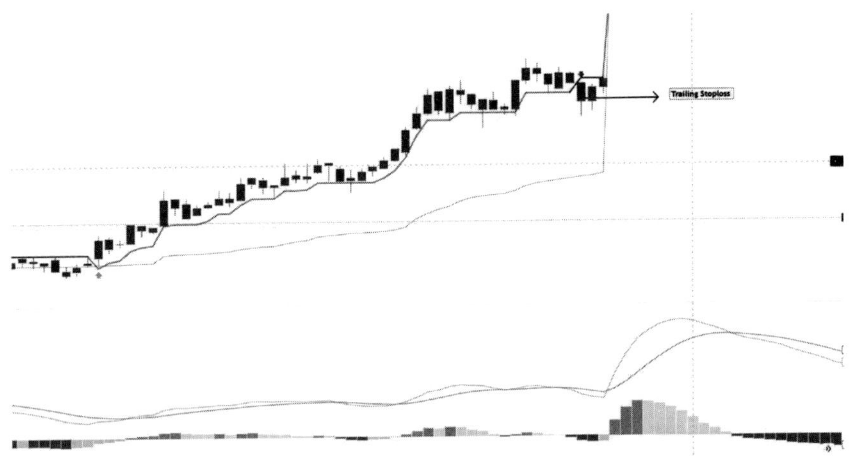

If you wish to take more risk, you can trail your stop loss, until you reach a point where the trend clearly changes. This is where you can book your final profits and exit.

ANOTHER EXAMPLE

Analyzing the given picture below, at the marked candle, we can observe the supertrend and MACD implying a decline in the trend. Here we can enter the market. Now the stop loss can be marked at the previous 3rd candle as shown below.

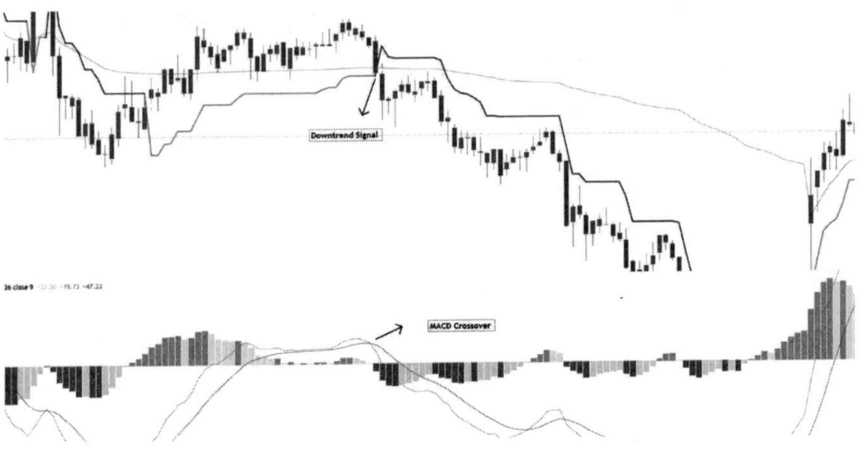

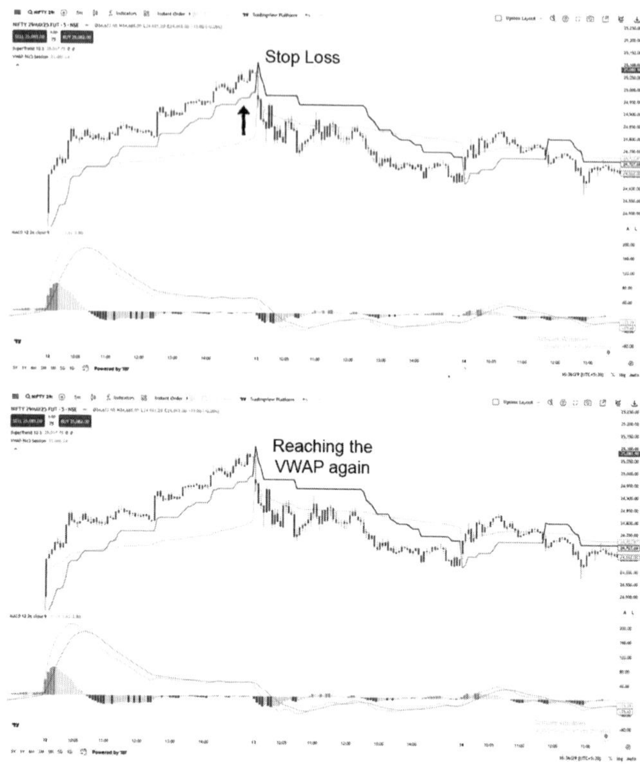

We can also see how the price went down but once again tried to reach the VWAP. Now the question arises, whether this would have leaded to a successful trade? Its clear that if the price goes below the VWAP; it'll try to reach back to it again. Hence, one thing to always keep in mind is that closer the price is to VWAP, the better it is.

Since we're using this strategy for Nifty Bank here, we won't carry it forward. If you analyse this overall, you can conclude that in buying the option, there wouldn't have been any profits and might lead to a small loss. This is because the Vix was low and that often leads to a sideways market.

EXAMPLE

As we can observe in the image below, at this particular candle the uptrend has begun, along with the MACD crossover below. At the same time, the VWAP falls on the same lines with the price too. This entry point can be assumed to be beneficial.

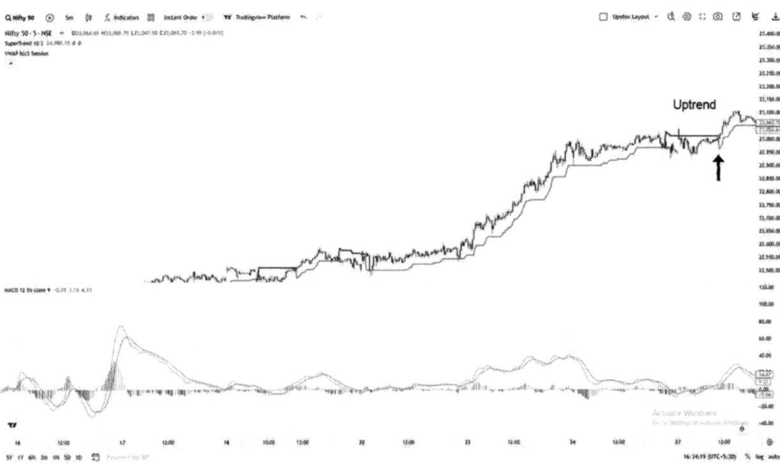

Stop loss can be marked as shown in the image below.

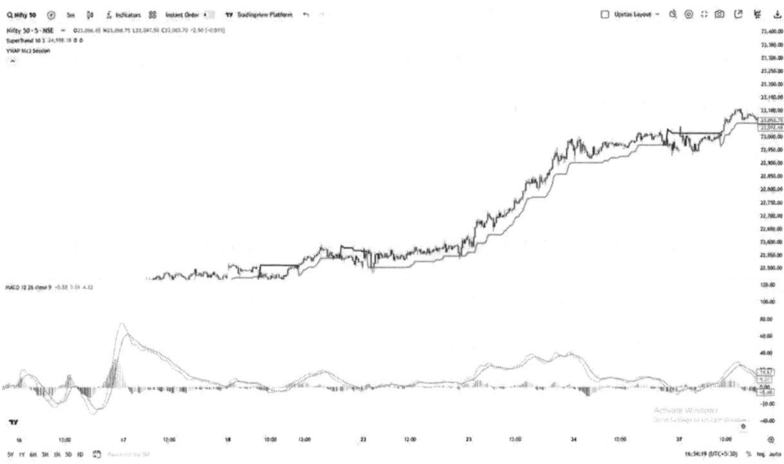

Now, you can exit when you encounter the first MACD crossover, or you can hold your position until the trend changes as shown in the below image.

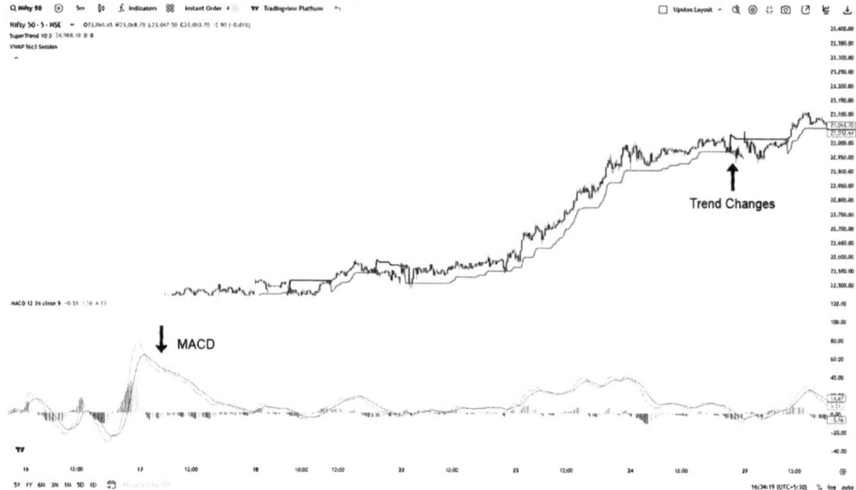

Despite the MACD crossover, you can take a risk, because chances are there that the trend won't suddenly change, but may assume a sideways trend causing theta decay. In the above image you can observe that the price more or less remained stagnant in a range after the MACD crossover had taken place. Its better to simply book the profits at MACD crossover there and then and move out.

NIFTY

Now moving on to Nifty, let's begin with the futures, since we cannot analyze the VWAP and volumes for the index graph. In the image below, we can observe a huge candle as well as MACD crossover right below. This is a good opportunity to enter the market; because the VWAP line is above the price. As we know the price tries to chase the VWAP line, if the price is below VWAP, it is a good time to enter. There is a high probability of the price rising above. Such trades often shoot up. Its imperative to keep your eye out for such trades.

EXAMPLE 2

In this example, the MACD crossover takes place before the supertrend has indicated a change in trend. Hence, this is not a beneficial time to enter. The three indicators should align in order to begin with the trade.

EXAMPLE 3

In the image below, we can observe the MACD has given a crossover, whereas the supertrend also indicates a change. The price is going up, but the VWAP line is still below the price. As per our strategy, this won't turn out to be much successful trade, because at any point the price will try to reach back to its VWAP.

EXAMPLE 4

In this scenario, we can observe the MACD is slightly placed before the supertrend, hence, we can still consider this trade opportunity because the VWAP is aligned with the price.

Now, if we enter here, we can mark our stop loss three candles before. Thereafter, we can book our profits at another MACD crossover.

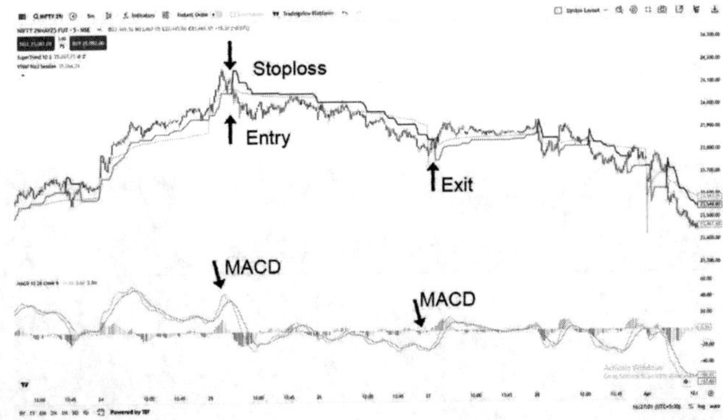

EXAMPLE 5

This is a perfect example of a good trade opportunity. As you can observe in the image below, the MACD crossover lies right under the change in supertrend. Moreover, the price is perfectly aligned with VWAP. Hence, there is a probability of the price shooting up, resulting in a successful trade.

You should observe many more such examples before initiating to implement this strategy right away. Moreover, you can also start with paper trading for the purpose of practice. Thereafter, you can start trading in small lots, and slowly build your experience as well as profits. Beginners often start with a lot of money only to incur losses. Hence, start small and practice diligently.

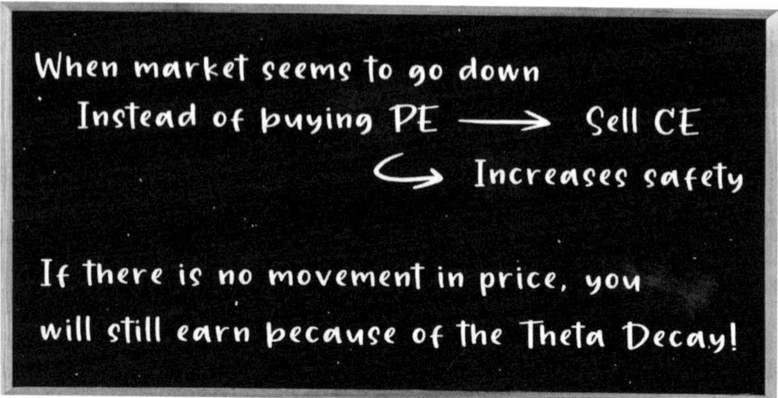

Lastly, when we see the market going sideways or the Volatility reduces, do not buy options. People often assume the market will fall and buy Put Options. Instead, go for selling your Call Options, in order to increase your security.

If you see a trend forming, and you decide to buy Call Option, do the opposite and sell the Put Option. This is done in case there is no significant movement in a sideways market, hence, you'll be able to earn because of theta decay.

Chapter 17

WHAT IS FUTURE & OPTIONS TRADING IN SHARE MARKET?

This particular chapter may have been highly anticipated by readers. Futures and options are considered to be one of the riskiest financial instruments, unless you have a solid understanding of how they work. Unfortunately, about 90% of people who invest in these instruments end up losing 90% of their invested capital within the first 90 days.

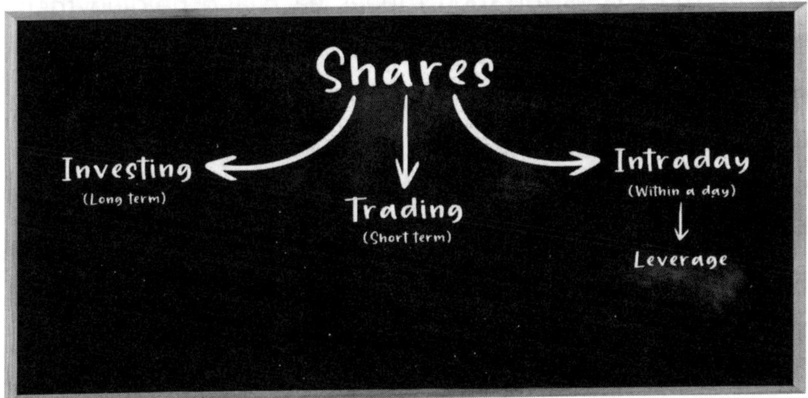

This statistic alone highlights the significant risk associated with these instruments, particularly for beginners. However, if you learn and understand how these instruments work, you can convert this risk into profit. For most people, trading means buying and selling shares. You purchase a share, and if its price increases, you earn a profit. If it decreases, you incur a loss. This process is not too risky for an investor since the money is invested for an extended time period, which balances out market movements. This investment type is known as delivery.

But what makes investing risky? This is where intraday trading comes into play. Although intraday trading carries a high level of risk, it has some benefits as well.

INTRADAY VS DELIVERY TRADING

- **PROFITS**

Typically, trading involves buying shares and waiting for their price to increase before selling them. However, in intraday trading, you have the option to sell first and then buy when the price goes down. For instance, in delivery trading, buying 100 shares for 1000 rupees each and holding them until the price rises to 1200 rupees each results in a profit of 20,000 rupees. But if the price falls to 800 rupees, you would incur the same amount in losses. In contrast, intraday trading works differently. Here, you can sell the 100 shares for 1200 rupees each and then buy them back when the price falls to 1000 rupees each, making a profit of 20,000 rupees. Therefore, intraday trading can be profitable in both upward and downward price movements.

Generally,
We buy → Price go up → We sell
Rs 1000 → Rs 1200 → Rs 200 Profit
In future & options,
We sell → Price go down → We buy
Rs 1200 → Rs 1000 → Rs 200 Profit
If 1 share = Rs 1000 & you bought = 100
then 1000*100 = 1 Lakh (was your investment)
And earned,
200*100 = Rs 20,000

- **LEVERAGE**

Further elaborating on the previous example, earning a profit of 20,000 rupees with 100 shares requires an initial capital of 100 x 1000 = 100,000 rupees. Unfortunately, not everyone has such a substantial amount to invest. In such scenarios, an individual can still earn a profit of 20,000 rupees using a capital of just 20,000 rupees through intra-day trading. This can be achieved by utilizing leverage, which is when the required margin decreases to one-fifth of the initial amount. The number of shares remains 100, but the required margin is reduced to 20,000 rupees. Brokers provide leverage to traders.

- **LOSSES**

The use of intraday trading can result in significant profits, but at the same time, it can also lead to substantial losses. As seen in the above example, if the share price falls from 1000 to 800 rupees, a loss of 20,000 rupees would be incurred. This is why intraday trading provides features such as stop-loss orders, which enables a trader to exit a position at a predetermined level of risk. Stoploss orders are particularly useful in intraday trading because they can help prevent the occurrence of complete losses. For example, if the maximum loss that a trader can tolerate is 20,000 rupees, a stop loss order could be set at a lower amount, such as 4000 or 5000 rupees. The specific level of stop loss can be determined based on the trader's calculation of the risk-to-reward ratio. Ideally, the risk-to-reward ratio should be at least 1:2, which means that for every 1000 rupees risked, the expected gain should be 2000 rupees.

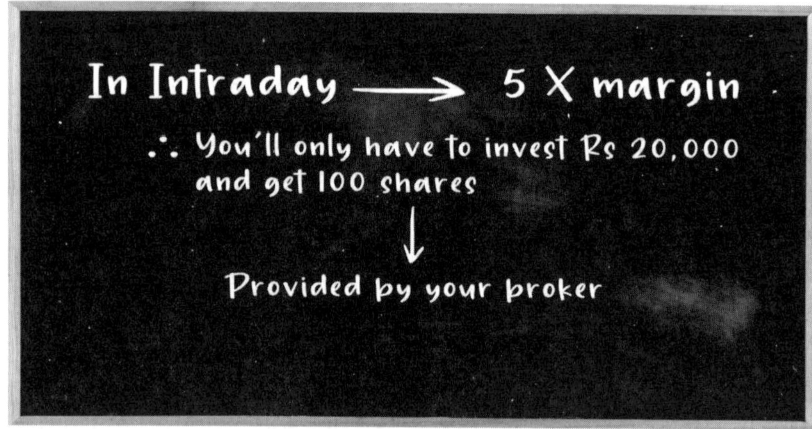

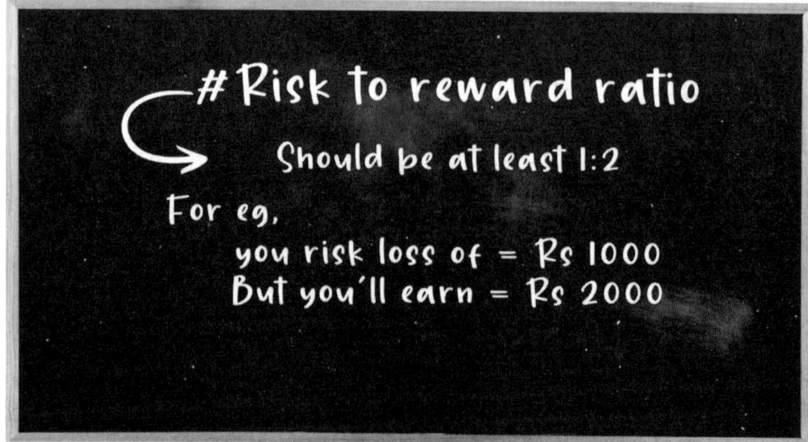

After the discussion above, you must have gained a decent understanding of intraday trading. Now, let's return to the primary query: What exactly is Futures and Options trading?

Taking the same example from intraday, suppose a person aims for a profit of 20,000 with capital investment of 20,000 but now he wants to trade for a longer period for:

- **Better margins**
- **Better leverage**
- **Time flexibility as in three expiry terms**

To get a better understanding, you can explore a trading platform, where you can view the listed futures and experiment with margin calculating tools using different combinations. Futures are typically classified into three expiry term contracts, namely the current month (the month of investment), near month (the approaching month), and far month (the second month after the near month).

The different expiry term contracts for futures have varying prices. This is because futures and spot shares have different intrinsic natures and intended uses. Additionally, futures trading requires a specific lot size, which can result in large numbers when combined with the share price. For instance, if you wish to trade in TATA Motors shares, your required margin could be as high as 6 lakhs. But if you choose futures, for the same share, your required margin comes down to around 1.5 lakhs for the same lot.

Considering not everyone has the required amount of capital to invest in futures trading; the stock brokers came up with a solution to this problem. They provide leverages on required margins, which can be calculated using margin calculators on trading platforms. It is important to note that leverage on futures is much lower than on options. For example, NIFTY shares with a lot size of 50 are priced at around 8 lakhs, while NIFTY futures are priced at around 86,000 and options are priced at around 12,000.

Hence, I always emphasize that Futures and Options can be profitable only if you have a clear understanding of the trading strategies and techniques to be employed.

Chapter 18

OPTIONS TRADING FOR BEGINNERS IN SHARE MARKET

I am sure a lot of beginners are enthusiastic about this chapter, eager to learn how to trade in options. Many people find options to be an attractive investment instrument. However, I always caution that futures and options can be risky endeavors unless a person fully understands what they are doing. It is important to focus on learning the fundamentals first. Once you have gained sufficient knowledge, options trading can be a profitable venture rather than a risky gamble.

Option trading is a complex subject, and many people have limited knowledge of it. There is often confusion about terms such as ITM, ATM, and OTM, as well as uncertainty about which to choose.

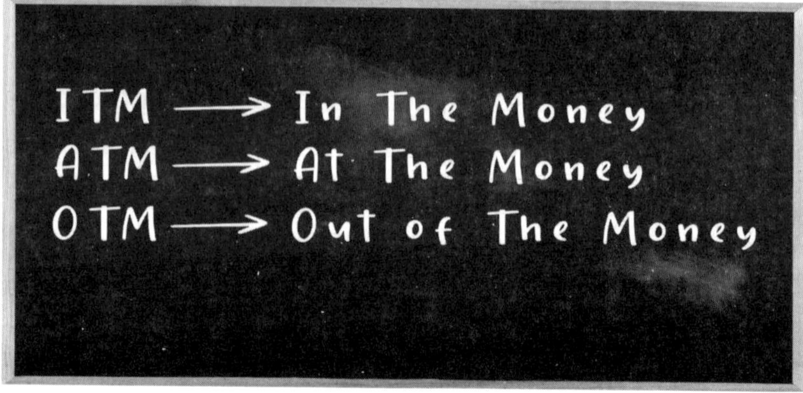

When discussing options, the conversation usually revolves around two types of assets: stocks or indices. Many traders prefer to trade in indices for options, such as NIFTY or Bank NIFTY. As we have previously discussed, the quantity of options trading is typically measured in terms of lot sizes. In the case of NIFTY, the lot size is 50, while for Bank NIFTY it is 25. Therefore, the price of an option is calculated by multiplying the value of ITM, ATM, or OTM by the lot size. For instance, an option for Bank NIFTY would be priced at lot size (25) multiplied by the value of ITM/OTM/ATM (100), which equals ₹2500.

WHY ARE OPTIONS OPTED FOR?

Suppose you want to purchase a stock with a price tag of ₹10,000, but you don't have the necessary funds to do so. In this case, there is an option that allows you to purchase only the premium value of the stock, which is significantly less than the actual share price. This is one of the main reasons why options trading appears to be so appealing.

In options trading, investors commonly purchase call options when they anticipate that stock prices will rise and put options when they expect a decline. This approach is also commonly used when trading in indices. However, this is not the only way that options trading works. In addition to purchasing call options, investors who anticipate a rise in stock prices can also sell Put options. Similarly, when anticipating a dip, investors can purchase Put options or sell Buy options.

Option trading is a zero-sum game, meaning that if a buyer profits, the seller incurs a loss, and vice versa. When trading with a call option, there is a 33% chance that the trade will be in the buyer's favor and a 67% chance that it will be in the seller's favor. The reason behind this will become clearer in the next chapter. While the seller has a slight advantage over the buyer, the potential for capital gains is higher for the buyer.

For example, suppose a share of NIFTY is priced at ₹18,000. Buying a future of the same share would also be costly. However, if an option for the same share is purchased, the price of the option would be (lot size x value of option) = 50 x 100 = ₹5,000. On the other hand, if you were a seller, the same option would be worth D1 lakh. Since most people have limited funds to invest, they tend to buy options more often. Because buyers invest less money overall, sellers tend to dominate in this relationship, benefiting them more.

Now that we have a better understanding of the underlying workings of option trading, let's turn our attention back to the types of options. There are two main types of options: Call and Put.

CALL OPTION

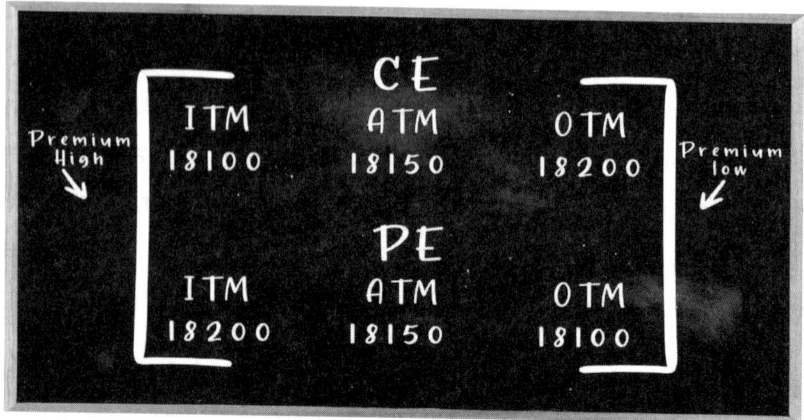

Options in trading rely on three main instruments known as ITM, ATM, and OTM. Despite sounding intimidating, these are simple terms that refer to the position of the price in option trading.

For example, let's consider NIFTY. If we check its current price, let's say it is ₹18,145, then ITM, ATM, and OTM can be defined based on this price. NIFTY lists its strike prices at intervals of 50 basis points, so ₹18,150 becomes its ATM (at the money) price, which is the current price. ₹18,200 becomes its OTM (out of the money) price, which is the price it is expected to move towards, while ₹18,100 becomes its ITM (in the money) price, which is the price it has already surpassed.

PUT OPTION

When it comes to Put options, the definitions of ITM and OTM are slightly different. Let's consider NIFTY as an example again, where the ATM is ₹18,145. In this case, the OTM is ₹18,100, as the prices are expected to fall. The ITM is ₹18,200, as the prices have already fallen beyond the ATM.

At times, people may speculate about the OTM price strikes. For instance, if the price is hovering around the above margins, one may speculate that the price will reach D19,000. In such cases, a seller may offer buy options to this person, and option trading occurs at the OTM. It's important to note that premiums at OTM are generally the cheapest, while ITM premiums are the costliest.

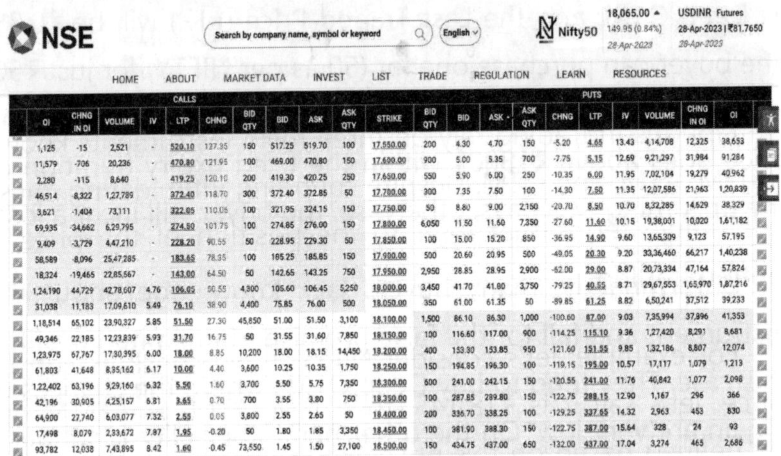

CALLS											PUTS									
OI	CHNG IN OI	VOLUME	IV	LTP	CHNG	BID QTY	BID	ASK	ASK QTY	STRIKE	BID QTY	BID	ASK	ASK QTY	CHNG	LTP	IV	VOLUME	CHNG IN OI	OI
1,125	-15	2,521	-	520.10	127.35	150	517.25	519.70	100	17,550.00	200	4.30	4.70	150	-5.20	4.65	13.43	4,14,708	12,325	38,653
11,579	-706	20,236	-	470.80	121.95	100	469.00	470.80	150	17,600.00	900	5.00	5.35	700	-7.75	5.15	12.69	9,21,297	31,984	91,284
2,280	-115	8,640	-	419.25	120.10	200	419.30	420.25	250	17,650.00	550	5.90	6.00	250	-10.35	6.00	11.95	7,02,104	19,279	40,962
46,514	-8,322	1,27,789	-	372.40	118.70	300	372.40	372.85	50	17,700.00	300	7.35	7.50	100	-14.30	7.50	11.35	12,07,586	21,963	1,20,839
3,621	-1,404	73,111	-	322.05	110.05	100	321.95	324.15	150	17,750.00	50	8.80	9.00	2,150	-20.70	8.50	10.70	8,32,285	14,629	38,329
69,935	-34,662	6,29,795	-	274.50	101.75	100	274.85	276.00	150	17,800.00	6,050	11.50	11.60	7,350	-27.60	11.60	10.15	19,38,001	10,020	1,61,182
9,409	-3,729	4,47,210	-	228.20	90.55	50	228.95	229.30	50	17,850.00	100	15.00	15.20	850	-36.95	14.90	9.60	13,65,309	9,123	57,195
58,589	-8,096	25,47,285	-	183.65	78.35	100	185.25	185.85	150	17,900.00	500	20.60	20.95	500	-49.05	20.30	9.20	33,36,460	66,217	1,40,238
18,324	-19,465	22,85,567	-	143.00	64.50	50	142.65	143.25	750	17,950.00	2,950	28.85	28.95	2,900	-62.00	29.00	8.87	20,73,334	47,164	57,824
1,24,190	44,729	42,78,607	4.76	106.05	90.55	4,300	105.60	106.45	5,250	18,000.00	3,450	41.70	41.80	3,750	-79.25	40.55	8.71	29,67,553	1,65,970	1,87,216
31,038	11,183	17,09,610	5.49	76.10	38.90	4,400	75.85	76.00	500	18,050.00	350	61.00	61.35	50	-89.85	61.25	8.82	6,50,241	37,512	39,233
1,18,514	65,102	23,90,327	5.85	51.50	27.30	45,850	51.00	51.50	3,100	18,100.00	1,500	86.10	86.30	1,000	-100.60	87.00	9.03	7,35,994	37,896	41,353
49,346	22,185	12,23,839	5.93	31.70	16.75	50	31.55	31.60	7,850	18,150.00	100	116.60	117.00	900	-114.25	115.10	9.36	1,27,420	8,291	8,681
1,23,975	67,767	17,30,395	6.00	18.00	8.85	10,200	18.00	18.15	14,450	18,200.00	400	153.30	153.85	950	-121.60	151.55	9.85	1,32,186	8,807	12,074
61,803	41,648	8,35,162	6.17	10.00	4.40	3,600	10.25	10.35	1,750	18,250.00	150	194.85	196.30	100	-119.15	195.00	10.57	17,117	1,079	1,213
1,22,402	63,196	9,29,160	6.32	5.50	1.60	3,700	5.50	5.75	7,350	18,300.00	600	241.00	242.15	150	-120.55	241.00	11.76	40,842	1,077	2,098
42,196	30,905	4,25,157	6.81	3.65	0.70	700	3.55	3.80	750	18,350.00	100	287.85	289.80	150	-122.75	288.15	12.90	1,167	296	366
64,900	27,740	6,03,077	7.32	2.55	0.05	3,800	2.55	2.65	50	18,400.00	200	336.70	338.25	100	-129.25	337.65	14.32	2,963	453	830
17,498	8,079	2,33,672	7.87	1.95	-0.20	50	1.80	1.85	3,350	18,450.00	100	381.90	388.30	150	-122.75	387.00	15.64	328	24	93
93,782	12,038	7,43,895	8.42	1.60	-0.45	73,550	1.45	1.50	27,100	18,500.00	150	434.75	437.00	650	-132.00	437.00	17.04	3,274	465	2,686

To remember the categories in option charts, I use a simple analogy of a milk and cream mixture. The yellow section represents the cream, which is costlier than the milk itself and corresponds to ITM. The white section represents the milk, which is cheaper and corresponds to OTM. This can be validated by the Last Traded Price (LTP) values for Call Option (CE) and Put Option (PE) premiums, as shown in the image above.

For example, the premium for CE ITM is ₹92.00 at the current market price of ₹18150. As we move towards ITM at ₹18100, the premium increases to ₹122.00 and keeps increasing up to

₹568.20 at the strike price of ₹17600. Conversely, as we move towards OTM, the premium reduces to D67.00 at ₹18200 and further decreases to ₹3.00 at the strike price of ₹18500. The same pattern is observed in PE, with ITM premiums being costlier, such as ₹394.0 at ₹18500.

Let's continue with the previous example where the seller wanted to sell for ₹19000. In this case, the option is considered as Deep OTM, and the Last Traded Price (LTP) will be ₹0.85. The buyer can purchase one lot (50 as per NIFTY) for just ₹50. However, in this case, the buyer will only make a profit if the price goes above ₹18801 within the fixed expiry duration of the upcoming two days, otherwise, the buyer will incur a loss.

Unfortunately, many buyers lack knowledge about the instrument and fall for the false promise of unlimited profit in this case. They tend to buy Deep OTMs where the chances of a gain are very low. On the other hand, the seller is seriously invested in the interplay and goes after the premium money to make profits.

EXAMPLES:

CE 18800 ⟶ Rs 1

Profit when Nifty reaches : 18801

Currently Nifty is : 18150

Days to expiry : 2 Days

Less chances ⟶ Less premium

Seller might get : 1*5 = Rs 50

Let's say

Nifty went to ⟶ 18200

Will premium reach Rs 50 ⟶ No

If,

18150 ⟶ ATM

Then margin ↑↑ ⟶ 2.5 points

Let's delve into the margin requirement of the seller in this scenario. If an individual buys the CE at ₹18800, the profit potential can be unlimited and the premium will be at 1 (with a loss potential of up to 50). The break-even point will be at ₹18801.

On the other hand, if the same individual decides to sell the CE at a profit of ₹50, the margin requirement will be approximately ₹75000. In the case of ATM (at the money) options, such as the one at ₹18150, the margin requirement for the seller will be 1 lakh and they will only earn a premium of ₹4600.

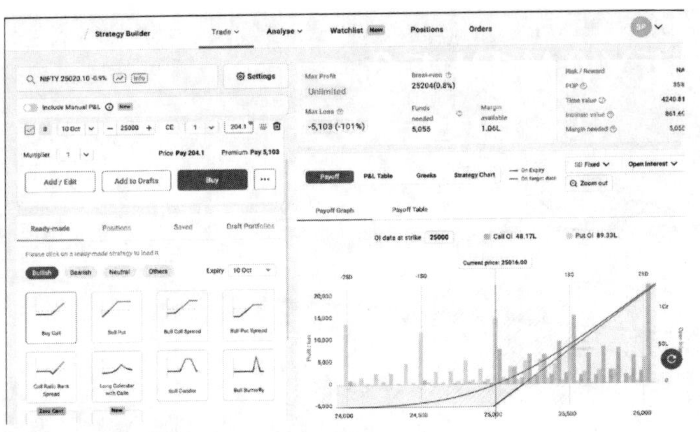

Let's take an example to understand the concept better. Suppose you purchase a CE for ₹18800 and the current NIFTY price is at ₹18150. If the NIFTY price goes up to ₹18200, the premium will increase only up to D1 and not up to the required ₹50 to make a profit. This trade will not be profitable. However, if you had purchased a CE for ₹18150, then in that case, your premium would have increased by up to 25%.

From the above example, it is advised to avoid trading in deep OTM options. Another reason for this is Delta, which is the ratio of the change in the price of the option to the change in the price of the underlying asset. Delta is a value between 0 and 1 for call options, and between 0 and -1 for put options. Delta helps to understand the increase in NIFTY by 1 point with respect to the increase in our premium ratio. The Delta for ATM is approximately ±0.5, for INM it varies from 0.5 to closer to 1, and for OTM it varies from 0 to a maximum of 0.5.

In a nutshell , one should take the INT and ATM option as the movement will help you gain profit.

Chapter 19

To Open Free Demat Account, Just Scan the QR Code

OPTION GREEKS DELTA, GAMMA, THETA, VEGA EXPLAINED

This chapter holds great significance for individuals engaged in options trading. Option Greeks form a crucial aspect of option trading fundamentals. We will begin by addressing a few questions that we will explore through option Greeks.

#1st Scenario
Suppose, during weekly, expiry,
on friday,
X Bought ⟶ 18000 CE at Rs 200
X keeps it till monday
on monday ⟶ price falls to : Rs160
But market stayed at 18000
X had paid ⟶ 200 x 50 (Lots) = Rs 10,000
#2nd Scenario
Now, 160 x 50 = Rs 8000 (Loss of Rs 2000)
Suppose,
If Nifty moves 18000 ⟶ 18100
Then premium ⟶ ?

Suppose a trader purchased a call option of ₹18000 Nifty at the money for ₹200 on Friday when the actual price of Nifty was also at ₹18000. However, instead of selling the option on Friday, he carried it forward. Subsequently, he noticed that the call option price had dropped to ₹160, although the price of NIFTY was still at ₹18000. Since the lot size of NIFTY is 50, his initial investment was 50 * 200 = ₹10000, which has now reduced to 50 * 160 = ₹8000, resulting in a loss of ₹2000. The question arises as to why he suffered a loss of ₹2000 despite the price of NIFTY remaining unchanged at ₹18000.

On the other hand, let's assume that a trader purchased a call option of ₹18000 NIFTY at the money for ₹200 on Friday, and the actual price of NIFTY also stood at ₹18000 on that day. Now, on the same day, the price of NIFTY increased to ₹18100. The question that arises is, by how much will the premium increase from ₹200? Also, will the premium increase by 100 points as NIFTY did, or will it gain in price by a different amount?

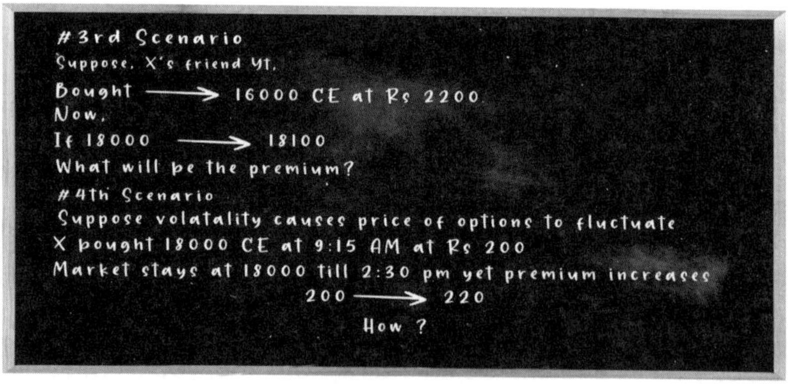

Now, let's Suppose a trader purchases a ₹16000 Nifty at-the-money call option for ₹2200 on Friday, and the current price of Nifty is also at ₹18000. Now, suppose the price of Nifty rises to ₹18100 on the same day. The question is, what will be the increase in the premium from the initial price of ₹2200?

DO OPTION PRICES VARY DUE TO THE VOLATILITY IN THE MARKET?

ANSWER 1.

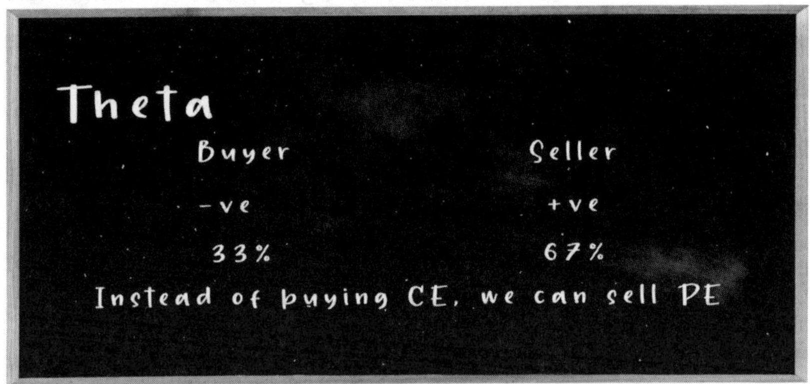

It is possible for the trader to suffer a loss of ₹2000 on their investment of ₹10000 even if the price of NIFTY remains constant at ₹18000. Furthermore, if NIFTY continues to remain at ₹18000 until Thursday, which is the weekly expiry day of the option, then the investment of ₹10000 will become ₹0, resulting in a complete loss for the trader.

This scenario arises due to the impact of the first Greek option called Theta, which refers to the rate of decline in the value of an option over time. Theta is positive for the seller and negative for the buyer. For instance, if you lend D10000 to your friend and charge an interest of ₹500, you as the seller make a profit of ₹500.

In options trading, the probability of winning on the buying side is only 33%, while it is 67% on the seller side. This is because if the market is consistent at a particular price range or moves sideways, the seller is always on the profitable side. To avoid losses due to Theta, traders can sell a put option instead of buying a call option. Selling a put option benefits from the direction of the market. If the market goes up, the buyer of the put option will be at a loss, but the seller will make a profit. Even if the market moves sideways, the seller of the put option can still make a profit.

On the day of weekly expiry, the trader who bought the ₹18000 NIFTY option and paid a premium of ₹200 will only break even if the market goes up to ₹18200. This means that the trader will only start making a profit if the market goes above ₹18200. On the other hand, the seller of the option will make a profit of ₹200 if the market remains consistent at ₹18000, and will break even if the market reaches ₹18200.

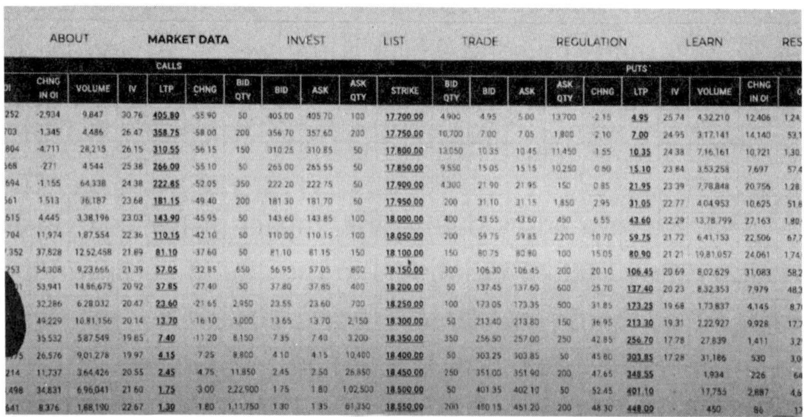

ABOUT MARKET DATA INVEST LIST TRADE REGULATION LEARN RES

	CALLS										PUTS									
OI	CHNG IN OI	VOLUME	IV	LTP	CHNG	BID QTY	BID	ASK	ASK QTY	STRIKE	BID QTY	BID	ASK	ASK QTY	CHNG	LTP	IV	VOLUME	CHNG IN OI	O
252	-2,934	9,847	30.76	**405.80**	-55.90	50	405.00	405.70	100	**17,700.00**	4,900	4.95	5.00	13,700	-2.15	**4.95**	25.74	4,32,210	12,406	1.24
703	-1,345	4,486	26.47	**358.75**	-58.00	200	356.70	357.60	200	**17,750.00**	10,700	7.00	7.05	1,800	-2.10	**7.00**	24.95	3,17,141	14,140	53.1
804	-4,711	28,215	26.15	**310.55**	-56.15	150	310.25	310.85	50	**17,800.00**	13,050	10.35	10.45	11,450	-1.55	**10.35**	24.38	7,16,161	10,721	1.30
568	-271	4,544	25.38	**266.00**	-55.10	50	265.00	265.55	50	**17,850.00**	9,550	15.05	15.15	10,250	0.80	**15.10**	23.84	3,53,258	7,697	57.4
694	-1,155	64,338	24.38	**222.85**	-52.05	350	222.20	222.75	50	**17,900.00**	4,300	21.90	21.95	150	0.85	**21.95**	23.39	7,78,848	20,756	1.28
561	1,513	36,187	23.68	**181.15**	-49.40	200	181.30	181.70	50	**17,950.00**	200	31.10	31.15	1,850	2.95	**31.05**	22.77	4,04,953	10,625	51.8
615	4,445	3,38,196	23.03	**143.90**	-45.95	50	143.60	143.85	100	**18,000.00**	400	43.55	43.60	450	6.55	**43.60**	22.29	13,78,799	27,163	1.80
704	11,974	1,87,554	22.36	**110.15**	-42.10	50	110.00	110.15	100	**18,050.00**	200	59.75	59.85	2,200	10.70	**59.75**	21.72	6,41,153	22,506	67.7
352	37,828	12,52,458	21.89	**81.10**	-37.60	50	81.10	81.15	150	**18,100.00**	150	80.75	80.90	100	15.05	**80.90**	21.21	19,81,057	24,061	1.74
253	54,308	9,23,666	21.39	**57.05**	-32.85	650	56.95	57.05	800	**18,150.00**	300	106.30	106.45	200	20.10	**106.45**	20.69	8,02,629	31,083	58.2
[illegible]	53,941	14,86,675	20.92	**37.85**	-27.40	50	37.80	37.85	400	**18,200.00**	50	137.45	137.60	600	25.70	**137.40**	20.23	8,32,353	7,979	48.3
[illegible]	32,286	6,28,032	20.47	**23.60**	-21.65	2,950	23.55	23.60	700	**18,250.00**	100	173.05	173.35	500	31.85	**173.25**	19.68	1,73,837	4,145	8.7
[illegible]	49,229	10,81,156	20.14	**13.70**	-16.10	3,000	13.65	13.70	2,150	**18,300.00**	50	213.40	213.80	150	36.95	**213.30**	19.31	2,22,927	9,928	17.7
[illegible]	35,532	5,87,549	19.85	**7.40**	-11.20	8,150	7.35	7.40	3,200	**18,350.00**	350	256.50	257.00	250	42.85	**256.70**	17.78	27,839	1,411	3.2
75	26,576	9,01,278	19.97	**4.15**	-7.25	9,800	4.10	4.15	10,400	**18,400.00**	50	303.25	303.85	50	45.80	**303.85**	17.28	31,186	530	3.0
214	11,737	3,64,426	20.55	**2.45**	-4.75	11,850	2.45	2.50	26,850	**18,450.00**	250	351.00	351.90	200	47.65	**348.55**	-	1,934	226	64
498	34,831	6,96,041	21.60	**1.75**	-3.00	2,22,900	1.75	1.80	1,02,500	**18,500.00**	50	401.35	402.10	50	52.45	**401.10**	-	17,755	2,887	4.6
641	8,376	1,68,190	22.67	**1.30**	-1.80	1,11,750	1.30	1.35	81,350	**18,550.00**	200	450.15	451.20	200	48.30	**448.00**	-	450	86	17

Whenever we pay a premium for the option, the premium consists of two things:

- Time value
- Intrinsic Value

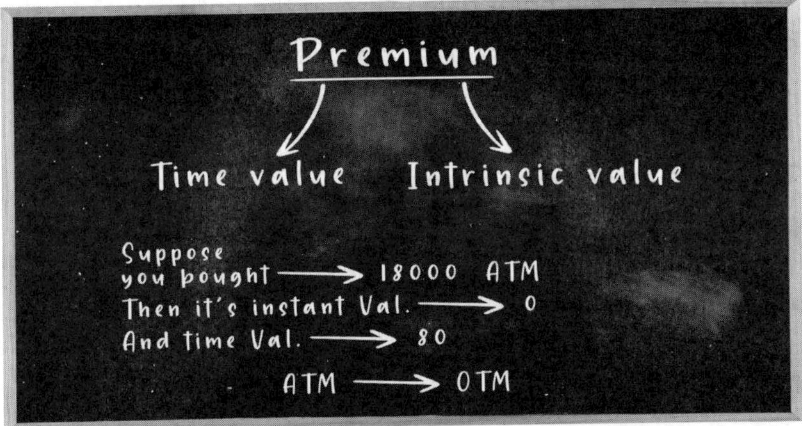

If an option of ₹ 18100 of NIFTY is bought at ₹ 80 and the price of NIFTY is also ₹80. Then, The intrinsic value will be ₹0 (18100-18100) and the time value will be ₹80

Option Premium - Intrinsic Value = Time Value

If the option of ₹ 16000 is bought at the premium of 2200 and the value of NIFTY is ₹ 18000. Then, the intrinsic value will be ₹ 2000 (18000-16000) and the time value will be ₹ 200 (2200-2000)

ANSWER 2

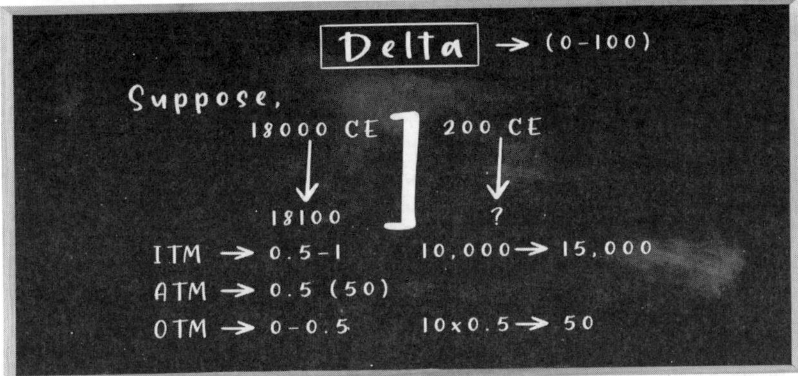

To answer the point gain asked in the option, we use the Greek called **Delta.** ₹18000 call option was bought at the price of 200. The market has moved to 18100 that is by 100 points.

There are three types of option

- In the money
- At the money
- Out of the money

The value of the delta is 0-1

The delta for in the money is 0.5 -1

The delta for at the money is 0.5

The delta for out of the money is 0-0.5

As the we have at the money delta of 0.5 and the point gain is 100

The gain in premium is delta*Gain in points i.e. 100 * 0.5 = 50

The premium now will rise to ₹250 from ₹200

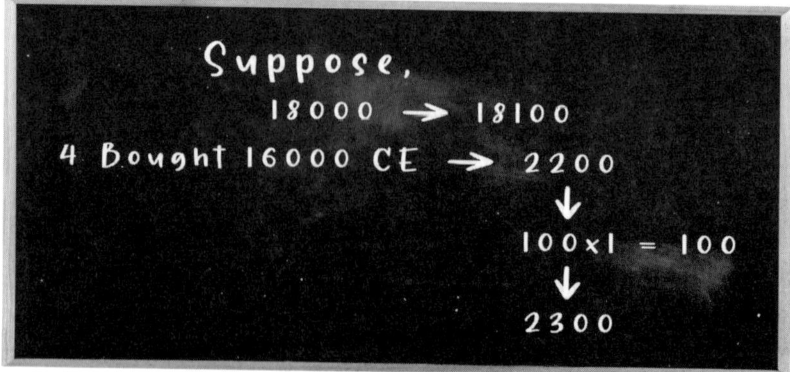

ANSWER 3

A 16000 call option was bought at the premium of ₹2200 and the NIFTY at the time was ₹18000. The NIFTY now has gained 100 points i.e., it has reached a value of ₹18100 from initial ₹18000.

In this case the trade has been made deep in the money. Therefore, the delta here will be close to 1.

The gain in premium is delta*Gain in points i.e., 100 * 1 = 100

The premium will now rise to ₹2300 from ₹2200

UNDERSTANDING GAMA

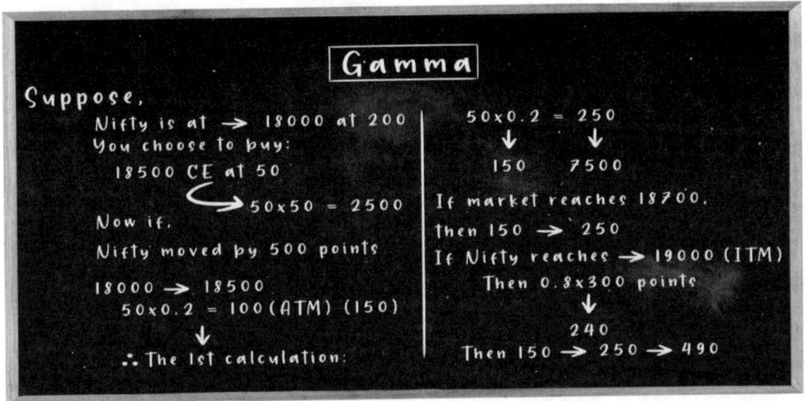

Assuming the below trade:

NIFTY was at ₹18000. With a lot size of 50, the total investment was ₹2500. If the NIFTY rises from ₹18000 to ₹18500, a gain of 500 points, the option is considered out of the money with a delta of 0.2. The gain in premium will be 0.2 multiplied by 500, resulting in a gain of ₹100. The premium will rise from ₹50 to ₹150, and the total value of the investment will be ₹7500, which is three times the initial investment. If the NIFTY further rises from ₹18500 to ₹18700, a gain of 200 points, the option is now in the money, and the delta increases to 0.5. Thus, the gain in the premium will be 0.5 multiplied by 200, resulting in a gain of ₹100. The premium will rise from ₹150 to ₹250. If the NIFTY continues to rise from ₹18700 to ₹19000, a gain of ₹300, the option is further in the money, and the delta increases to 0.8. The gain in the premium will be 0.8 multiplied by 300, resulting in a gain of ₹240. The premium will rise from ₹250 to ₹490. Gamma refers to the rate of change in delta, which can be observed in the above example as the delta changes with the movement of the NIFTY.

ANSWER 4

Option prices are subject to fluctuations due to volatility in the market, which can be observed in the options chain with the term IV or implied volatility. IV reflects the market's level of volatility. If a call option is purchased and the IV increases, the premium will also increase. Similarly, if an option is sold and the IV increases, the premium will increase as well. However, if the IV decreases, the premium will also decrease for both buyers and sellers. It is advantageous to purchase an option at a low IV, specifically below 10, because the price will increase when the IV increases. In contrast, if the IV is high, it is recommended to sell the option and take profit as there is a likelihood that the IV will decrease. This market volatility is also known as Vega.

Chapter 20

To Open Free Demat Account, Just Scan the QR Code

OPTION CHAIN ANALYIS

Often when the topic of trading and investing in the stock market comes up, we hear statements and stories like "It's equivalent to gambling," "My friend lost all his money," or "People lose everything they have." Undoubtedly, we too may have a certain resistance within us because of the conditioning we have gone through in our lives. After reading this article, there will be a shift in your notions and how you perceive the stock market, and similarly, you'll be able to change the perception of others around you.

According to me, the stock market is nothing like gambling; rather, it is one of the most calculated businesses ever. Suppose you bought 1 crore worth of gold from the market because your analysis indicated that the price of gold will be rising in the near future. In case the price goes up, you'll earn a profit, and in case it goes down, you'll incur a loss. It's a simple calculated concept; this is not gambling but called trading. Similar to the above gold example, such trading has been a part of human society for ages. Shares or stocks are like any other commodity that is commonly traded, be it metals, groceries, grains, etc.

In the options market, 90% of people lose their money in the first 90 days of their trading. The risk factor only exists when the trader does not know what is going to happen next. Most people have no logic or strategies behind their trades. When calculations and analysis increase, the risk itself becomes nominal. Since option trading is deemed as one of the riskier markets, let's unravel how you can make it much less risky. The key is to understand how to analyze the option chain.

In order to analyze an option chain, you simply have to go to Google and type "NSE Option Chain." Open the first official link of NSE, and a set of data will appear before you with some filters and options above. You can select the Nifty option or Bank Nifty and choose the expiry.

When you take a look at the option chain page, there are call options on the left side, and put options on the other side. The ones marked in white are 'out of the money', and the ones marked in yellow are 'in the money'. Then come the three most important columns: Open Interest (OI), Change in Open Interest, and Implied Volatility.

Open Interest or OI is a highly important aspect because it represents how many lots are standing or created here. The number of lots is visible there. For example, for the strike amount of 18,200 in the below picture, the OI is 1,84,000, which represents the number of lots. For instance, Nifty has a lot of 50. Now if you multiply this amount by 50, you'll get the number of shares. Moreover, we also know that if we wish to sell a lot of Nifty, we will require approximately a lakh rupee of margin.

Similarly, if we look at the strike of 18,100 (at the money), the OI created is 1,67,000. For every different strike price, we see a different OI amount mentioned. These numbers are an important indication that we have to decode.

One of the most important aspects of option trading is support and resistance. When you're observing OI, you must understand that in order to create these OIs, crores of money have been put in. Hence, there is no way one can leave this to chance and not be sure. By these values mentioned above, you get an idea of support and resistance. Support refers to that particular line from where the falling price will pick up its pace or bounce back. In case the falling price breaks the first support line, then the support 2 and support 3 lines come into the picture accordingly as shown in the image below.

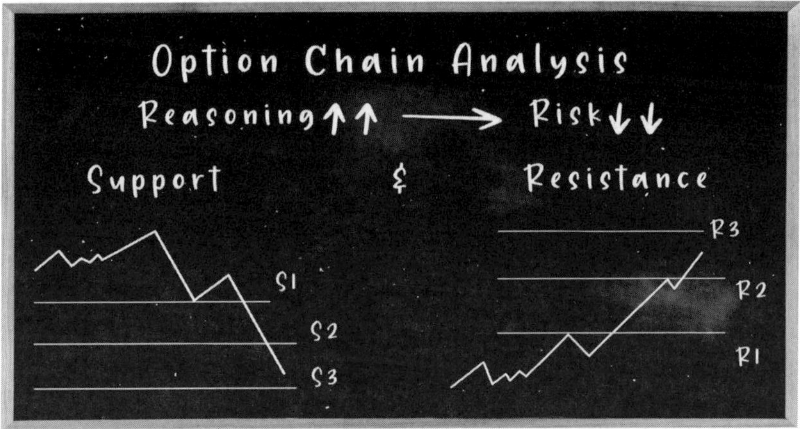

If we are analyzing the Nifty, we will need to observe the various support lines. Once we figure this out, we will know that the chances of the price reaching its third support line are quite low, and it is almost impossible for the price to reach the 4th support line.

Resistance refers to the line that the price attempts to reach but is unable to break through and bounces back. If the price breaks the resistance, it might move higher to its second resistance and subsequently to the third resistance.

When checking the strike prices, always avoid those in multiples of 50 because the Open Interest (OI) is low for them. For example, the OI for the 150 strike price is just 96, whereas the OI for the 200 strike price is 184. You must understand that the market has both buyers and sellers. If the seller has put crores of money into creating these, they wouldn't want to incur a loss.

If the Nifty begins to rise from here, the very first resistance is standing right there: for the strike price of 18,100 (at the money), the strike price of 18,200 becomes its resistance with a lot of 1,84,000. Moreover, at the strike price of 18,300, there is a lot of 1,56,000, and this continues ahead. As we scroll down, the quantities reduce.

The biggest resistance for the market, assuming 18,500 here, is the line which is impossible to reach by the price. The reason it won't cross the resistance is that, at the end of the expiry, there are lots of 1,64,000, which won't let the money go any further down. Here, the chances of the Nifty even crossing 18,300 have a very low probability because a lot of 1,56,000 is created here.

The first and the biggest resistance for the Nifty here will be to cross the strike price of 18,200 because there are lots of 1,84,000 at the same place.

In case the Nifty crosses the resistance of 18,200, I am sure it won't cross the resistance of 18,300 because the expiry is just tomorrow. The Nifty at this moment is at 18,100. Now that we know all about our resistance levels, let's start observing the other side to deduce the support levels.

At the money, the lot size is 1,74,000 quantity, with a margin of 1 lakh over 1 lot. Now you can calculate. These are the lots that the seller has sold and are bought by people, who incur a loss as you know. On the strike price of 18,000, there is an OI of 1,80,000. This quantity seems like a significantly strong support. If we go another level above, my analysis says that Nifty won't break the price of 17,900 with the OI of 1,28,000.

The current price of Nifty is 18,100, and with certainty, I can say that Nifty won't be able to break the support price of 17,900 and neither the resistance price of 18,300. What does this imply? If Nifty remains in this particular range, it will lead to profits. Hence, option chain analysis is one of the greatest tricks of the stock market that I have learned. Undoubtedly, it is one of the simplest yet most powerful tools.

Since we deduced that Nifty won't go beyond 18,300 or 17,900, we sold both of them without making the strangle or straddle, as shown in the table in the image below. In this trade of mine, LTP is 24, average price is of 27, and net quantity is of 9000.

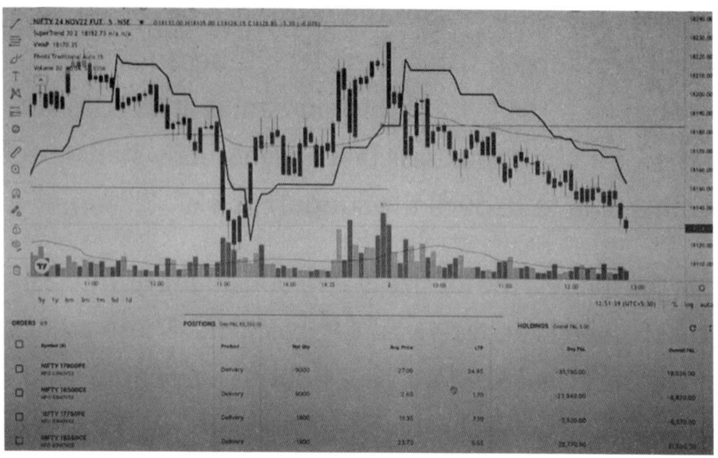

What we need to understand here is that regardless of what the profits are right now, when I square this off, there will be almost 3 to 4 Lakhs in here because it was all calculated. The price action in the above image looks good, which can also be the basis of your trade if you wish. Generally, I recommend not trading in large amounts solely using price action. This is because I understand the probability of Nifty staying in a particular range. Therefore, it is better to trade in a calculated manner as shown above.

In the image, we can clearly see that if the price breaks its pivot, it will go down until it reaches its first support line. If it breaks the first support line, it will try to reach the second support line. This is a simple price action taking place. How you can gain profits from such trends has been illustrated in the previous chapters. Just remember, if India Vix and ADX are low, sell instead of buying.

In the image below, you can enter at this particular candle when it breaks the previous low. At the same time, we can observe that the price is near its VWAP, and the MACD crossover is also coinciding with volumes. This confirms the trend and its strength.

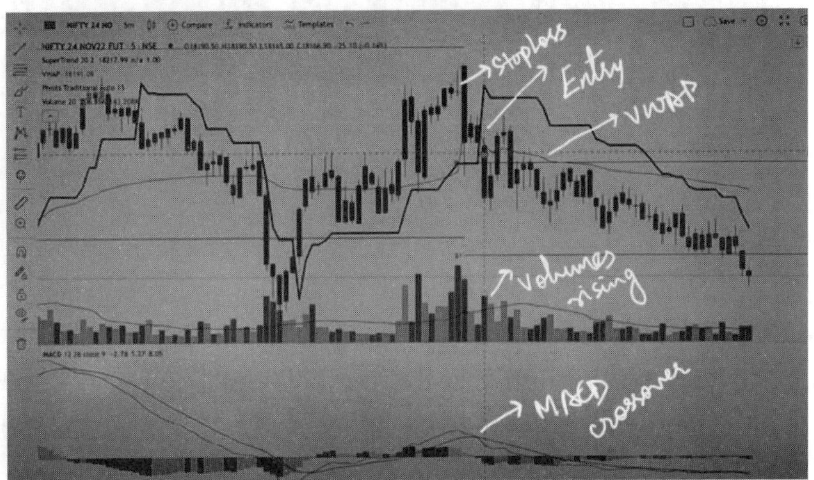

Another confirmatory tool you must use before entering this trade is checking the PCR. The PCR may appear to be negative and showing the status as "sell." This will help you curate your shared view and how you can approach the market in order to gain better returns. Trend trading should always be done with a correct and foolproof approach.

We can observe the Nifty option data, that comprises of number shares instead of number of lots. The column of Change In Open Interest (OI) and a separate column for the change in OI. All these values are automatically calculated for you. But there are so many strike prices, how do you which one's relevant for you? This is where PCR helps. PCR is elaborated as Put Call Ratio, it is calculated by taking the change in OI of both the sides of Put and Call; as shown below.

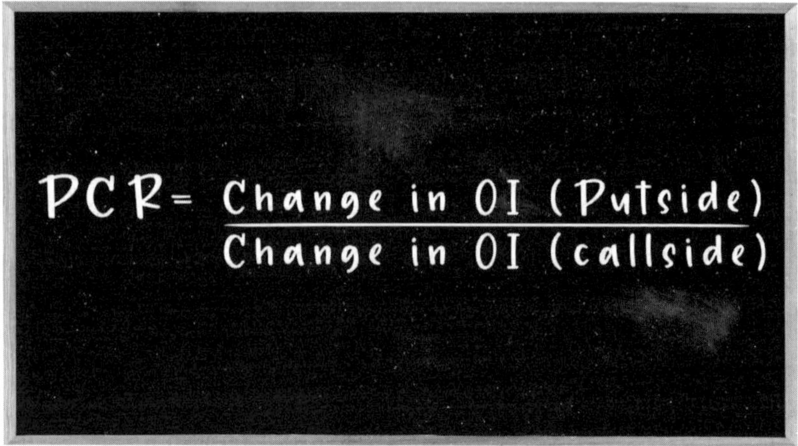

If you go through this thoroughly, you'll come to know that Change in OI never gives its total. Total is only available for OI. This Change in OI is significant because the sellers keep changing their position in the market according to their convenience.

PCR does not follow the price, yet it is one of the most powerful indicators. This type of analysis falls under the purview of quantitative, instead of technical analysis. We have understood by now that sellers make the most profit here.

When you see a significant Change in OI of the Put side, its relevancy ranges from eight strike prices above and eight strike prices below. Suppose the change in the above OI appears to be 2 crore, and the change in the below one appears to be 1 crore. After calculation, the ratio comes out to be 2. This implies that there is more probability of the price going up.

If this ratio keeps increasing above 1, it implies that the

market is going to remain in a bullish phase. If this ratio keeps decreasing below 1, it would mean that the market is going to follow a bearish phase. Let's understand the reasoning behind it. Let's assume there has been a significant change in the OI of the put side; this means that people are buying put options. People who think the market is going down are the only ones who buy put options. At the same time, there is some activity on the call side. Here, the sellers will look where they can gain more money. Hence, they will try to increase the PCR and push the price upwards.

You can use several platforms that calculate PCR for you, or you can calculate it on your own as well. Nothing is impossible! The only problem you'll face in calculating is that the values given by the NSE are always changing. Hence, the use of platforms and websites comes in handy that calculate the change in OI on a time frame of 5 minutes.

If the PCR remains negative for a while, you can deduce that the probability of the price going up is also low. Since the PCR was negative in previous images, hence, we can see a significant downfall in the below image. As soon as the price had taken a dip, it tried to come back above. At this point, people bought call options only to incur a loss because the price went down again.

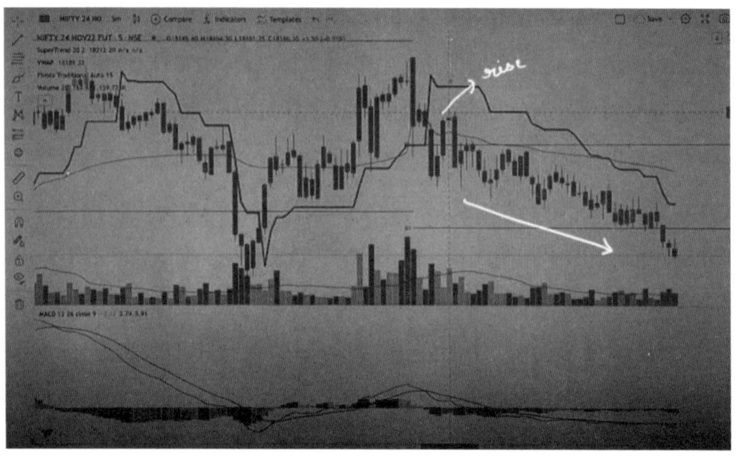

When using the 'Brahmastra' strategy, one thing you must keep in mind is that the ADX must be increasing, which will provide further confirmation regarding the strength of the trend. In the image below, the price breaks its support and tries to reach its next support line. At the same time, the ADX can be seen increasing, implying that this trend is gaining strength. Due to small volumes, the probability of a decrease in price increases.

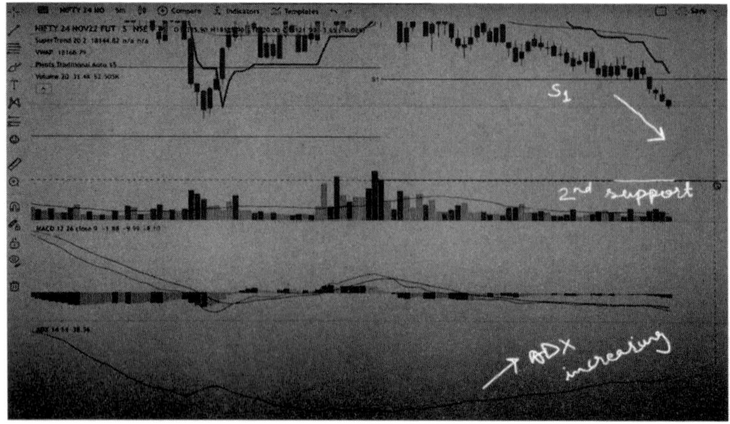

In this same example, there are at least five support lines that the price will have to break for me to incur a loss. Hence, incurring a loss seems almost impossible now. But how do I know this? The NSE option chain told us when we calculated our support and resistance earlier in the chapter. Hence, there is no need to worry because we already know the range in which the price will stay. In this case, only something as drastic as a world war will send the price into a frenzy causing a loss. Until that happens, I'll focus on the profits. On the day of expiry, all these premiums will go back to zero, and we'll see what we earned.

In order to increase your accuracy in price action for option analysis, you must also check the average delivery percentage and current delivery percentages, which have been explained in detail in the 15th chapter.

Chapter 21

To Open Free Demat Account, Just Scan the QR Code

EXPIRY SPECIAL STRATEGY

In this chapter we'll learn a very special strategy, hence, named as Expiry Special Strategy. Special because, it rarely ever misses from generating profits once it is mastered. The probability of profit of this strategy is certainly high. There's a possibility that this strategy might not make sense to you now, but down the lane; you'll thank me for it. I emphasize upon this one, because it has assisted me a lot in my trading endeavors.

The first thing you ought to check before implementing this technique is: India Vix. As you must've read in earlier sections of the book, India Vix is a volatility index that represents how volatile the market currently is. If it is below 25, it is less volatile. Whereas, anything above 25 is like a party for the trend trading strategies to do their magic.

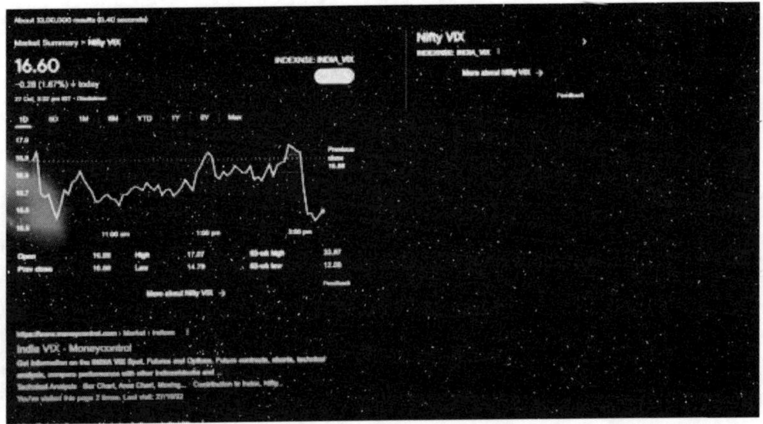

As we check, we can see the India Vix to be of 16.60 in the below image. What does this mean? This implies that the market is less volatile, and might follow a sideways trend. It is for such situations, that this strategy steps in to save the day when you cannot do the trend trading.

When we carry out trading in case of Nifty and Bank Nifty, we have to find out the value these indexes could reach. Since I usually trade with Nifty, let's begin with its example in order to understand this strategy. Since we already know the Volatility is ranging at 16; instead of trying to figure out where Nifty might reach, we have to figure out the point that it won't reach. Let's see how we will do this!

We can employ this strategy as soon as the market opens, so keep your calculations done already. So as per the image below, we have the current value of Nifty = 17,783 as well as Vix = 16.88. Taking these exact figures, we'll make our calculations.

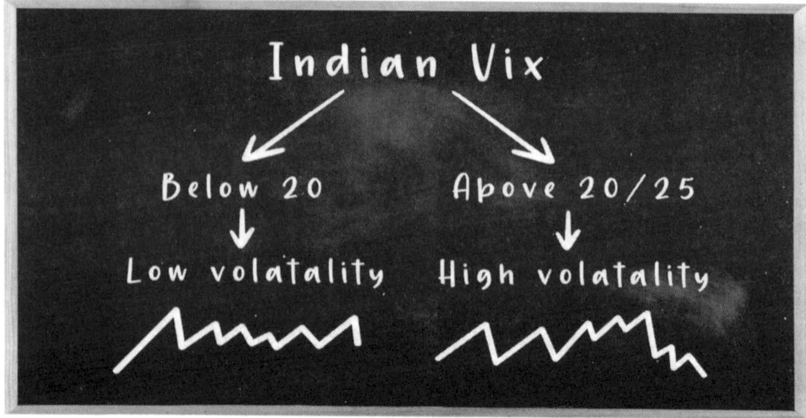

The first thing to be calculated is: how much higher or lower will the Vix index go? Go ahead... use a calculator. For this one, you simply need to calculate the square root of 365 (No. of days in a year) After calculating this, you get a value of 19.10. Now simply divide the Vix by this number, you get 16.88÷19.10 = 0.88.

Suppose,
Vix = 16.88
Nifty = 17783

Square root of 365 days
$\sqrt{365} = 19.10$

Now,
$\frac{16.88}{19.10} = 0.88\%$
17783 + 0.88% = 17932 (possible increase)
17783 - 0.88% = 17626 (possible decrease)

Rounding off the numbers
Max → 16.88
Min → 17783
] at Rs 5
So,
5x50(no. of lots) = Rs 250
to find out the range for 1
Week: $\sqrt{52}$ → 7.2
Month: $\sqrt{12}$ → 3.46
$\frac{16.88}{7.2} = 2.34\%$
$\frac{16.88}{3.46} = 4.87\%$

This value of 0.88 signifies how much the Volatility index can rise up or decline further.

Moving ahead, lets divide the Nifty price by 0.88, you

get 17,783 + 0.88% = 17,939. And boom! Now we know the market won't move ahead beyond the value of 17,939.

Let's find out how much can it decline; 17,783 - 0.88% = 17,626. Now, we know the Nifty won't decline beyond this point. By now, we have deduced a range for our trade. This range is highly important because the entire strategy depends upon this.

How to implement the strategy?

First thing to do is - rounding off and slightly increasing the range. So we take lowest of 17,600 and the highest of 18,000. You must've heard that traders turn their money to zero on the days of expiry, because they trade in the Out of Money Options. When the price is 17,783, they will buy the same at 18,000 or at 17,600.

Since the premiums are super low on days of expiry, suppose you get the same in Rs. 5. Even if you buy a single lot, that'll be 5 × 50 = Rs. 250 only. If it turns out to be a good trade, this money can double too. As a seller, we only need this Rs. 250 only. Because the buyer has zero money in his pockets now, the money will have to go somewhere! And we need this money in our pockets. Since one lot is of 250, it'll depend on how much money we have and how much can we earn.

By using the India Vix value, you can also calculate the probable range of market over a period of a week too. Instead of calculating square root of 365 days, you calculate the square of 52 for a week. For the purpose of calculating the range for a month, you calculate the square root of 12.

Using these calculations, square root of 52 is equal to 7.2. Now, using the earlier value of Vix as 16.88, we can now divide 16.88 by 7.2, which is equal to 2.34, this implies the the market can increase or decrease by 2.34% in a week.

In case of deducing the range of market over a month, we will calculate the square root of 12, which is equal to 3.46, now dividing the Vix by this value, we'll get 4.8 – this implies that the market can increase or decrease by 4.87% over a period of month.

At this point, people often make a mistake. Since they know of the range, now they short the strangle, meaning - they sell both the Options of Rs. 17,600 and Rs. 18,000. But margin requirements is very high in the latter price. As a businessman or a trader, what matters is how much you invest and how much you gain.

Let's see how it all actually takes place through Sensibull, using this unique strategy. How much amount you profit from this strategy is not important, whats important is – the percentage you gain over the amount of capital invested. Starting with the strategy builder, you can use this strategy for the upcoming expires too.

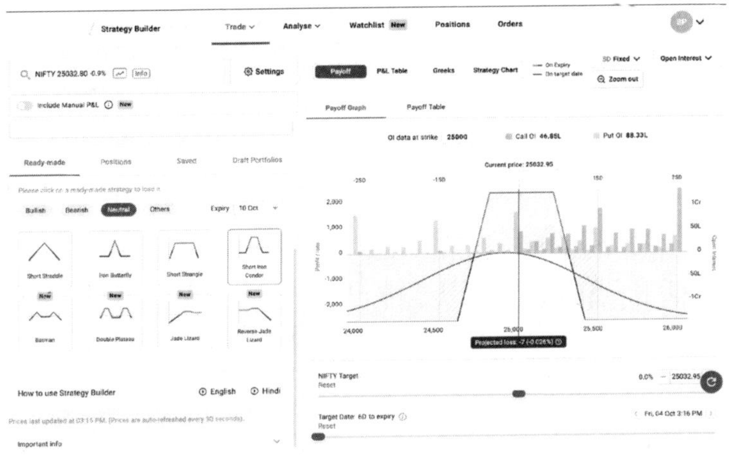

Some trading platforms also provides ready-made strategies too. We will now click on the option on the left below, wherein we will select the neutral category, where we will finally select 'short iron contour'. We change the expiry as per our requirement. Here, we can the profit appearing to be 8%, whereas on the day of expiry; the maximum profit appears to be less than 0.5% right when you'll be executing this strategy.

Next important thing to note is the maximum loss, here it appears to be 12% against the maximum profit of 8% with the probability of making this profit is 56%. Whereas, on the day of expiry; the maximum profit will be of 0.5% but the maximum loss remains the same at 12%, but here, the probability of making the profit increases to 80%.

Once you have calculated the range for the particular time period, you can accordingly shift the values on the left panel. As we create the strangle, we will sell on both the sides, while earning the profit of 6% and the probable loss will be limited.

In case, the market increases or decreases too drastically, the loss can be unlimited, whereas the probability of making profits would be 64%.

In case of iron candour, suppose you were selling at Rs. 17,550 out-of-the-money, the premium of which is Rs. 66. At the same time, you can also buy deep-out-of-the-money at Rs. 17,350 with the premium of Rs.30. The difference between these values becomes your profit.

Similarly, If look at the call option of Rs. 17,950 is coming with a premium of Rs.64. The another one is of Rs.18,150 (deep-out-of-the-money) with the premium of Rs. 20. Hence, you'll have to give Rs. 20 from your pocket while gaining Rs. 64.

When we go by this strategy, the probability of profit increases and the margin requirement lessens. Therefore, we can say that we'll be earning Rs.4000 after putting Rs.48000. On the day expiry, you'll barely earn 0.5%, this means if you will invest a crore rupees; you'll earn Rs.50,000.

Irrespective of the funds you have and how much you'll earn, one thing is for sure that you'll earn! Even if you earn 0.5% per week, and 2% every month, by the magic of compounding; you'll be able to double your money in a period of 4 years just by using this strategy. The profits may seem low but it is such stable and secure profits that fill your pockets overtime. We can use this benefit of theta decay over the week and use this strategy on Tuesday, Wednesday and Thursday. In case you don't wish to take any risk, you can simply use this strategy during the expiry. On the day of expiry, you can click on the trade all option and then check your positions from the above panel.

People often use this strategy because they don't wish to lose such big amount of money, as this is one of the simplest and safest strategies. If you don't have big chunk of money to invest in this one, you can try your hands at option trading.

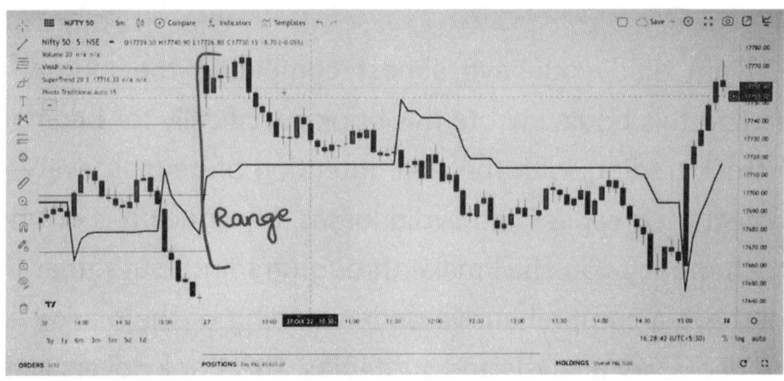

In the above image, we can see how the market is moving in a particular range. Whenever I use this strategy, I definitely check the PCR, after 10am the PCR can give you certain idea in regards to your probability of making profits or loss. This is a quick way to simply gain a additional confirmation. When the PCR rises, the price rises too. Vice versa, when it decreases or goes negative, the price goes down too. This strategy makes sure you earn no matter where the market closes within the range. Your view in regards to the market and this strategy must be clear. In case, the market it too volatile, you can avoid this strategy and use other ones instead. If the market in not volatile, you can comfortably use this one as per your convenience.

Chapter 22

TRADE WITH PSYCHOLOGY AND RISK MANAGEMENT

I am glad you have almost completed the journey of reading this book. I wrote this book specifically for beginners in stock trading, with the clear intention of helping everyone protect their capital and avoid losses. My concern is not how much money you shall make through trading, but rather that you have a comprehensive understanding of the market and the necessary analysis and strategies. This book covers all the essential aspects of the stock market that a beginner needs to learn. As you read this chapter, I urge you to take some time to review all the previous chapters, so that the information becomes even more firmly embedded in your mind.

Let's begin by discussing the psychology of trading. Trading involves the buying and selling of assets, and just like any art form, it requires patience. As a beginner reading this book, I urge you to prioritize learning patience first, as it is the key to generating profits and making the trading process smoother. These three P's - patience, profits, and process - are crucial in the world of trading.

Hence, the first lesson is to refrain from short-term trading.

1. Avoiding Scalping
2. How much can you lose?
3. How much you want to gain?

One important lesson for beginners is to avoid scalping, which is a trading strategy aimed at making quick profits by opening and closing trades within a very short time frame, often just seconds or minutes. Scalping may train our brains to focus only on short-term profits and is generally not suitable for beginners. Instead, it is advisable to focus on long-term investment strategies that employ the principle of compounding, which can lead to significant growth over time. As Warren Buffett famously said, trading is about taking money from impatient people and giving it to patient people for growth.

HOW MUCH CAN YOU LOOSE?

When you make the decision to invest money, the first thing you need to consider is how much money you can afford to lose. This will define your risk appetite - the amount of money you can bear to lose even if it goes to zero during the investment process. Different individuals have different risk appetites - one person may be able to handle a loss of D50,000, while another can take a loss of D1 lakh, D10 lakh or even D1 crore. Therefore, it is important to invest according to your own risk appetite.

HOW MUCH GAIN YOU WANT TO MAKE?

During the initial phase of trading, it is important to aim for a gain target of 5% of your capital investment, regardless of your expectations. Although a 10% gain would be excellent, 5% should be your initial target. When you think in terms of percentage gains, you need to consider larger numbers. For instance, someone trading with 10 crores is targeting to make 50 lakhs a month with a 5% gain, while someone trading with 100 crores is targeting 5 crores a month. If you wish to earn 10,000 a month, you will need a capital investment of 2 lakh rupees to start with. However, it is important to refer back to point number 2, which is determining your risk appetite, as your expected gain and required capital are dependent on it. If you cannot afford to risk 2 lakh rupees, your prospects of earning 10,000 a month will be dim.

Similar to any other business, investing in the stock market also requires capital. Just as you need to invest in stocking up a shop with products after buying it for 2 lakh rupees, the stock market is a business that demands both initial capital and consistency to yield results.

4. Never Average
5. Analyze before trading
6. Never copy ⟷ Always learn

NEVER AVERAGE WHEN IT COMES TO STOCKS

Let's understand with the help of an example. Suppose you bought shares for Rs. 10,000 at a price per share of Rs. 100, but the share price drops to Rs. 80. To reduce your loss, you might consider buying more shares at the new rate to average out your loss. However, if the share price drops further to Rs. 40, your loss will increase even more. This is why it is never wise to average out in stock trading. For instance, take Yes Bank as an example, where the stock price fell from Rs. 400 to Rs. 5. If someone had been averaging the trade price throughout the whole drop, their entire investment would have become worthless. The only way to avoid this is by analyzing before trading.

ANALYSIS SHOULD BE DONE BEFORE TRADING

Make it a rule to analyze before trading and then stick to either stop loss or target achievement. Always conduct your analysis before investing your money to reduce the likelihood of incurring losses. Be wise with your money and thoroughly investigate where you intend to invest it. While it is true that no one knows everything, we can make a more informed judgment by delving deeper into the subject matter.

NEVER IMITATE

I often emphasize that trading and investment are highly personal endeavors. Your risk tolerance, earning potential, analysis methods, and individual circumstances are unique to you, and should determine your approach to trading. While some traders may achieve incredible gains, their success is not necessarily relevant or feasible for everyone. It's essential to prioritize self-discovery, recognize your own limitations and strengths, and invest accordingly based on your personal truths.

KEEP LEARNING AND GROWING

Finally, it is possible to reach a point where trading becomes comfortable and the market seems like a friend. However, it is important not to become complacent and assume that your strategy is foolproof. Instead, always strive to learn and expand your perspective. Similarly, if you experience a string of losses, it is important to analyze and learn from your mistakes instead of becoming disheartened. Balancing your risk-to-reward strategy and being patient can lead to greater growth.

Chapter 23

SEVEN GOLDEN RULES TO MAKE MONEY

This chapter is of utmost significance in this book as it contains essential rules that will not only aid you presently but also in your future endeavors. These rules are gathered from years of experience in the market and business and are considered golden for both investing and trading. So, let's commence with the golden rules of investing

RULE 1 : THINK FOR THE LONG-TERM TERM AND LET COMPOUNDING DO THE MAGIC.

I am certain you have heard this saying countless times, and while it may seem cliché, it is still the most crucial rule for anyone who wishes to make long-term profits. It is important to understand that investing is always a long-term game. You must always keep your future goals in mind when deciding to invest in any company. If you know that you will need the invested money in the near future, it is best to refrain from investing, as the stock market is a volatile industry. The moment the market goes down or remains stagnant, you may believe that all your investments are lost.

Recently, while shopping with my wife, a man recognized me and began asking several questions about the current state of the stock market: where do you think the economy is headed? How do you think the ongoing Russia-Ukraine conflict will impact the stock market? Should I sell and withdraw my money? Should I stay put?

The man was convinced that it was a good time to sell and cash in his profits. This prompted me to ask him one simple question: do you need the invested money right now? He was taken aback by the question and proceeded to explain that he did not require the money at present, how his business was performing well, and also, the sum he had invested was not significant anyway.

I inquired why he believed that it was a good time to withdraw his money, to which he explained his prediction of an upcoming market downturn. I then asked him how long he anticipated the market to remain in a slump and what would happen if it rebounded soon after. He rightly said that it'll end up creating a FOMO!

DO YOU KNOW WHAT FOMO MEANS IN THE STOCK MARKET WORLD?

FOMO or Fear of Missing Out is a market scenario, wherein people assume that the market is booming, hence, they come back with their money and begin investing or trading to not miss out on the profit. One of the greatest examples of this is the Dutch Tulip Craze, where the price of one tulip rose by more than 50,000 dollars. Where-after, the market soon crashed.

I told the man: in the long run market will only go upward, regardless of any short-term fluctuations for while in between.

Often, people go through their portfolios, see a minor decline, and spiral into thinking that they're going to lose their money. Well, I say you haven't incurred a loss until you've sold your shares for less. Similarly, you haven't made a profit until you've sold your shares for more. Hence, the game is still on!

I often advise people to not sell until they really need that money, instead, keep on investing more with time. According to my years of experience in this field, I believe that the Indian economy has a lot of scope for growth in the coming time. The Indian economy is nowhere near its peak point yet.

People often invest impulsively when they see the market doing well, owing to their fear of missing out. As soon as they observe a fluctuation or a dip, they spiral into overthinking about incurring a loss.

Instead of relating dips to a probable loss, take them as a chance to make more in the long term. You can buy more during the dip, keeping in mind the long-term goals. If so, you can also try your hands on SIPs.

The Power of Compounding : Rule of 15: 15: 15

Investors and traders aspire to become multimillionaires, and it is possible to achieve this goal by investing Rs. 15,000 per month for 15 years with an interest rate of 15%. The power of compounding can help you accumulate Rs. 15 crores over this period. Go on, do the math, or play around on a

SIP calculator, and you won't be able to neglect the power of compounding anymore.

RULE 2 : DONT HOLD LOSING TRADES: Respect your StopLoss

One of the most common mistakes made by traders and investors is holding onto losing trades even when it's clear that they shouldn't. It's understandable that people find it difficult to accept a loss and move on. Despite seeing a stock declining, there is a tendency to hold onto it in the hope of a revival. However, if you're experiencing continuous losses and still holding on, it's an indication that there is something wrong with your approach. Holding onto a losing trade is not the best solution. It's one of the hardest lessons to learn and accept, but it's necessary. It's important to accept the loss and put a stop to it in the early stages before it gets worse. Consider this - you quickly book a profit of Rs. 500, but you continue to hold onto a stock that has incurred a loss of Rs. 5000. If you find yourself in such situations, it's time to rethink and start respecting your stop loss. Always keep in mind your risk-to-reward ratio.

RULE 3 : THE TREND IS YOUR FRIEND!

Novice or overconfident traders often make this mistake where they make trend predictions without any valid reason and go against the current trend, eventually resulting in losses. Identifying the trend is one of the fundamental tasks that one must undertake before investing or trading. Conducting basic research can help you easily identify the trend, and then you can buy and sell accordingly instead of acting on unverified tips from acquaintances. Once you understand the nature of the trend, your trades are more likely to be successful. Remember to never go against the trend!

RULE 4 : IF YOU'RE TOO ANXIOUS, RECHECK YOUR POSITION SIZING

If you experience a surge of anxiety and fear after buying a trade, it's essential to revisit your position sizing, especially if you've invested a large sum. Exceeding your trading capacity can significantly increase your heart rate and negatively impact your trading decisions. To safeguard your capital, it's crucial to determine a suitable position size that allows for a probable stop loss within your financial means. As Warren Buffet aptly stated, "Protect your capital." Running out of capital entirely would impede your ability to trade or invest, making it critical to preserve your capital by respecting the probable stop-loss. Keep in mind that success results from a disciplined approach that accumulates over time to achieve desired outcomes.

For instance, suppose you usually trade in lot sizes of 500, but you deviated from your strategy and purchased a lot size of 2500 based on your instincts for a particular stock. This lack of discipline exposes you to an excessive amount of risk, which may result in irreparable losses. Develop a disciplined approach that prioritizes risk management over arbitrary gambling to enhance your chances of success.

RULE 5 : TRADE ONLY WHEN YOUR SETUP ALLOWS

It is important to remember that trading should never be done just for the sake of it. Only trade when your financial situation permits or when you have a clear understanding of the potential for success. Avoid the temptation to jump into the market based on unfounded speculation, tips, or unrealistic expectations. Many people make the mistake of investing more than their financial means allow, only to end up bankrupt. It cannot be emphasized enough: never take a loan to trade or invest. It is essential to trade or invest within your financial means and follow a particular strategy diligently.

RULE 6 : FOLLOW A MAXIMUM OF THREE STRATEGIES

Having too many trading techniques is akin to having too many cooks spoil the dish. It leads to a lack of focus, confusion, and prevents you from mastering a specific technique. Remember that being a jack of all trades means you are a master of none. It is advisable to know or follow a maximum of three strategies, with a focus on mastering them. Some trades may only be successful with one strategy and not possible with another.

It is better to follow a specific strategy with a logical approach as it yields better results over time rather than frequently changing strategies after experiencing a loss. Calculating your risk-to-reward ratio can be helpful in this regard. If a strategy works at least 50% of the time, with practice and mastery, it can be made to work 100% of the time.

RULE 7 : INVESTING AND TRADING IS A PERSONAL GAME!

This principle is not limited to your stock market activities but also applies to how you manage your finances in general life. Never trade just to show off and always keep your financial situation to yourself. Often, people lose sight of using their money wisely while seeking attention or validation. They create a delusion for themselves by only noticing the profits earned by others, while remaining oblivious to their own capacity to take probable risks and losses. As a result, they try to initiate their strategy with a large sum of money and end up going bankrupt because they didn't calculate the risk and potential loss. I can assure you that no one generates profits every day, and there are always risks and losses. However, you can choose to avoid risks and losses that you know you cannot afford. This is where the power of discipline comes into play and pays off in the long run.

NOTE

1. Never go beyond your budget.
2. Never take a loan for the purpose of trading
3. Never trade for the sake of showing off
4. Never give way to unsubstantiated speculations or tips
5. Follow a minimum number of strategies and master them
6. Always keep the Risk to Reward Ratio in mind
7. Accept the defeats and respect the stop loss
8. Think for the long run and trust the magic of compounding

Doubts & Queries:

If you have faced any challenges in understanding any of the concepts or chapters in this book, we would love to inform you that you can also watch comprehensive videos on each topic in form of complete playlist. It will also help you for revision and better clarity of strategies.

Just Scan the QR CODE below and watch the Free Playlist on Stock Market Crash Course!

http://bit.ly/CrashCourseStockMarket

NOTE

Doubts & Queries